Neoliberal Policies and Inequality

This book explores the discourse on urban and regional inequality within the framework of neoliberalism. It analyzes the widespread application of neoliberal policies in Asian city regions and identifies their influence on rising inequality. The book captures inequality through spatial and non-spatial policy narratives with empirical evidence from India, Japan, South Korea, Taiwan, and Thailand. The book uses analytics, narratives, and simulation to unfold the opportunities and threats to urban regions that bear the impacts of globalization and neoliberal policies.

Lucid and topical, this book will be an essential read for scholars and researchers of urban economics, urban and regional planning, urban studies, urban sociology, political economy, public policy, governance, development studies, and Asian economy.

Arindam Biswas is Associate Professor at the Department of Architecture and Planning, Indian Institute of Technology (IIT) Roorkee, India.

Tetsuo Kidokoro is Professor at the the Department of Urban Engineering (DUE), School of Engineering,The University of Tokyo, Japan.

Fumihiko Seta is currently Associate Professor at the Department of Urban Engineering (DUE), School of Engineering, The University of Tokyo, Japan.

Neoliberal Policies and Inequality

Evidence from Asian City Regions

Edited by Arindam Biswas,
Tetsuo Kidokoro and Fumihiko Seta

Routledge
Taylor & Francis Group
LONDON AND NEW YORK

First published 2025
by Routledge
4 Park Square, Milton Park, Abingdon, Oxon OX14 4RN

and by Routledge
605 Third Avenue, New York, NY 10158

Routledge is an imprint of the Taylor & Francis Group, an informa business

British Library Cataloguing-in-Publication Data
A catalogue record for this book is available from the British Library

ISBN: 978-1-032-11329-6 (hbk)
ISBN: 978-1-032-24949-0 (pbk)
ISBN: 978-1-003-28086-6 (ebk)

DOI: 10.4324/ 9781003280866

Typeset in Sabon
by Deanta Global Publishing Services, Chennai, India

Contents

Figures

Tables

Author Biographies

Editors

Arindam Biswas is Associate Professor at the Department of Architecture and Planning, Indian Institute of Technology (IIT) Roorkee, India. He has a doctorate in Urban Planning from the University of Tokyo. He is a recipient of the Institute research fellowship for outstanding young faculty, the ASEM Duo-India Fellowship, the DAAD Fellowship (Germany), and the MEXT Scholarship (Japan). He has also undertaken a Certificate Program on International Environmental Leadership (Asian Program for Incubation of Environmental Leadership, APIEL) from the University of Tokyo. He is presently pursuing research sponsored by different research foundations of the Government of India like the Department of Science and Technology (DST), the Ministry of Education, the Indian Council of Social Science Research, the Ministry of Environment Forest and Climate Change, and the National Building Construction Company. He is also working on research sponsored by the Royal Academy of Engineering, the British Council, and GCRF-UKRI, United Kingdom. He has published four editorial books and contributed to six book chapters. He has also extensively published peer-reviewed articles on urban infrastructure, inclusive growth, resilience, housing and informality, innovation, and regional development.

Tetsuo Kidokoro is Professor at the University of Tokyo. Prof. Kidokoro Specializes in urban planning and governance, international development, and regional planning. He acquired Ph.D. from the University of Tokyo (Urban Planning) in 1993. His job experiences include being Visiting Professor at the United Nations University; Visiting Lecturer at the Department of Urban and Regional Planning, Chulalongkorn University, Thailand; Associate Expert at the Human Settlements Unit, UNESCAP; and National Expert, at the United Nations Center for Regional Development (UNCRD). He also worked as Consultant for the World Bank and Asian Development Bank and as Expert for OECD. He wrote many books in the field of urban and regional planning, including 'Transit-Oriented Development Policies and Station Area Development in Asian Cities' in *Handbook on High-Speed Rail and Quality of Life* (2020); 'Creation of Collaborative Networks at the City-Regional Level: Two Innovative Cases in Japan', in *Sustainable Landscape Planning in Selected Urban Regions* (2017); *Understanding African Urbanization: Discourse, Representation and Actuality* (2013); *Sustainable City Regions: Space, Place and Governance* (2008); and *Vulnerable Cities: Realities, Innovations and Strategies* (2008).

Fumihiko Seta is currently Associate Professor at the Department of Urban Engineering (DUE), School of Engineering, the University of Tokyo. He was born in 1972 in Tokyo, graduated from the University of Tokyo in 1995, and worked at the University of Tokyo from 1998 to 2005 and Osaka City University from 2005 to 2012. He was also tentatively assigned as a senior research associate of the Asian Institute of Technology (AIT) (2000), a short-term expert of Japan International Cooperation Agency (JICA) (2000, 01, 02), and a visiting researcher at Stuttgart University, Germany (2003, 2004–2005) and a visiting researcher of Stuttgart Technology University of Applied Science (HFT Stuttgart), Germany (2018–2019). His major is regional and urban planning in Japan and foreign countries for growing and depopulating cities and towns. His contributions to publications include *Japan's Population Implosion: The 50 Million Shock* (ed. Yoichi Funabashi, 2018) and *Community Livability Second Edition* (ed. Fritz Wagner and Roger W. Caves, 2019). He is currently a member of some committees to support the central government of Japan regarding national spatial strategies and national land use plans in the Ministry of Land, Infrastructure, Transport and Tourism (MLIT).

Contributors

Arindam Biswas is Associate Professor at the Department of Architecture and Planning, Indian Institute of Technology (IIT) Roorkee, India. He has a doctorate in Urban Planning from the University of Tokyo. He is a recipient of the Institute research fellowship for outstanding young faculty, the ASEM Duo-India Fellowship, the DAAD Fellowship (Germany), and the MEXT Scholarship (Japan). He has also undertaken a Certificate Program on International Environmental Leadership (Asian Program for Incubation of Environmental Leadership, APIEL) from the University of Tokyo. He is presently pursuing research sponsored by different research foundations of the Government of India like the Department of Science and Technology (DST), the Ministry of Education, the Indian Council of Social Science Research, the Ministry of Environment Forest and Climate Change, and the National Building Construction Company. He is also working on research sponsored by the Royal Academy of Engineering, the British Council, and GCRF-UKRI, United Kingdom. He has published four editorial books and contributed to six book chapters. He has also extensively published peer-reviewed articles on urban infrastructure, inclusive growth, resilience, housing and informality, innovation, and regional development.

Arun Natarajan Hariharan is currently working as Assistant Professor at the Manipal School of Architecture and Planning and is Architect and environmental planner with doctoral-level experience in regional planning. Arun's choice of eco-friendly and ecological aspects at the built environment level stimulated choosing environmental planning at the postgraduate level to explore the organic growth of Indian cities and towns at a regional level. One of his research interests is location choice factors in determining the industrial cluster development within a city. Additionally, Arun has published about the development of knowledge-based industry at national and regional levels through international peer-reviewed article publications.

Tetsuo Kidokoro is Professor at the University of Tokyo. Prof. Kidokoro Specializes in urban planning and governance, international development, and regional planning. He acquired Ph.D. from the University of Tokyo (Urban Planning) in 1993. His job experiences include being Visiting Professor at the United Nations University; Visiting Lecturer at the Department of Urban and Regional Planning, Chulalongkorn University, Thailand; Associate Expert at the Human Settlements Unit, UNESCAP; and National Expert, at the United Nations Center for Regional Development (UNCRD). He also worked as Consultant for the World Bank and Asian Development Bank and as Expert for OECD. He wrote many books in the field of urban and regional planning, including 'Transit-Oriented Development Policies and Station Area Development in Asian Cities' in *Handbook on High-Speed Rail and Quality of Life* (2020); 'Creation of Collaborative Networks at the City-Regional Level: Two Innovative Cases in Japan', in *Sustainable Landscape Planning in Selected Urban Regions* (2017); *Understanding African Urbanization: Discourse, Representation and Actuality* (2013); *Sustainable City Regions: Space, Place and Governance* (2008); and *Vulnerable Cities: Realities, Innovations and Strategies* (2008).

Hwajin Lim is Associate Professor at the Graduate School of Environmental and Information Studies, Tokyo City University. She has extensively researched spatial policy and information science, including big data and social network analysis. She was previously appointed as Special Researcher at the Center for Socio-Environmental Systems Research, National Institute for Environmental Studies; a Senior Researcher at the Chungnam Development Research Institute (Korea); and a Senior Researcher at the Future Strategy Research Center, Korea Advanced Institute of Science and Technology (KAIST). Her primary research interests are the comparative study of Korea and Japan, DX and spatial planning, innovation networks, social network analysis, big data analysis, urban dynamics, and urban and regional policy.

Shraddha Pandit is Doctoral Student in the Department of Architecture & Planning, Indian Institute of Technology Roorkee, Uttarakhand, India. She completed Bachelor in Architecture (B. Arch) from Jadavpur University, Kolkata, and thereafter earned a master's in Regional Planning from the School of Planning and Architecture, New Delhi. She is also a recipient of the prestigious Prime Minister Research Fellows (PMRF) award from the Government of India. Her research interests include urban and regional growth dynamics, regional inequality, regional economics, and socio-spatial challenges within urban areas.

Vanitha Putta is Ph.D. Research Scholar at the Department of Architecture and Planning, IIT Roorkee, India. Her research examines the residential segregation of internal migrants in urban India and investigates spatial inequalities and their dynamics. Her research interests include residential segregation, spatial inequalities, and migration networks.

Nikita Ranjan is Doctoral Student at the Department of Architecture and Planning, Indian Institute of Technology, Roorkee, Uttarakhand, India. She earned a master's degree in urban and Rural Planning. She also received the Combined Study and Practice Stays for Engineers from Developing Countries (KOSPIE) scholarship from the German Academic Exchange Service (DAAD). Her research interests include urban resilience, climate resilience, urban governance, and urban and regional development. She is a recipient of the Prime Minister's Research Fellowship (PMRF).

Fumihiko Seta is currently Associate Professor at the Department of Urban Engineering (DUE), School of Engineering, the University of Tokyo. He was born in 1972 in Tokyo, graduated from the University of Tokyo in 1995, and worked at the University of Tokyo from 1998 to 2005 and Osaka City University from 2005 to 2012. He was also tentatively assigned as a senior research associate of the Asian Institute of Technology (AIT) (2000), a short-term expert of Japan International Cooperation Agency (JICA) (2000, 01, 02), and a visiting researcher at Stuttgart University, Germany (2003, 2004–2005) and a visiting researcher of Stuttgart Technology University of Applied Science (HFT Stuttgart), Germany (2018–2019). His major is regional and urban planning in Japan and foreign countries for growing and depopulating cities and towns. His contributions to publications include *Japan's Population Implosion: The 50 Million Shock* (ed. Yoichi Funabashi, 2018) and *Community Livability Second Edition* (ed. Fritz Wagner and Roger W. Caves, 2019). He is currently a member of some committees to support the central government of Japan regarding national spatial strategies and national land use plans in the Ministry of Land, Infrastructure, Transport and Tourism (MLIT).

Kojiro Sho is Associate Professor at Kyushu University. He specializes in urban planning and landscape design, participative planning and community empowerment, and dynamics of urban space transformation. He received his Ph.D. from the University of Tokyo (Urban Planning) in 2017. His job experiences include being Engineering Official in Construction and Planning Agency, Ministry of Interior and Taipei City Government, Taiwan; Project Assistant Professor at the Tokyo Metropolitan University; and Lecturer (Assistant Professor) and Associate Professor at the Osaka City University, Japan. He is also involved in several committees regarding urban planning and community policy in Osaka and Fukuoka, Japan. His recent publications in urban and regional planning include 'Urban centre revival and the changing locations of condominiums', Geographical Research (2022); 'Formation of the Tokyo West Creative Industry Cluster and Gentrification in Tokyo', International Journal of Urban and Regional Research (2022); and 'From stigma to pride: New practices of housing-based welfare for regenerating disadvantaged communities in Taipei City, Taiwan', in Mizuuchi, T. et al. (eds.), Diversity of Urban Inclusivity (2022).

Ankita Sood graduated from the Department of Architecture and Planning, Indian Institute of Technology, Roorkee, Uttarakhand, India. She is a working professional as Urban Planner and Disaster Risk Reduction Specialist. Her research area resonates with climate change adaptation and mitigation, disaster resilience, and sustainable urban/regional planning.

Kristi Verma is Architect–Urban Planner. She grew up in Delhi but counts Jaipur and Ahmedabad as her homes. She completed her bachelor's degree in architecture from Malviya National Institute of Technology and her master's degree in urban planning from CEPT University. Kristi is a registered architect and a member of the Institute of Town Planners, India. She is passionate about working around the synergies between urban spaces and people. She practices urbanism through social work and has demonstrated it for the last eight years as an active member of the wildlife NGO Hope and Beyond. Whilst graduating, she published her articles in academic journals and international conferences. During three years of professional experience, she engaged in prominent transdisciplinary projects in the country. Her recent engagement at CEPT University includes the formulation of 'Local Area Plans' and 'Town Planning Schemes' for cities covered under the Smart City Mission. She contributed notably to academia during her term as Guest Faculty at IIT Roorkee. Her research on 'Urban Inequality Modelling as Story Telling' with IIT Roorkee evolved as a chapter in this book.

Acknowledgments

The purpose of this book is more exploratory in nature, where we seek to inspire the readers, whether academic, students, professionals, or citizens, with thought-provoking insights from our research outputs on the trends, patterns, and reasons for inequality in the neoliberal policy era. We certainly raise more questions that we can answer, but this is undoubtedly a positive development in our spectacle. All the contributors restricted themselves not to put forward their own values and perspectives in the discussions but rather relied on drawing conclusions from the research findings. As editors, we have also tried to maintain a similar method of articulation and refrain from any such additional inputs in any of the chapters. Honestly, sometimes we are baffled by the findings, while on other occasions, the output corroborates our research hypothesis. Our intent is not to impede innovative debate or contradicting viewpoints but rather to motivate it in our academic discourse. We believe that the discussions presented in the book will be useful and helpful for readers to formulate their own hypotheses and widen their research perspectives.

Many institutions and individuals are directly and indirectly responsible for the book's ideas. As editors, much of our research work and academic thoughts are captivated by this publication. In addition to our own research output, we reached out to the potential contributors to enhance the diversity and incorporate varied viewpoints. While the research output in the form of structured manuscripts took some time to emerge, none would have occurred unless we received a research grant from the Ministry of Education, Government of India, under the Scheme for Promotion of Academic and Research Collaboration (SPARC) program (Grant code: SPARC/2018-2019/P222/SL, dated March 15, 2019, project code P222). The project focusing on 'narrative and storytelling to study urban and regional inequality' allowed and motivated us to bring together a pool of researchers, inspired to contribute their insights and research findings through this book. We also owe to our affiliated institutes and the staff, i.e., the Indian Institute of Technology (IIT) Roorkee, India, and the University of Tokyo, Japan, for continuously inspiring us to achieve academic excellence. Sincere thanks to CRC Press and Taylor and Francis Group for supporting this project and publishing it under its flagship publishing house. Many personnel read and suggested important parts that helped us write, edit, and compile this book. We would like to thank them all. During the development of this book, we experienced an unprecedented global disaster of COVID-19 threatening the entire human civilization. Millions of people all over the world endured personal and collective loss due to the pandemic. We hope that the world will overcome the evil of the pandemic and embrace a healthy, happy, and peaceful life. We would like to thank our families for supporting us during this journey, particularly during the difficult phase of the pandemic. We hope the book will inspire many souls worldwide through its novel work and inspire them to research these fields.

Arindam Biswas
Indian Institute of Technology (IIT) Roorkee, India.
Fumihiko Seta,
The University of Tokyo, Japan.
Tetsuo Kidokoro,
The University of Tokyo, Japan.
June, 2024

Preface

This book discusses neoliberal policies and their impacts on inequality in Asian cities. Inequality at the urban and regional scale is becoming pervasive and profound. This book aims to analyze the widespread application of neoliberal policies in Asian city regions and identify its influence on rising inequality. Countries, irrespective of their level of development, have embraced globalization to gain from global connections. Globalization is conceptualized as the internationalization of goods, services, capital, and knowledge. Presenting urban regions as the location of globalization's impacts allows us to visualize and analyze the actual consequences of globalization in different geographic and policy environments. Neoliberalism as an incentive of globalization infers market deregulation, privatization, anti-union, and withdrawal of the welfare state by encouraging market-oriented policy fundamentals within the state-controlled institutional regime, which has a deepening connection with globalization, particularly propagated by international organizations. It also encourages competition to facilitate innovation and growth rather than a monopoly of capital among select elites. Such multiplicity of economic, social, policy, and cultural shifts has widespread ramifications on the overall opportunities of individuals, households, and societies. Some people and places benefit from their ability to access opportunities, while much of the population cannot access them and benefit from such a policy. Such conditions create spatial dispersal of economic activities, evolving new forms of territorial polarization and rising inequality.

The central concern of our work is inspired by our continuous efforts over a combined experience of 60 years to investigate inequality, exclusion, and eccentricity of economy and society and their underlying reasons. This new economic geography of city regions reconstructs inequality as the output of neoliberal policies. Spatial inequality is deeply embedded within the characteristics of their economy, sometimes disconnected from the region and even the nation. The extent of such inequality is prompting distortions in market operations from investments in housing, physical and social infrastructure, and welfare programs. The ascendance of finance and restructuring economic activities in profit-making and worker-earning capacities in service sectors contribute to inequality through cumulative causations. The emergence of a new urban economy enables social and economic restructuring, producing new social forms and class alignments, which reflect the different forms of inequalities, i.e., dualization of economic organizations, steep rise of homelessness and slums, residential and commercial gentrification, and rapidly expanding informal economy.

The book consists of ten chapters capturing inequality through policy narratives with empirical evidence from India, Japan, South Korea, Taiwan, and Thailand. It also visualizes inequality through spatial modeling and simulation from multiple metropolitan cities in India. The first chapter analyzes the emerging challenges due to neoliberal policies and privatization in the urban housing sector in India. While completing the objectives of this chapter, the article also appraises the expression of neoliberalism as it unfolds from the global sphere to the Indian realm. Neoliberalism is considered a loose set of philosophical, institutional, and political principles to safeguard individual and collective freedom, like private property rights, exchange of goods and services, and movement of capital and labor. The neoliberal policy promotes free markets and free trade to free the creative potential and the entrepreneurial spirit through efficient utilization of resources and upbringing of human well-being. In a neoliberal regime, cities compete to attract talented people, capital, and resources to achieve newer economic and social benchmarks. However, the constant pursuit of excessive achievements lets some negativities grow within. Large-scale inequality, deprivation, social unrest, and meager quality of life affect the sustainable and holistic development of seemingly most developed cities worldwide. Drawing on a wide range of literature across social sciences, urban planning, and development studies, this chapter focuses on the Indian manifestation of neoliberalism and its impact on urban housing.

The second chapter examines the impacts of gentrification under neoliberal urban policy regimes and the resultant spatial inequality from the empirical evidence of Tokyo and Mumbai. The chapter highlights the urban planning systems of Tokyo and Mumbai, which are transforming toward a market-friendly zoning system under the neoliberal urban development policies. Along with the formation of hybrid development and state-neoliberalism regimes, FAR bonus schemes have been introduced to promote state and property-led urban regeneration projects in Tokyo and Mumbai. Large-scale gentrification projects (luxury high-rise condominiums/ apartments) have increasingly been implemented in these cities following the global city policies to enhance their global status. The study finds Tokyo's urbanization process as the concentration of wealth and wealthy people in the city center through gentrification and Mumbai's urbanization through simultaneous suburbanization and re-centralization through gentrification, i.e., high-rise suburban developments and high-rise gentrification developments.

The third chapter scrutinizes gated communities and the fragmentation of urban green space, threatening urban resilience during the neoliberal urban development process. Urban resilience is a popular point of deliberation in contemporary urban planning. With the influence of neoliberal development agendas, contemporary resilience programs often focus primarily on innovation and specialized infrastructure solutions. Without considering inclusion, resilient initiatives limit infrastructure access to the elite and push the vulnerable population further under stress. This chapter presents a new perspective on the neoliberal development of urban green spaces and its effects on cities' resilience. Investment of private capital in urban development leads to the progressive replacement of public open and green spaces with gated/enclaved green spaces, affecting their accessibility and co-benefits and, thus, the resiliency of urban residents. This chapter inspects the missed opportunity of developing inclusive urban green spaces as a resilience-building tool owing to lost ecological and functional benefits due to fragmentation and gating. The study relies primarily on existing literature, secondary data, and case studies to evolve an analytical narrative of how the neoliberal development of urban green space in Indian cities affects urban resilience. It reflects on plausible strategic options for restructuring the green spaces within the gated communities using a case example from Noida, India. While the chapter limits itself to the specific discussion of gated urban development in detail, it opens the scope for further academic discourse on the effect of various neoliberal development phenomena on a city's resilience.

The fourth chapter researches migration as a metaphor for regional inequalities. The study attempts a critical exploration of migration and inequalities. An evident yet hardly acknowledged interlink between inequalities and migration is complex and overlapped by multiple layers. Migration, prominently known as a phenomenon occurring due to imbalances present in a location, can also cause a rise in inequalities at the destination of migrants. The chapter presents the data analysis to understand the state-level disparities concerning movement patterns through the lenses of gender and age and the correlation between migration and socio-economic variables of the states of India. In the chapter, linear regression and correlation analysis examined the association between migration and socio-economic variables.

The fifth chapter reviews how the Thai government has dealt with the regional disparity between urban and rural areas through national spatial planning from a medium- and long-term perspective and describes how the regional disparity between urban and rural areas has changed using the identified economic indicators. Then the chapter briefly shows how the accumulation of industrial locations causes the concentration of regional disparity. After the extreme concentration and expansion in the capital city Bangkok and surrounding provinces, industrial locations have been expanded to provinces where the Eastern Seaboard (ESB) development program has continued since the 1990s. While the central government has continuously identified such a situation in successive national plans, the government's actual policies have prioritized the manufacturing-oriented economy following the trend of globalization. The three eastern provinces are designated as the new center of economic development of high-value-added industries. The chapter finally introduces the kind of spatial strategies the Thai government will likely pursue in the near future based on the recent economic growth strategy called 'Thailand 4.0' and anticipates future developments.

The sixth chapter investigates spatial polarization in Indian urbanization in the neoliberal era. The chapter studies the city of Hyderabad, India, as an example of spatial polarization. After globalization, the Andhra Pradesh development model suggested technology-intensive development, which led to a high concentration of labor and capital in Hyderabad. In this technology-intensive development, an intensive process of residential and commercial enclave formation was initiated specifically along the city peripheries to reimagine Hyderabad as a global city. While these enclaves have effectively connected themselves with the global network, they have fallen behind in establishing interconnectedness with their immediate surroundings. As a part of the policy initiatives, these enclaves have been provided with all the world-class amenities to support highly skilled labor. However, these glittering urban pockets exist simultaneously, with most of the population struggling from extreme poverty, and informality failing to secure even basic needs to survive. The study finds that post-1991, Hyderabad and its surrounding peri-urban areas experienced polarization at two levels: Firstly, a growing disparity between the old city core and the newly developed urban peripheries. Secondly, pockets of spatial disparity in the urban peripheries between the highly skilled labor and the traditional settlements. Post-1991, the spatial growth of the city highlights significant changes in its growth pattern and reflects the continuing spatial polarization. The research, thus, attempts to address the spatial changes caused by the changing economic conditions in the city and interprets its connection with spatial polarization at a metropolitan scale.

The seventh chapter studies Korea's urban policy against the backdrop of the administrative and political influence of the national election every five years. Korean urban policy is institutionalized to follow the trend of the central government. The current central government has adopted an urban renewal policy and supports urban development activities in more than 200 cities nationwide. On the other hand, real estate policy in Korea has been changing rapidly since the Asian financial crisis (IMF crisis). In particular, the increase in household debt and the rapid rise in real estate prices due to the foreign capitalization of the housing finance market are progressing and are a source of concern for the current government. The current macro-spatial disparity in Korea is further aggravated by a complex concentration pattern in the Seoul metropolitan area and regional decline. This chapter introduces the currents of national land and urban policies in Korea, their relevance to neoliberalism, and recent initiatives. The characteristics of promoting neoliberalism while maintaining the national system of developmentalism in Korea's urban policy.

The eighth chapter uses simulation as a narrative for studying Bangalore's (India) inequality. Inequality has always existed in human habitations in some forms. With the increasing population and complexity of the urban systems, the scale of inequality is increasing at an alarming rate. The spatial spread of inequality can be observed regarding income, resource distribution, infrastructure accessibility, housing, etc. These inequalities appear more acute in developing nations due to resource and capacity constraints, polarization, weaker financial conditions, and preferential treatment toward the affluent class. This research aims to study the spatial inequalities due to urban infrastructure using statistical and mapping techniques in Bangalore City to showcase the principal objectives. Bangalore is chosen because of its urban character and its diverse population structure, creating a visible divide between the affluent class and the poor, especially after the advent of neoliberalism. The city's urban fabric is extracted using high-resolution temporal imageries to understand the startling differences in the built form. Temporal data is captured for three decades, from 1989 to 2021, to understand the growing differences in these areas. Machine Learning models are trained to capture the extent of emerging inequality by integrating remotely sensed and statistical data. The results aid in understanding the underlying causes of spatial inequalities and the expressions of disparities in accessing urban infrastructures.

The ninth chapter explores housing inequality as one of the most critical issues driven by the neoliberalism-oriented housing market in Taiwan. Facing the situation of a low rate of public housing stock and the rising price of private housing, housing affordability has naturally become a serious concern in Taipei City, Taiwan. Many social movements have recently emerged in Taipei to counteract the housing inequality caused by the neoliberal shift in housing policies. As the output of continuous community development activities to support socially vulnerable groups in the community, three major community facilities have been developed in the community of the 'Nanjichang resettlement housing complex'. Among them, Nanjichang Food Bank supports improving the quality of life of socially vulnerable groups by offering daily necessities. It also provides an opportunity to enter the circle of mutual trust among community members by incentivizing them to participate in community activities.

The final chapter discusses globalization and innovation as crucial attributes for enterprises in the information and communication technology era. The chapter argues that the advent of ICT and the globalization of production activities have impeded offshoring innovation activities into developing economies. Cost-effective skilled labor and novelty in knowledge augmented the scope for developing economies to attract much of the innovation expenditure by multinational enterprises (MNEs). USA-based MNEs are the dominant players in spending knowledge-based innovation (KBI) activities. Countries like China and India have joined Taiwan and South Korea in augmenting knowledge production through patent publication in ICT industries. Developing economies have succeeded in attracting the KBI due to dynamic liberalization and export-oriented economic policies. This chapter utilizes the OLI (Ownership, Location, Internalization) framework of John H Dunning to understand the role of nations like India and China in the regional location of the USA-based MNEs.

Arindam Biswas,
Indian Institute of Technology (IIT) Roorkee, India.
Fumihiko Seta,
The University of Tokyo, Japan.
Tetsuo Kidokoro,
The University of Tokyo, Japan.
June 2024

1 Neoliberalism and the Urban Housing Conundrum in India

Arindam Biswas

1.1 Introduction

The neoliberal thought deciphered as a free assertion of state, market, and citizenship; technological rise and promotion of competition; and economic consideration are the central features of neoliberal urbanism (Pinson & Journel, 2016). Cities and regions incorporate massive public goods and are thus substantially regulated, particularly land use and housing. Even in policymaking, urban policy change depends on complex pragmatics of the urban system shaped by changing technologies, migration processes, lifestyles, economic structure, and development rather than by the macro-outlook (Storper, 2016). An urban system functions as the space for neoliberalism, where people live, work, and interact and are influenced by the norms and actions of different hierarchical public institutions. A complete absence of the state in an urban system is unlikely because the capitalist sector looks for business opportunities only in the profitable segments of an urban economy, whereas it shies away from conflicting or loss-making public services. There is hardly any state in the world that can sustain complete market-friendly or competitive urban policies. Invariably, the state extends welfare provisions and subsidies to safeguard the interests of the urban commons and the weaker sections of society. The delivery of public services and public goods and the implementation of development projects in cities are comprised of different combinations of models. A state may choose to develop joint ventures to extend public services in the neoliberal regime rather than privatize entirely. Public-private participation in cities has become a new norm for the service delivery of public goods and the implementation of urban development projects.

Emerging economies like India experience more challenging situations, whether to encourage more privatizations in housing and urban development or to safeguard the large section of homeless and deprived people. The opportunities in the growing real estate ventures due to the rising incomes and expanding neo-middle class employed in service sectors create a trade-off between the capitalist form of housing and housing supply in all (Gopalan & Venkataraman, 2015; Hariharan & Biswas, 2019; Singh, Kumar, & Prasad, 2014). The increased investment in housing supply to financial elites creates

DOI: 10.4324/9781003280866-1

a real estate and rental process, making it impossible for even middle-class families to afford houses (Sangma, 2006). The chapter's objective is to analyze the impact of neoliberal policies on the urban housing sector in India. In the process, the chapter begins with a concise note on neoliberalism and its eventual introduction into India's policy sphere. The objectives of the research are as follows:

i. To comprehend the evolution of neoliberalism in India's urban housing;
ii. To record the ramifications of neoliberalism on urban housing in India.

The first objective is responded to by a systematic literature review of macro-data. The second objective is answered by analyzing the macro-data and 'case study' analysis of Indian cities.

The chapter is structured into seven sections. Section 1.2 records the literature review, specifically relieving the advent of neoliberalism as a policy fundamental in India. Section 1.3 presents the research methodology adopted to build on a logical narrative of the urban housing dilemma and neoliberalism in India. Section 1.4 evaluates the influence of neoliberalism on the Indian urban housing sector. Section 1.5 analyzes the performance of urban housing policy during its evolution from socialist to neoliberalism. Section 1.6 postulates empirical evidence from India to manifest the existing pattern of housing development because of neoliberalism. Finally, Section 1.7 commences the chapter with the relevant discussion and conclusion from the analysis. The research contributes to specifying the evolution of neoliberal principles in Indian urban development and the consequences of neoliberalism on urban housing in India. The major limitation of the research is fewer empirical evidence. Future research may focus on more empirical analysis to learn about the on-ground impact of neoliberalism on India's urban housing scenario. It will help to address the policy reform needed to address the urban housing challenges in India.

1.2 Evolution of Neoliberalism and Its Critics

After independence, India's economic and social policy was focused on the state-led development process. The state was extremely interventionist with protective policies, sizeable public sector industries, and strict measures to prevent privatization, especially in infrastructure and basic industries. Consequently, India's transformation to a liberal and open industrial policy regime in 1991 was historically significant (Chandrasekhar, 2010). Neoliberalism also garners much acceptance in the Indian economy, policy planning, and the drive for privatization. The ascendance of neoliberalism in India is characterized by its integration with the new international economic order (Adduci, 2012). In India, neoliberalism is recognized through economic reforms and the new economic policy (Das, 2015). Neoliberalism in India primarily refers to economic liberalization or economic reforms rather than a cosmopolitan social order with political, behavioral, religious, and cultural freedom.

The 1991 economic reforms are considered the lynchpin for India's connection with the globalized world and neoliberal economic principles.

> The liberalization did away with the investment licensing and myriad entry restrictions on 'Monopolies and Restrictive Trade Practices (MRTP) firms by the statement of industrial policy, commonly referred to as the new industrial policy. It also ended the public sector monopoly except for eight sectors selected on security and strategic grounds. It initiated a policy of automatic approval of foreign direct investment up to 51 percent. All other sectors were opened to private enterprises. In the subsequent years, the list of restricted public sector monopolies has been trimmed further.
>
> (Panagariya, 2004)

However, many authors argue that India's path toward neoliberalism started with the 1980s reforms. The 1980s reforms instigated confidence among conservative Indian politicians on the opportunities and threats associated with the policy shifts toward devaluation, trade liberalization, and de-licensing of investment, spurring continuous growth. Desai (1999), Panagriya (2004), and Virmani (1997), among others, have argued that the 1980s reforms facilitated the much structured and systematic reforms in 1991 (Desai, 1999; Panagariya, 2004; Virmani, Economic Development and Transition: India, 1997). Bhagwati and Desai (1970) documented India's interventionist policies from the onset of independence to economic liberalization (Chandrasekhar, 2010; Panagariya, 2004). Gordon and Gupta (2003) argue that the reasons for India's growth were fast-growing telecommunication, financial, and community services. The correlation between growth acceleration and deregulation of communication, financial, and business services is quite evident (Gordon & Gupta, 2003).

Many scholars and authors critic India's failure in many aspects, e.g., lopsided structural distribution toward the service sector in the overall macroeconomic settings, inability to create enough jobs in the economy, deepening regional inequality, extremely slow rate of poverty reduction, and the rising disparity between the capitalists and ordinary citizens, especially the rural citizen (Patnaik, 2007; Walker, 2008). Das (2015) cites that the neoliberal economic and industrial policies have mostly benefited the capital-intensive sectors, including finances, information technology (IT), real estate, and minerals (Das, 2015). The advantages and predicaments of liberalization are vehemently debated in India. Liberalization has ushered in corporatization, commodification, and privatization of public monopolies and achieved its primary objective of starting new avenues for capital accrual previously regarded as exclusive to the public domain and beyond profitability. Public utilities (i.e., water, telecommunications, transportation), welfare (housing, education, health care, pensions), and public institutions (e.g., universities and research laboratories) have all been privatized to some degree (Harvey, 2007). Evidence suggests that the complete withdrawal of state control in public utilities and housing can have a contradictory impact at the city level.

1.3 Research Approach

Even though social research is primarily descriptive or qualitative in nature, it plays an important role in reorienting housing research around the concept of dwelling units, where the preliminary method of accumulating information is counting. Various kinds of housing programs carried out in developing countries reveal a set of typical problems that require a qualitative approach, particularly during an understanding of the impacts of policies and economic conditions. Qualitative research is predominantly beneficial in comprehending important issues relevant to processes and connections. It also allows rediscovering facts between the program design and the complicated history of institutional evolution (Peattie, 1983). This research uses the 'case study approach'[1] to understand the housing systems under neoliberalism's influence and analyze, describe, and map the processes. The approaches allow us to understand social reality by focusing on evolving a negotiated view of social order and emphasizing the processes and meanings that are not measured rigorously. The methods help to identify the meaning, intent, and motivation of human actions (Dandekar, 2005).

One way of considering informational requirements requires to consider housing as a process. The other way of considering the informational requirements of the new approaches to housing is to consider the invisible structures that govern the resource flow into and out of housing and thus control how institutionalized groups and people utilize housing (Peattie, 1983). The methods are categorized in the milieu (Biswas, 2008). Section 1.4 uses methods to facilitate comprehension and interpretation through a 'thick description' of policy contents largely collated from five-year plans and census. Section 1.5 uses temporal data on housing performance indices to understand the neoliberalism process and its consequences on urban housing in India. It helps to identify the components and anatomies of systems. Section 1.6 synthesizes existing information and analyzes a specific case of Delhi-Ghaziabad to validate through empirical evidence.

The rationale or motivation underlying each approach, key characteristics, limitations, cost indicators, and their potential for application in planning and design are suggested, and some planners who utilize or subscribe to the specific method are identified. This research method illustrates how planners use various qualitative methods, drawn broadly from various fields within and outside the social sciences, and how these contribute to practice and theory to understand the relationship between physical outcomes and the economic functioning of cities and city regions.

1.4 Impacts of Neoliberalism on Urban Housing in India

The service sector offers more job opportunities in cities – these working-class agglomerate in certain parts of the city regions. The social, cultural, and behavioral properties determine the choice of housing locations, particularly for incoming migrants. Sassen (1991) finds that the financial sector's growth is geographically agglomerated in a few areas of a city. Its labor force concentrates in and around that region, creating an economic hierarchy of people with high incomes, competing for housing, and affecting the gentrification (Sassen, 1991). Cities, including the urban peripheries, have become important locations for public-private enterprises, business incubators, and new forms of local boosterism as the outcome of neoliberal policy. The land at the urban periphery and suburbs mobilizes space for development or redevelopment schemes for market-oriented output and supporting elite consumption activities (Brenner & Theodore, 2002). Few urban governments have taken note of the increasing difficulty with gentrification through new housing policies to ensure enough percentage of social housing among the total housing stock at neighborhood levels and negotiated constantly with the developers to integrate low-income housing in their projects (Pinson & Journel, 2016). However, the difficulty of integrating different social classes always remains as gated communities create physical and psychological barriers. It's like a city made of numerous townships with very few shared amenities. While neoliberalism promotes privatization and profits for private enterprises, the private enterprises' desire for more profit even out necessary commodities and services (Nelson, 2019). Rampant commercialization of essential commodities like housing and urban development may fetch more capital for the capitalist sectors but fails to safeguard the interests of urban commons. A city requires proper policy and regulations to mitigate the interests of urban commons in a neoliberal policy regime.

In neoliberalism, housing privatization and urban development continue to reduce public housing size, while the states lack fiscal resources and expertise to support the sector (Tsenkova & Polanska, 2014). Neoliberalism also shifts a government's housing policy approach from direct provisions to strengthening institutional capacity, allowing private enterprises to supply housing and delegating housing supply responsibility to local and state administration without much resource allocation. The ascent of neoliberalism is generally taking place against the erosion of the welfare state. A welfare state focuses on state support for the inseparable commodities of land and housing along with labor market restructuring. A secured land tenure ship facilitates capability enhancement with or without using the land as a commodity or resource (Mazer, 2019).

India abolished all titles while becoming a republic after independence and initiated land reforms to restructure land holdings prevalent with the erstwhile landlords. During the post-independence tenure, often called nation-building, the government had to explore the massive demand for housing with a specific focus on urban housing. The state had to intervene in the early phase, as there was no institutional mechanism or private investment in the urban housing sector. A centralized institution named the 'Planning Commission' was bestowed with the administrative and financial power to plan the country's development roadmap by efficient resource utilization. The Planning Commission published 'five-year plans' to envision the country's development roadmap, indicating its long-term strategies. A review of the five-year plan gives a better understanding of the country's evolution process (Government of India, 2014). A think tank named 'NITI Aayog' replaced the Planning Commission without financial allocation and policy implementation power in 2014. Along with other sectors, the five-year plans unveil urban housing policy and programs, financial allocations, distribution among different states, and working modules. The urban housing program primarily consists of housing schemes, legislative backup, and loan schemes. The chapter reviews all the five-year plans chronologically and categorizes all the relevant urban housing policies by the government of India.

India witnessed prolonged government control in the housing sector after its independence. The initial three five-year plans (1951–1956, 1956–1961, and 1961–1966) mostly focused on institutional capacity development and direct support for urban housing provision. These three plans also recognized the need for individual and cooperative housing. Accessibility to cheap land was a major constraint for urban housing, even during the early nation-building phase. India's fragmented monarch system of governance before the 200-year-long colonial rule created extremely lopsided land ownership among its citizens. Many Indian citizens were deprived of land even after the abolition of monarchic titles and becoming a republic. In the absence of a structured post-independence land policy, the polarization of land tenure is a persisting national distress. The much-needed land reform was elusive except in the state of Kerala, where the agricultural worker-tenant was granted land rights as part of this reform process (Rao, 2004). The fourth (1969–1974) and fifth (1974–1979) five-year plans continued the direct intervention by the state to provide urban housing. The government associated public sector support to urban housing provision among government employees, plantation laborers, Dock laborers, etc. Housing for industrial workers and public sector employees constituted the largest share of urban housing stock, which took care of migrated workers and public sector employees' housing woes (Tiwari & Rao, 2016).

Sibal (2012) notes that during the period between 1965 and 1981, regulatory restrictions in India increased with the regulation of domestic businesses by the 'Monopolies and Restrictive Trade Practices Act 1969', nationalization of the banking sector by the 'Banking Companies Act 1969', productivity control by the 'Industrial Licensing Acts 1970 and 1973', limiting foreign investment by the 'Foreign Exchange Regulation Act 1973, curb on land value increase, and promotion of low-income housing by the urban land socialization through the 'Urban Land (Ceiling and Regulation) Act 1976'

(Acharya, 1987; Sibal, 2012). 'Therefore, the 30-year period from 1950-51 to 1979-80 is better described as the "Indian-socialist" period' (Virmani, 2004). India was growing fast by the late 1980s. Still, it borrowed heavily from its future, amplifying its fiscal deficit and international debt beyond an untenable debt-service ratio (Basu & Maertens, 2007).

The first instance of liberalism in the Indian economy came along in the 1980s with the increasing internationalization of trade and services. It subsequently influenced the urban housing sector from the sixth five-year plan (1980–1985). The sixth (1980–1985), seventh (1985–1990), and eighth (1992–1997) five-year plans provided greater incentive and support to private housing even for the middle- and lower-income groups and institutionalized housing finance for the state housing boards and retail borrowers. The ninth (1997–2002) and tenth (2002–2007) five-year plans paved the way for a sweeping transformation of urban housing toward neoliberalism and privatization. During these periods, urban housing transformed from a 'basic need' or a commodity to a sector for trade, investment, and employment generator. The government also benefitted from increased direct and indirect tax revenue. The economic liberalization that removed government control over a wide range of industries and services and connected India with the wider globalized world came along in the year 1991. Following the economic liberalization, the government's focus on the eighth (1992–1997), ninth (1997–2002), tenth (2002–2007), and eleventh (2007–2012) five-year plans was restricted in creating an enabling environment through modification of the existing legal, regulatory, and financial regime. The government restricted its role as a direct housing provider and facilitated privates and cooperatives to play leading roles in providing urban housing. Direct housing provisions are transformed into various enabling strategies like subsidy, long-term credit, land allocation through leasehold or proprietorship mode, and cross-subsidization, which are linked with housing for economically weaker sections. The government also encouraged business opportunities in urban housing through crucial legislation like the 'Real Estate (Regulation and Development) Act 2016' and financial policies like liberal 100% foreign direct investment (FDI) for the integrated townships.

After reviewing the urban housing strategies from the five-year plans, the next section focuses on analyzing its performance during the gradual shift of policy from socialist principles to neoliberalism.

1.5 Performance of Urban Housing Policy from Socialist to Neoliberalism

To analyze India's performance in the urban housing sector over the past seven decades, the chapter considers five variables – decadal change in percentage of urbanization, percentage of net rural-urban migration, the urban homeless population as a percentage of the total urban population, slum population as a percentage of the total urban population, and plan outlay in urban housing as a percentage of GDP (Office of the Registrar General & Census Commissioner, India, 2001; Mohanty & Mohanty, 2005; Census of India, 2011; National Buildings Organisation, 2013; Sattar, 2014; Aijaz, 2017; Singh, 2019; Office of the Registrar General & Census Commissioner, India, 2020). Urban policy directly impacts urban homelessness and improvement from slum-like situations, while plan outlay in urban housing as a percentage of GDP shows whether the government focuses on the socialist or neoliberal approach to policymaking. The decadal change in the percentage of urbanization and net rural-urban migration substantiates a continuous growth of urbanization and steady population flow from rural to urban areas. A significant part of these migrants is low and semi-skilled labor (Table 1.1).

In the past five decades (1961–2011), the decadal change in the percentage of urbanization continue to reduce except in 1971–1981, whereas the net rural-urban migration continues to grow. It implies that rural-urban migration is influencing much of urban growth more than the natural growth process in India. During the same period, both the slum population and urban homeless people as a percentage of the total urban population remained almost the same. The urban population amplified from 44.2 million in 1941 to 377.1 million in 2011 during this period. Although the percentage of urban homeless and slum people in Indian cities remains similar, the massive increase in the urban population transmits into a considerable increment of urban homeless and slum people.

Interestingly, the plan outlay in urban housing as a percentage of GDP reduced gradually during this period, after its peak in 1971–1981. It is particularly alarming as much of the rural-urban migration occurs due to the movement of low-skilled and semi-skilled labor in the informal and semi-formal sectors. This phenomenon causies a significant housing challenge for Indian cities as the cities struggle with severe housing deficits for the vast number of migrants earning extremely low wages. The high land cost hinders adequate investment in housing for the economically weaker section. The high land price in urban areas is the primary reason for our inability to 'build our way out' of the current crisis, either by relaxing regulations or by extending tax incentives to private developers (Nelson, 2019) (Table 1.2).

After the abolition of the Planning Commission in 2014, India formally introduced a centralized and executive approach to public policymaking. Currently, the state's intervention in the housing market occurs through the 'Pradhan Mantri Awas Yojana' (The Prime Minister's Housing Scheme) aiming to provide housing for all by the year 2022. It follows four strategies – in-situ slum redevelopment, credit-linked subsidy scheme, affordable housing in partnership, and beneficiary-led individual house construction/enhancements. The strategies limit the government's role as an enabler of institutional, legal, and financial provisions rather than a direct housing provider. The government also encourages private enterprises to supply housing stocks by utilizing any of its four strategic functions. Currently, profits or gains arising from building affordable houses are exempted from tax. Additionally, self-occupied house owners can claim a tax deduction of up to INR 150,000

Table 1.1 Performance indices of urban housing in India

Census decade	*Decadal change in percentage of urbanization*	*Percentage of net rural-urban migration*	*Urban homeless population as percentage of total urban population*	*Slum population as percentage of total urban population*	*Plan outlay in urban housing as a percentage of GDP*
1961–1971	10.78	18.70	0.43	–	1.30
1971–1981	15.97	19.60	0.39	1.88	2.53
1981–1991	10.47	21.70	0.33	1.96	2.45
1991–2001	9.08	21.20	0.28	1.83	2.1
2001–2011	12.04	24.10	0.25	1.73	1.17

Table 1.2 Evolution of urban housing during the past seven decades in India

Census decade	*Decadal change in percentage of urbanization (%)*	*Percentage of net rural-urban migration (%)*	*Urban homeless population as percentage of total urban population (%)*	*Slum population as percentage of total urban population (%)*	*Plan outlay in urban housing as a percentage of GDP (%)*
1941–1951	24.60	–	–	–	–
1951–1961	3.96	–	0.25	–	2.30
1961–1971	10.78	18.70	0.43	–	1.30
1971–1981	15.97	19.60	0.39	1.88	2.53
1981-1991	10.47	21.70	0.33	1.96	2.45
1991–2001	9.08	21.20	0.28	1.83	2.1
2001–2011	12.04	24.10	0.25	1.73	1.17

(#USD 2000) on interest paid on loans. The tax exemption for both these schemes was valid till March 31, 2021 (Mishra, 2019). Housing for the affluent or even middle class is left to the market-driven demand-supply mechanism that takes care of the social obligation of housing and creates economic opportunities. The real estate and construction sector contribute significantly to revenue generation and employment creation in the economy.

In a significant urban housing financial restructuring, the central government reduced 69% of its budgetary support to state governments during 2018–2019 and 2020–2021. During the same period, the central government's financial support for the economically weaker section (EWS) and the middle-income group (MIG) experienced a 31% and 17% reduction, respectively (Mishra, 2019). The actual capital expenditure from the government allocation falls much short of the actual budgetary allocation of the urban housing scheme (Table 1.3). The matching grant emanates from the state, and the local governments substantiate the national government's funding

Table 1.3 Key components of Pradhan Mantri Awas Yojana (Prime Minister's Housing Scheme)

	2018–2019 actual	*2019–2020 RE***	*% change 2019–2020 RE**/2018–2019 actual*	*2020–2021 BE**	*% change 2020–2021 BE*/2019–2020 RE***	*% change 2020–21 BE*/2018–2019 actual*
Interest payment against loan raised through EBR	–	3,000	–	5,000	67%	–
Central assistance to states/UTs	4,192	2,681	-36%	1,301	-51%	-69%
CLSS-I for EWS/LIG	1,300	600	-54%	900	50%	-31%
CLSS-II for MIG	600	400	-33%	500	25%	-17%
Others	43	172	300%	299	74%	595%
Total	6,135	6,853	12%	8,000	17%	30%

*BE – budgetary estimate; **RE – revised estimate.

but fail to match the desired funding requirements. For rental housing provisions, the national government is also in the process of deriving a model tenancy law to promote rental housing, bring harmony to the landlord-tenant relationships, and balance the scale for both parties (Mishra, 2019).

The scarcity of marketable land parcels, rising costs of land and construction materials, and regulatory constraints are some of the factors that affect housing affordability in Indian cities (Gopalan & Venkataraman, 2015). The major obscurity of the government is to promote and support land cost rationalization in the new policy. As a result, the developers maximize profits by developing housing for the high-income group (HIG). In this kind of housing market, the government needs to intervene through legislative and financial instruments like cross-subsidy of land, flexible development rights, and tax benefits to the developers for a constant supply of affordable housing to EWS and MIG (Nelson, 2019). The increasing unaffordability of housing among all segments of society is validated by India's nominal house price index, which is growing at the fastest rate in the world (Palayi & Priyaranjan, 2018). Credit-financed consumption and investment contribute to keeping an elevated level of industrial demand. Credit serves as a stimulus to industrial demand (i.e., construction materials) using housing and real estate investment. Financial liberalization facilitates this sharp increase in the credit-financed housing industry (Chandrasekhar, 2010). The non-performing asset (NPA) ratios of public sector banks and housing finance companies have increased with the sharp rise in loan disbursements and the number of beneficiaries in the affordable housing segment. Housing loans up to INR 200,000 (USD 2,700) had the highest level of NPAs, ranging at 10.4% in 2016–2017 among all socio-economic categories (Palayi & Priyaranjan, 2018). The persisting level of NPAs shows some serious concern over the government's approach to supporting housing only as an enabler and no intervention in supply-side constraints (e.g., land supply and cost, cost and supply chain management of construction materials, housing price inflation, etc.). The neoliberal policy results in a unique pattern of urbanization and housing development, which differs from the traditional neighborhood and organic clusters (Biswas, 2021) of Indian cities.

1.6 Empirical Evidence from Housing Pattern Post Neoliberalism in India

'Spatial patterns are affected by various contextual attributes, which in turn reflect in shaping city's images and their social, cultural, and physical expression' (Seta, Biswas, Khare, & Sen, 2017). Many Indian cities planned to integrate urban infrastructure within the organic growth process. The brownfield urbanization pattern aims to regenerate urban areas with infrastructure infusion to sustain increasing population density and modernize infrastructure support systems. Chandigarh, planned as a greenfield city, is the most prominent Indian example of state-led urban development.

Chandigarh's neighborhood planning, housing strategy, and density accommodate the socio-economic diversity with proximity between serving and recipient Indian urban society (Banerjee, 2009). It showcases methods for integrating informality and social hierarchy into space planning, neighborhood planning, and housing design (Biswas, 2008, 2019). Government-aided housing continued to control India's urban development process. Although the government realized its limitation in supplying adequate housing to all citizens from the first five-year plan and invited private participation, the private sector's response to the housing market was limited to ownership and cooperative housing. Large-scale investment and corporate-aided real estate ventures in the housing market are a recent neoliberal phenomenon that started during the seventh five-year plan (1985–1990).

Housing, which constitutes approximately 50% of urban land use, immensely influences the urban growth pattern (MoUD, 2014; Ramachandran, 2017). The urban transformation over the past five decades reminiscences the changing pattern of growth and housing development. The neoliberal housing growth is reminiscent of what Florida (2018) refers to as urbanized knowledge capitalism instead of knowledge-based capitalism. In such cases, the erosion of urban cohesion between different service and economic classes creates social and spatial polarization, gentrification, inequality, slums, and ecological crises. An urban ecosystem finds it hard to sustain functional social networking, where teachers, nurses, hospital workers, police officers, firefighters, restaurants, and service workers can no longer afford to live reasonably by commuting to their workplaces (Florida, 2018). The neoliberal urban development process polarized the pattern of urbanization with bourgeoning numbers of gated communities and insulated townships. These insulated townships contain their own amenities like lawns, greenfields, jogging trails, swimming pools, gymnasiums, community centers, and grocery shops for their exclusive use. Thus, cities are developing as isolated islands of private housing colonies with limited public interaction between housing colonies or communities. Society became more individual and fragmented, which led to extremely low usage of public goods provisions (e.g., urban parks, plazas, footpaths, lakes, and riverfront) at the city level (Figure 1.1).

The chapter presents a case of Delhi, which developed very fast through the traditional greenfield development and densification of the urban core (Figure 1.2). Urban outgrowths such as Ghaziabad and Faridabad emerged organically after the independence and continued to grow and densify to support Delhi as the primate city. Noida and Gurugram were envisioned as self-sustained new towns bordering Delhi with mixed land use combining residential, commercial, institutional, public, semi-public, and industrial usages. These new towns were expected to support Delhi as a center for habitation, livelihood, commerce, and enterprise.

The state and the private enterprises acquired land (mostly erstwhile agricultural land) and developed the land with the access road before auctioning

Figure 1.1 Gated townships as seen in Rajnagar extension near Ghaziabad.
Image credit: Author.

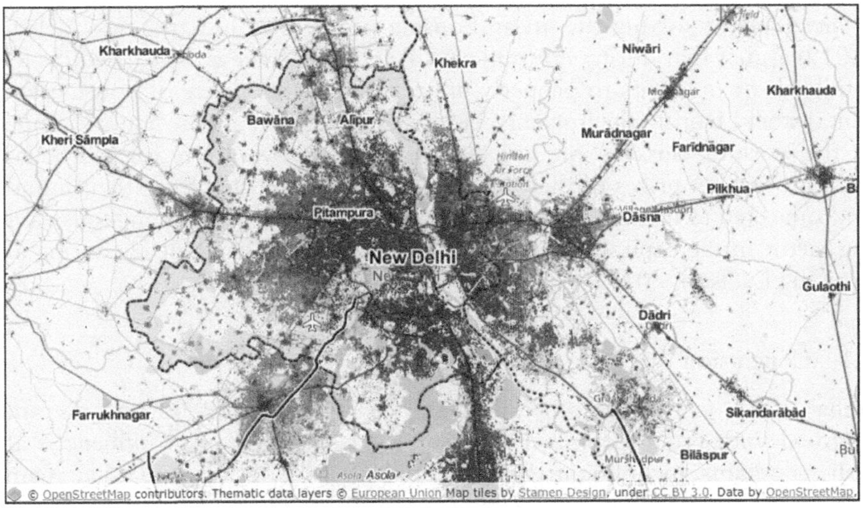

Figure 1.2 Delhi's urban agglomeration and the surrounding towns as developed over the past Reproduced from the original publisher, licensed by Creative Common 3.0. map originally produced by Stamen Design.

it among the developers for a leasehold user right. Some of the townships are so big that they contain thousands of apartments, reflecting small towns with a population of 5,000 or more. After 1990, many new towns developed near Delhi along the high-speed transit corridors. Unlike Noida and Gurugram, these new towns (e.g., Greater Noida, Rajnagar extension, and Sonipat) serve as the dormitory/satellite town to Delhi and Noida (Figure 1.2). These dormitory towns follow similar private enterprise-led development patterns like Noida and Gurugram. Being a dormitory town, residential land use with few city-level infrastructures like schools, shopping arcades, and clinics dominate its land use. People who cannot afford the high apartment or rental costs of

Noida and Gurugram choose to locate in the dormitory towns and commute daily by private car for livelihood and other amenities. The massive scale of real estate is quickly transforming the landscape and emancipating large-scale gentrification of the local communities. Although the housing supply to the middle-income and higher-income categories is relentless, a large percentage of the housing remains unsold. In 2019, the collective unsold housing stock in Noida, Greater Noida, and Ghaziabad was 27% (Haidar, 2019).

Even though housing stock for the affluent class remains unsold, rationalizing housing prices or improving the supply of housing stock to economically weaker sections remains elusive. The reason for such high housing prices is due to the excessive land and development costs, which do not incentivize private enterprises to reduce housing unit prices. The state's reluctance to intervene comprehensively in land price subsidization in the extensively privatized housing market has created a housing enigma that is incapable of solving the urban housing problem of Indian cities. Nelson (2019) argues that during housing prices' collapse, there is little incentive for landlords or investors to properly upkeep and maintenance of housing and rental stock. During the housing price rise in the urban areas, bank accounts of the working-class people are squeezed as they owe more for mortgages than the market prices of their homes. They are displaced from their homes and subjected to intense policing. The profit motive is a dominant constraining factor in the capitalist society's ability to meet housing needs during an upswing (Nelson, 2019).

1.7 Conclusion

India's path toward neoliberalism started with the 1980s reforms and matured with the sweeping reforms in 1991. Neoliberalism influenced all policy domains, including urban development and housing. India, like many developing countries, adopted neoliberal ideology and privatization to automate urbanization and economic prosperity, aiming to improve its citizens' standard of living. However, the simple consequence followed and benefitted the USA, much of Europe, Japan, Korea, and China, which did not transmit enough benefit to India. It is puzzling yet prominent that innovative and thoughtful policymaking is needed to derive an impressive development trajectory rather than blindly following the path of rapacious capitalism.

The chapter shows that irrespective of the combined effort by the government to raise private investment and public-private collaboration, the percentage of urban homeless and slums remained unchanged over the past seven decades. India needs massive investment in urban infrastructure and housing, and as Krugman (2014) argues, the government can borrow incredibly cheaply to build urban infrastructure and housing; what has happened is the reverse (Krugman, 2014). Public investment in housing has been reduced with the adaptation of neoliberalism, which also transforms the national government's housing policy from direct provisions to strengthening institutional capacity, allowing private sectors for housing supply and delegating authority to local and state administration without much resource allocation. Local governments, too, are forced to slash property taxes despite heavily relying on them to fund social services (Nelson, 2019). Financial deregulation is also transforming housing into a financial asset, affecting housing booms and busts in cities (Storper, 2016). The trend of private sector investment in housing for the EWS dwindles in the absence of direct government spending. Housing oversupply to HIG and the affluent class continues to hover in the urban housing market largely due to the extreme clustering of economic activity in very limited parts of cities and fierce competition over them. This competition, in turn, shapes a related economic consequence (Florida, 2018). Nelson (2019) believes governments may conveniently eliminate the middleman and construct or finance affordable urban infrastructure and housing for anyone (Nelson, 2019).

India's approach to urban housing strategies combined with direct support in the initial phase after the independence to facilitate housing affordability through incentivizing private enterprises. The traditional social housing policies prevalent in Europe and western countries are less applied in India. Nelson (2019) argues that

> this kind of publicly built and publicly run 'social housing' is far superior to the privately owned and publicly subsidized 'affordable housing'. He concludes that subsidized housing is also confronted by the pressures of the profit motive. These developments will be less likely to undergo proper maintenance, and if the underlying land continues to rise in value, there will be pressure to convert those units to market-rate rent or sell them off as condominiums.
>
> (Nelson, 2019)

Reducing infrastructure costs to facilitate cheaper housing for all economic classes is an ideal investment. On the contrary, the Indian approach to urban infrastructure with an expensive strategy like the smart city program creates more dysfunction and puzzle about the strategic decision-making of the government. One may argue about the relevance and need for such an expensive program, which benefits venture capitalists and consultants (middlemen) in the short term more than the immediate needs of the city. The overreaching goal of expanding basic urban infrastructure and augmenting private investment has not been achieved at all (Seta, Sen, Biswas, & Khare, 2017). A cohesive amalgamation between the neoliberal principles and people's benefit is urgently needed in India, instead of following the traditional footsteps of capitalism. The research provides an understanding of neoliberalism's impact on the Indian urban housing sector. However, it needs more empirical analysis to substantiate the finding. In the future, researchers may emphasize empirical analysis from different categories of cities to create robust evidence and support appropriate urban policymaking.

Note

1 A case study method focuses on business systems to explain why certain systems are successful and why some end up as a failure. It reveals the concepts of efficiency.

References

Acharya, B. P. (1987). The Indian urban land ceiling act: A critique of the 1976 legislation. *Habitat International, 11*(3), 39–51.

Adduci, M. (2012). Neoliberalism and class reproduction in India: The political economy of privatisation in the mineral sector in the Indian State of Orissa. *Forum for Social Economics, 41*(1), 68–96.

Aijaz, R. (2017, December). Measuring urbanisation in India. *Observer Research Foundation, Brief no. 218*, pp. 1–14.

Banerjee, T. (2009). US planning expeditions to postcolonial India: From ideology to innovation in technical assistance. *Journal of the American Planning Association, 75*(2), 193–208.

Basu, K., & Maertens, A. (2007). The pattern and causes of economic growth in India. *Oxford Review of Economic Policy, 23*(2), 143–167.

Bhagwati, J., & Desai, P. (1970). *India: Planning for industrialization.* Oxford University Press.

Biswas, A. (2008). Research techniques in housing. *Journal of 'The Indian Institute of Architects'.*

Biswas, A. (2019). Why Indian cities are so chaotic? Decoding from the urban development efforts of Chandigarh. *Smart and Sustainable Built Environment, 8*(5), 438–456.

Biswas, A. (2021). Continuity in tradition – A narrative on the cultural heritage of Para and Adda in Kolkata. *Urban Design and Planning, 174*(4), 145–156.

Brenner, N., & Theodore, N. (2002). Cities and the geographies of "actually existing neoliberalism". In N. Brenner & N. Theodore (Eds.), *The urbanization of neoliberalism: Theoretical debates* (pp. 349–379). Blackwell Publisher.

Census of India. (2011). *Provisional polupation totals.* New Delhi: Office of Registerar General and Census Commissioner, India.

Chandrasekhar, C. P. (2010). From dirgisme to neoliberalism: Aspects of the political economy of the transition in India. *Development and Society, 39*(1), 29–59.

Dandekar, H. C. (2005). Qualitative methods in planning research and practice. *Journal of Architectural and Planning Research, 22*(2), 129–137.

Das, R. J. (2015). Critical observations on neo-liberalism and India's new economic policy. *Journal of Contemporary Asia, 45*(4), 715–726.

Desai, A. V. (1999). The economics and politics of transition to an open market economy: India. *Working Paper, 155*, 1–73..

Florida, R. (2018). *The new urban crisis: Gentrification, housing bubbles, growing inequality, and what we can do about it.* Oneworld Publications.

Gopalan, K., & Venkataraman, M. (2015). Affordable housing: Policy and practice in India. *IIMB Management Review, 27*, 129–140.

Gordon, J., & Gupta, P. (2003). Understanding India's services revolution. In *A tale of two giants: India's and China's experience with reform* (pp. 1–34). IMF-NCAER Conference.

Government of India. (2014). *Five year plans.* Government of India.

Haidar, F. (2019, November 4). Unsold housing inventory reduces by 27% in Noida, greater Noida, Ghaziabad: Report. *Economic Times.* India.

Hariharan, A. N., & Biswas, A. (2019). A critical review of knowledge-based industry location policy against its theoretical arguments. *Regional Science Policy and Practice*. https://doi.org/10.1111/rsp3.12257

Harvey, D. (2007). Neoliberalism as creative destruction. *The Annals of the American Academy of Political and Social Science, 610*, 22–44.

Krugman, P. (2014, October 26). Ideology and investment. *Opinion – Ideology and Investment*.

Mazer, K. (2019). Making the welfare state work for extraction: Poverty policy as the regulation of labor and land. *Annals of the American Association of Geographers, 109*(1), 18–34.

Mishra, P. (2019, July 9). Retrieved March 6, 2020, from prsindia.org: https://prsindia.org/parliamenttrack/budgets/demand-grants-2020-21-analysis-housing-and-urban-affairs

Mohanty, L. N., & Mohanty, S. (2005). *Slum in India*. S.P. Nangia, A.P.H. Publishing Corporation.

MoUD. (2014). *URDPFI guidelines - Volume I*. Government of India.

National Buildings Organisation. (2013). *Sate of slums in India: A statistical compendium*. Ministry of Housing and Urban Poverty Alleviation, Government of India.

Nelson, R. (2019). *Capitalism can't give us affordable housing*. Retrieved December 21, 2019, from https://jacobinmag.com/2018/11/capitalism-affordable-housing-rent-commodities-profit

Office of the Registrar General & Census Commissioner, India. (2001). *eCENSUSIndia: Issue number 3: 2001*. Retrieved March 5, 2020, from http://censusindia.gov.in/Census_Data_2001/Census_Newsletters/Newsletter_Links/eci_3.htm

Office of the Registrar General & Census Commissioner, India. (2020, March 3). *Population enumeration data (Final Population)*. Retrieved March 5, 2020, from http://censusindia.gov.in/2011-Documents/slum_data_census_2011.xls

Palayi, A., & Priyaranjan, N. (2018). *Affordable housing in India*. RBI Bulletin. Reserve Bank of India.

Panagariya, A. (2004). India in the 1980s and 1990s: A triumph of reforms. *IMF Working Paper, 4*(43), 1–37.

Patnaik, U. (2007). Neoliberalism and rural poverty in India. *Economic and Political Weekly, 42*(30), 3132–3150.

Peattie, L. (1983). Realistic planning and qualitative research. *Habitat International, 7*(5/6), 227–234.

Pinson, G., & Journel, C. M. (2016). The neoliberal city – Theory, evidence, debates. *Territory, Politics, Governance, 4*(2), 137–153.

Ramachandran, H. (2017). Intensity of use of land in urban residential areas. *ISID working Paper, 199*, 1–13.

Rao, P. (2004). *Transformation of housing policy in India – The trend towards market mechanisms*. Retrieved February 27, 2020, from https://www.housingauthority.gov.hk/hdw/ihc/pdf/rhk.pdf

Sangma, C. (2006). *Housing in urban India*. Welsh School of Architecture.

Sassen, S. (1991). *The global city: New York, London, Tokyo*. Princeton University Press.

Sattar, S. (2014). Homelessness in India. *Shelter, 15*(1), 9–15.

Seta, F., Biswas, A., Khare, A., & Sen, J. (Eds.). (2017). *Understanding built environment*. Springer.

Sibal, R. (2012). *India: The next superpower?: The untold story of India's economy*. IDEAS reports – special reports. London School of Economics.

Singh, A. K. (2019). India's urban development policy: Retrospect and prospect. In *City, space and politics in global south* (pp. 341–368). Manohar Publishers and Distributors.

Singh, C., Kumar, L., & Prasad, H. (2014). *Housing market in India*. IMF Presentation.
Storper, M. (2016). The neo-liberal city as idea and reality. *Territory, Politics, Governance, 4*(2), 241–263.
Tiwari, P., & Rao, J. (2016). *Housing markets and housing policies in India*. ADBI Working Paper Series. Asian Development Bank Institute.
Tsenkova, S., & Polanska, D. V. (2014). Between state and market: Housing policy and housing transformation in post-socialist cities. *GeoJournal, 79*, 401–405.
Virmani, A. (1997). Economic development and transition: India. *Tokyo Dialogue on Alternatives to the World Bank-IMF*. IMF.
Virmani, A. (2004). India's economic growth: From socialist rate of growth to Bharatiya rate of growth. *Working Paper, 122*.
Walker, K. L. (2008). Neoliberalism on the ground in rural India: Predatory growth, Agrarian crisis, internal colonization, and the intensification of class struggle. *The Journal of Peasant Studies, 35*(4), 557–620.

2 The Neoliberal Shift of Urban Planning in Asian Megacities

Gentrification and Spatial Inequalities in Tokyo and Mumbai

Tetsuo Kidokoro

2.1 Neoliberal Shift of Urban Planning

Spatial inequality is one of the major issues in Asian cities. This chapter examines the impacts of gentrification under neoliberal urban policy regimes and the resultant spatial inequality in Tokyo and Mumbai. Gentrification and resultant spatial inequality have been brought about on a massive scale by neoliberal urban development policies in Asian cities (Shatkin, 2007; Hyun, Lees, & Lopez-Morales, 2016; ; Kidokoro et al., 2021; Kidokoro et al., 2022). In both Tokyo and Mumbai, urban planning systems are transforming toward a market-friendly zoning system under neoliberal urban development policies. While Tokyo has followed a market-friendly zoning system under the new Urban Planning Law 1968, urban planning regulations have been relaxed to a large extent and various FAR bonus systems have been introduced during the past two decades. Various measures to promote large-scale urban regeneration projects have also been introduced. Mumbai follows the planning permission system and the restriction on urban development hitherto had been rather strict. Yet, since economic liberalization in 1991, various relaxation measures of urban planning regulations have been introduced, including the FAR bonus scheme for redevelopment projects, promotion of the development of former mill sites, transferable development rights (TDR) system, etc.

The key idea of the urban development policies of Tokyo was welfare oriented-decentralization policy before 2000. Yet, the Tokyo Metropolitan Government (TMG) changed urban development policies drastically to neoliberal, growth-oriented re-centralization policies after 2000. The National Government of Japan also enacted the Urban Renaissance Special Act (URSA), 2002, to facilitate large-scale urban regeneration projects in Tokyo and other major cities in Japan. Under URSA, the real estate developers can propose a broad range of relaxations of urban planning regulations including massive relaxation of FAR regulation in exchange for public contributions such as open space, public infrastructure, etc. (Figure 2.1). In Mumbai, under the Mumbai Metropolitan Regional Plan 1995, the decentralization policy was changed to a re-centralization policy to enhance the status of Mumbai as a global city (Pacione, 2006; Vedula, 2007).

DOI: 10.4324/9781003280866-2

Tokyo Mumbai

Figure 2.1 Urban redevelopment under the deregulation of urban planning in Tokyo and Mumbai

(*Image credit:* author).

The role of real estate developers has been significant both in Tokyo and Mumbai under the abovementioned neoliberal shift of urban planning. In Japan and India, a close relationship between the government and private sectors was created under the development state regime (Shatkin, 2007). The formation of a hybrid developmental state neoliberalism has worked as a basis for the recent massive urban transformation and resultant spatial inequality in both Tokyo and Mumbai (Figure 2.1). We observe the same situations in other Asian megacities.

2.2 Urbanization Process and Spatial Inequality

Besides suburban real estate projects targeting the wealthy and upper-middle-class people developed as gated communities, massive gentrification projects in existing built-up areas have been implemented under the abovementioned neoliberal shift of urban planning in many Asian megacities. Table 2.1 shows the trends in the construction of high-rise building with over 100 m in selected Asian cities. Although there are some differences between cities, a growing number of high-rise condominiums/apartments have been constructed, particularly since the 2000s in Asian megacities. These high-rise residences generally target the new middle. It may be inferred that gentrification is rapidly progressing in Asian megacities.

As a result, while luxury gated communities in suburban areas and massive, high-quality gentrification projects are in progress, a large extent of low-standard self-shaped urban areas (SUAs)[1] often resided by lower-income people remain in Asian megacities. This process has deepened the spatial disparity between planned urban areas (PUAs) and self-shaped urban areas (SUAs) in Asian cities.

In case of Tokyo, the population in the city decreased drastically during the bubble economy period in the latter half of the 1980s, while population of the city center has grown significantly after the latter half of the

Table 2.1 Newly built buildings with the height of over 100 m height in selected Asian megacities (numbers in the past four decades)

	Type	*1980–1989*	*1990–1999*	*2000–2009*	*2010–2019*	*Total*
Tokyo	Residential	4	10	74	32	120
	Office/Hotel/Others	14	43	66	43	166
	Mixed-use	0	4	25	19	48
	Total	18	57	165	94	334
Seoul	Residential	0	1	37	24	62
	Office/Hotel/Others	5	15	14	14	48
	Mixed-use	0	0	10	7	17
	Total	5	16	61	45	127
Shanghai	Residential	0	2	18	8	28
	Office/Hotel/Others	4	45	47	66	162
	Mixed-use	0	5	16	12	33
	Total	4	52	81	86	223
Bangkok	Residential	0	4	14	54	72
	Office/Hotel/Others	2	16	13	14	45
	Mixed-use	0	3	1	6	10
	Total	2	23	28	74	127
Jakarta	Residential	0	10	23	35	68
	Office/Hotel/Others	4	20	19	36	79
	Mixed-use	0	2	3	6	11
	Total	4	32	45	77	158
Mumbai	Residential	0	0	22	48	70
	Office/Hotel/Others	1	0	2	6	9
	Mixed-use	0	0	1	2	3
	Total	1	0	25	56	82

Source: Compiled based on the data collected from the website of the Council on Tall Buildings and Urban Habitat: https://www.skyscrapercenter.com/buildings (accessed on December 2, 2020).

1990s. Large corporations and developers grabbed land for speculation in the city center areas, and original residents in SUAs moved out voluntarily or involuntarily during the bubble economy period. After the latter half of 1990s, the urban redevelopment projects massively occurred in city center areas targeting the higher income class. This process can be regarded as a typical gentrification process, i.e., the replacement of original residents by higher-income people.

On the other hand, in Mumbai, the impacts of the re-centralization policy are not so clear, unlike Tokyo. Certainly, the decreasing population trends in the city center during the decentralization period before liberalization in 1992 stopped under the re-centralization policy and subsequent relaxation of urban planning regulations. Yet, the population of the suburbs is still increasing at high rates at the same time (see Figures 2.2–2.4). It can be said that gentrification and suburbanization processes are ongoing at the same time unlike Tokyo.

Next, I shall examine the spatial inequality in Tokyo and Mumbai. In Tokyo, the city center areas have been largely reconstructed by applying the planning principles of the West as planned urban areas (PUAs) through the reconstruction after the Great Kanto Earthquake in 1923 and the reconstruction of bombed areas during World War II. On the other hand, SUAs are widely spread in the 5–15 km range, namely *Misshu Shigaichi* (literally high-density built-up areas). *Misshu Shigaichi* were formed after the Great Kanto Earthquake in 1923 and the post-WW II period in an unplanned manner. These areas are characterized by narrow roads/alleys with less than 4 m width and dense two-story old wooden-made houses (Figure 2.3). TMG evaluated the level of earthquake vulnerability of neighborhoods[2] in the Tokyo Metropolitan Area (TMA) from 1 (low) to 5 (high), based on the possibility of collapse by earthquakes as well as the possibility of the spread of fire (Report of the Eighth Earthquake Risk Assessment Study in 2018). Indices used in this evaluation reflect the actual conditions of *Misshu Shigaichi*

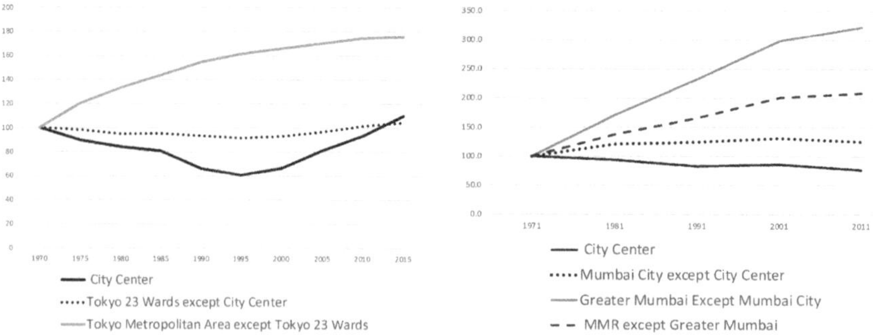

Figure 2.2 Population trends of Tokyo and Mumbai

(*Source:* National Census of Japan and the Census of India).

SUA in Tokyo

SUA in Mumbai

Vibrant Shopping Street in SUAs in Tokyo

Vibrant Shopping Street in SUAs in Mumbai

Figure 2.3 Scenes in SUAs in Tokyo and Mumbai
(*Image credit:* Author).

Tokyo Metropolitan Area

1 City center; 2 Tokyo 23 Wards; 3 Tokyo Metropolitan Region (TMR)

Tokyo 23 Wards Area

1 City center; 2 Western adjoining areas of the city center; 3 Southern inner city; 4 Western inner city; 5 South-western suburb; 6 Eastern adjoining areas of the city center; 7 North-eastern suburb

Figure 2.4 Area classification of Tokyo
(*Source:* Depicted by author).

(narrow roads/alleys, insufficient access to major roads, concentration of old wooden houses). Areas with a rank of more than three generally correspond to *Misshu Shigaichi* areas (Table 2.2).

As shown in Table 2.3, more than 50% of the population is living in SUAs in inner-city areas (refer to Figure 2.4 for the location). The percentage of low-income people is more than 50% in these inner-city areas of SUAs, which is significantly higher than the city center in its vicinity. Notably, almost one-fourth of the population living in these areas is vulnerable to multiple physical and socio-economic threats. The percentages of households living in high-rise residences and their continuous growth are observed in these areas. This reflects the fact that high-rise condominiums-led gentrification is in progress in the central areas of Tokyo.

In the case of Mumbai, when the slum areas noted by the State cover a wide variety of SUAs (Figure 2.5). The inequality of basic infrastructure is

Table 2.2 Distribution of household income and the population living in SUAs in Tokyo (2018)

Area		*Share of Household Income Class (%)*a*			*Percentage of population living in SUAs (%)*b*
		Lower (less than 4 million JPY annually)	*Middle (4--10 million JPY annually)*	*Higher (over 10 million annually)*	
Center	City Center	33.8	42.3	24.0	6.5
West	Western adjoining areas of the city center	45.5	39.3	15.2	32.2
	Southern inner city	43.4	44.1	12.4	44.3
	Western inner city	50.1	38.8	11.1	59.3
	South-western suburb	41.6	40.6	17.8	24.3
East	Eastern adjoining areas of the city center	43.9	43.4	12.7	25.7
	Eastern inner city	50.0	42.6	7.4	52.6
	Northeastern suburb	50.7	39.6	9.7	21.4

Note: Median of annual HH income in 2018 was 4.23 million JPY. Less than 4 million means the income bracket of lower than approximately 50% of the total households. The percentage of households with over 10 million JPY annual HH income was 12.2% in 2018. *Source*: (a) Housing and Land Survey 2018 (Ministry of Internal Affairs and Communications), (b) The Report of the Eighth Earthquake Risk Assessment Study 2018 (TMG).

Table 2.3 Slum (SUAs) population in Mumbai

Area	*Percentage of slum population (%)*		*Increasing rate of slum population (%)*	*Raito of slum pop. of each area/ total slum pop. (%)*
	2001	*2011*	*2001–2011*	*2011*
City center	12.3	15.5	11.2	3.6
Adjoining areas of the city center	47.1	36.0	-27.2	12.9
Western suburb	57.0	35.5	-37.5	16.6
Eastern suburb	74.4	51.9	-23.8	38.2
Northern suburb	58.8	48.3	7.6	28.7

Source: Calculated from the data of Yadav & Bhagat (2017).

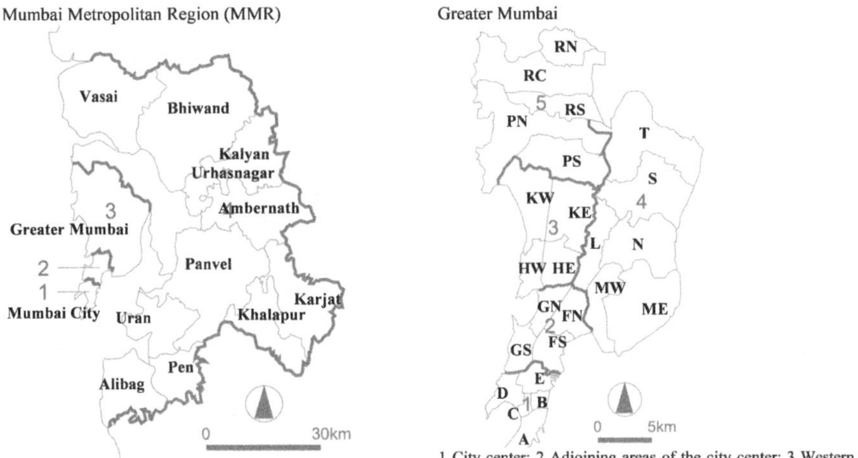

1 City center; 2: Mumbai City; 3 Greater Mumbai; 4 Mumbai Metropolitan Region (MMR)

1 City center; 2 Adjoining areas of the city center: 3 Western suburb; 4 Eastern suburb; 5 Northern suburb

Figure 2.5 Area classification of Mumbai

(*Source:* Depicted by author).

quite large between SUAs and PUAs. Yadav and Bhagat (2017) reported that the average percentage of households with latrines in slum areas was quite low (31%) in Mumbai in 2011 (Yadav & Bhagat, 2017).

SUAs and PUAs coexist like patchwork in Mumbai. Looking at the rate of slum dwellers to the whole population in each area, SUAs spread widely in the central and suburban areas. There is a growing number of high-rise residences not only in the central areas but also in suburban areas. In suburban areas, too, private gated community developments composed of luxury condominiums address the demand from wealthy people. The population living in SUAs decreased largely in the areas nearby the city center between 2000 and 2011 (Table 2.3). Yadav and Bhagat (2017) point out the impacts of infrastructure development as well as slum redevelopment as the backdrop of this reduction of slum population in the central areas. The Slum Rehabilitation Scheme (SRS) 1995 has promoted real estate developers to redevelop slum areas with FAR bonuses under the conditions that they provide relocation housing (SRH).[3] Yet, many scholars criticize SRH for its low standards and its inadequacy in improving housing conditions of slum dwellers because of low standards: e.g., narrow unit sizes, the narrow interval between buildings, the loss of social/workspace, etc. (Bardhan et al., 2015; Nijman, 2008; Debnatha et al., 2019).

2.3 Discussion and Conclusion

The coexistence of and conflicts between SUAs and PUAs characterize the urban expansion in Asian megacities. In Asian cities, the neoliberalism shift in urban planning has progressed during the past two decades. As discussed in Section 2.1, in both Tokyo and Mumbai, I observed the clear shift of the planning system to a more market-friendly system following the market-oriented neoliberalism doctrine. Along with the formation of hybrid development and state-neoliberalism regimes, FAR bonus schemes have been introduced to promote state and property-led urban regeneration projects both in Tokyo and Mumbai. Against this background, large-scale gentrification projects (luxury high-rise condominiums/apartments) have increasingly been implemented in the existing SUAs, supported by global city policies to enhance the global status of cities. Massive gentrification in SUAs is, therefore, rapidly occurring in both cities. As a result of gentrification amidst SUAs, the social and physical disparity is widening between PUAs (gentrification areas) and surrounding SUAs. In other words, the spatial inequality is deepening at the macro-scale between gentrification projects and surrounding SUAs.

Importantly, the actual process of urban development and the situations of spatial inequality vary significantly in Tokyo and Mumbai. As a post-suburbanization city, Tokyo's current urbanization process is characterized by the concentration of wealth and wealthy people in the city center areas through gentrification. On the other hand, in Mumbai, both suburbanization and re-centralization are ongoing simultaneously through gentrification: i.e., high-rise suburban developments and high-rise gentrification developments. It may also be noted that reflecting its characteristics as a central city of an emerging economy, the level of spatial inequality is much higher in Mumbai compared to Tokyo.

It is also noted that the situation in Indian megacities varies to a significant extent. In Delhi metropolitan areas, the redevelopment in city center areas is rather restricted due to strict planning regulations, yet the development in the peripheral areas such as Gurugram is massively in progress by private real estate developers under market-oriented planning policies (Figure 2.5).

Emergence of new CBDs in the outskirt of Delhi metropolitan areas (Gurugram)	Micro scale spatial inequality between gated community and surrounding areas in the suburban areas (Bengaluru)

Figure 2.6 Gentrification in the outskirts of megacities in India (Image credit:Author).

In emerging megacities such as Bengaluru, redevelopment demand in the city center areas is still not high because of the existence of abundant green fields in suburban areas. In these megacities, gentrification and spatial inequality emerge in the outskirts of metropolitan areas are ongoing on a massive scale, i.e., the clear contrast between the emergence of gated communities composed of luxury high-rise condominiums/offices and the concentration of low-income unskilled laborers in rental apartments in original villages (Figure 2.6).

As discussed in this chapter, the conflicts between SUAs and PUAs have been aggravated by the neoliberal shift in urban development policies both in Tokyo and Mumbai. Similar situations are observed in other Asian cities too. Although there is naturally no one-size-fits-all solution, there is an urgent need for a paradigm shift from the current neoliberal-oriented urban planning regime to a more inclusive one.

Notes

1 Self-shaped urban areas (SUAs) are defined as the areas shaped through individual, small-scale development attempts in an unplanned manner, while planned urban areas (PUAs) are defined as the urban areas developed in a planned way based on city master plans/zoning.
2 It is called Chou in Japanese. Chou typically covers an area of around 100–400 ha.
3 According to Bardan et al. (2015), more than 240,000 SRH units were constructed during the initial ten years.

References

Bardhan, R., Sarkar, S., Jana, A., & Velaga, A. R. (2015). Mumbai slums since independence: Evaluating the policy outcomes. *Habitat International, 50,* 1–11-.

Debnatha, R., Bardhan, R., & Sunikka-Blanka, M. (2019). Discomfort and distress in slum rehabilitation: Investigating a rebound phenomenon using a backcasting approach. *Habitat International, 87,* 75–90.
Hyun, B. S., Lees, L., & Lopez-Morales, E. (2016). Introduction: Locating gentrification in the Global East. *Urban Studies*, *53*(3), 455–470.
Kidokoro, T., Matsuyuki, M., & Shima, N. (2022). Neoliberalization of urban planning and spatial inequalities in Asian megacities: Focus on Tokyo, Bangkok, Jakarta and Mumbai. *Cities*, *130*, 103914.
Kidokoro, T., Hsiao, H., & Fukuda, R. (2021). Study on the polarization to megacity regions and the urban divide: Focusing on the case of Nishinari Ward, Osaka City, Japan. *Japan Architectural Review*, 4(1), 117–126-.
Nijman, J. (2008). Against the odds: Slum rehabilitation in neoliberal Mumbai. *Cities, 25,* 73–85.
Pacione, M. (2006). City profile Mumbai. *Cities*, *23*(3), 229–238..
Shatkin, G. (2007). Global cities of the South: Emerging perspectives on growth and inequality. *Cities, 24*,(1), 1–15.
Vedula, A. (2007). Blueprint and reality: Navi Mumbai, the city of the 21st century. *Habitat International, 31,* 12–23.
Yadav, V., & Bhagat, R. B. (2017). Changes in slum population and living conditions of slum dwellers in Mumbai. *Mumbai Reader.*

3 Threatening Urban Resilience during Neoliberal Urban Development

Gated Communities and Fragmentation of Urban Green Space

Nikita Ranjan and Ankita Sood

3.1 Introduction

The global rise in urban population and the discourse on sustainability have brought the concept of urban resilience into the foreground. Changing demographic patterns and the complex effects of climate change have pushed urban systems to adapt rapidly, thus making urban resilience one of the most influential precepts in contemporary urban planning and development (Leitner, Sheppard, Webber, & Colven, 2018; Meerow & Newell, 2016). The theory and concept of resilience are rife with multi-faceted analysis and critique, often intertwining with the subjects of disaster risk reduction, climate change adaptation, and sustainability. In a broad sense, urban resilience can be understood as

> the ability of urban systems (including its constituent socio-ecological and socio-technical networks) to maintain or rapidly return to desired functions in the face of a disturbance, to adapt to change, and quickly transform systems that limit current or future adaptive capacity.
>
> (Meerow & Newell, 2016)

This notion of contemporary resilience aligns with the neoliberal urbanism whose ideology 'prioritizes economic growth and advocates relaxation of regulatory frameworks, withdrawal of state intervention, and privatization of social resources to remove controls from the free market' (Vives-Miró, 2011). This concept of resilience emphasizes on change and adaptation to the prevailing shocks and stresses, thus promoting the ecological traits of 'growth, competition, and self-organization' in the urban systems. This concurs with the neoliberal ideology of becoming adaptive and entrepreneurial to seek opportunities for growth (Derickson, 2016). However, this method of resilience-thinking suffers from a critical gap. It places the source of the disturbance outside the control of the subjects of the system. While in cases with socio-spatial inequalities, many of the stresses on the system occur from within the system itself. It's not only the external pressures like climate change but also elements of the urban systems like socio-economic inequalities and exclusionary urban development that put people under stress. This resilience

DOI: 10.4324/9781003280866-3

ideology also focuses on economic growth, which is supposed to propel resilience-building and self-regulation by resilient subjects of the system. Thus, forgoing the inclination to cater to the issues of socio-spatial inequalities to alter the stresses through political action (Derickson, 2016; Leitner et al., 2018; Reid, 2013; Tierney, 2015).

With the influence of neoliberal development agendas, the present-day resilience programs often focus primarily on innovation and mainstreaming through the physical/ecological infrastructure (Gould & Lewis, 2018). Such resilience initiatives have complex effects on the urban fabric, often limiting the access of ecological infrastructure and resources to the elite and pushing the already vulnerable population further under stress (Anguelovski et al., 2016). These resilience-building schemes often lack the forethought for ensuring the inclusion of the needs of different socio-economic groups. One such component of resilience-building is the development of urban green spaces. With neoliberal reforms in urban development, the way urban green spaces and related amenities are developed and distributed in Indian cities has transformed. As private capital is invested into urban development, more and more public open and green spaces are replaced by gated/enclaved green spaces. This phenomenon is changing who can access and benefit from these green spaces, thus changing the resiliency of urban residents in complex ways. It is apparent that contemporary resilience planning requires greater thought and consideration of the aspects of social injustice and systemic inequalities often devised by the conflicting objectives of the neoliberal development agenda (Leitner, Sheppard, Webber, & Colven, 2018; Wilson & Jonas, 2018; Ziervogel et al., 2017).

3.1.1 Background

3.1.1.1 Privatized Urbanization and Its Impact on the Development of Green Spaces in India

A rapid urban population increase has followed India's economic reforms. The transformation of the country's economy from rural (agriculture-based) to urban (non-agricultural sectors) has been a key characteristic of the development process. Thus, after the mid-1980s, the development of urban centers became a focus area for supporting economic growth in India (Sharma & Shaban, 2006; Tripathi, 2018). After the neoliberal economic reforms of 1991, the policy and legislative initiatives propelled the phenomenon of privatized urbanization in Indian cities. While enabling the development of gated communities in the form of luxury housing complexes, townships, and privately funded greening projects, this process also contributed to eviction, expropriation, ecological degradation, and gentrification (Sood, 2015; Shaban & Sattar, 2016; Bose, 2013). Urban development plans like the Jawaharlal Nehru Urban Renewal Mission (JnNURM) and the Smart Cities Project followed in the following decades. These plans focused on the use of innovative infrastructure and technological solutions as a response to all the socio-economic needs of cities. However, in their execution through private players, these projects prioritize the needs of the elite, which results in supplementing the systemic patterns of gating and exclusion of the urban poor (Mahadevia, 2016).

In addition to the issues of social inequality, this pattern of urban development is essentially fragmented in nature. Instead of having a holistic view of urban-environmental management, fragmented environmental solutions and piecemeal projects have become commonplace (Mahadevia, 2016). This private-enterprise-led development has been repeatedly accused of non-alignment with the existing master plan and poor coordination with other concerned agencies for implementation (CSE, 2011). Several researchers have pointed out that the pace of actual urban growth often overtakes the capacity of the city administrations and development authorities for strategic environmental planning (Sankhe et al., 2010; Mell, 2017). This mismatch in the plan and pace of development has resulted in the fragmented planning and development of green spaces in Indian cities. The expansion and restructuring of urban habitats through private gated communities often take over the existing green spaces and limit the opportunity to develop continuous stretches of greenspaces within the city. The enclosed townships and housing complexes promise safe and accessible green spaces to the elite residents while compromising the continuous development of green spaces.

3.1.1.2 Green Infrastructure and Urban Resilience

Green infrastructure (GI) has become a key solution to healthier and more dynamic urban systems in recent years. The definition of GI has also been diversely outlined and debated by academics, practitioners, and policymakers (Wright, 2011). For this discussion, however, GI can be understood as 'the (interconnected) network of green spaces (both natural and engineered) that conserves natural ecosystem values and functions and provides associated benefits to human populations' (Benedict & McMahon, 2002). GIs are integral parts of any urban system and provide essential ecosystem services. They have been advocated as 'nature-based solutions', capable of addressing a variety of challenges at the same time. GI aids the absorption and storage of stormwater, reducing the risk of pluvial floods (Ellis, 2013; Liao, Deng, & Tan, 2017).

Urban green spaces are a subset of urban GI systems and provide essential ecosystem services. It is widely recognized that urban green spaces provide essential physical and mental health benefits to their users. Urban green spaces contribute toward essential ecological functions like stormwater management and reduction of local temperatures. Urban green spaces and green surfaces can help curb the formation of Urban Heat Islands (UHI) and reduce energy demand by reducing local temperature. They also act as carbon sinks enabling the offsetting of carbon emissions, thus increasing resilience to climate change (Foster, Lowe, & Winkelman, 2011; Alves, Gersonius, Kapelan, Vojinovic, & Sanchez, 2019). GI also has several socio-cultural co-benefits for urban communities. Thus, people's access and proximity to these urban greens is an important element in deciding their level of vulnerability and coping capacity toward climatic shocks and stresses.

GI is an approach to urban resilience that is especially sought after by policymakers and city-level decision-makers. In disaster management, it is also acknowledged as a crucial infrastructural element of cities' approach to resilience-building (Staddon et al., 2018; Foster, Lowe, & Winkelman, 2011). It provides on-ground targeted infrastructure solutions for short-term and long-term resilience (Kearns, Saward, Houlston, & Rayner, 2014; Meerow & Newell, 2016). However, the attributes related to the trade-offs between various co-benefits and the population groups benefiting from them are often either unclear or an afterthought in literature and practice (Meerow & Newell, 2016). Although GI is advocated as a multi-functional infrastructure, GI projects often overlook the comprehensive effects the GI has on the urban system (Meerow & Newell, 2017; Staddon et al., 2018). GI is often designed and implemented to cater to a specific purpose like creating a recreational space or stormwater management. Resilience building, however, is a systemic phenomenon. Therefore, the design and development of urban GI require the deliberation of comprehensive impacts of GI projects. Recent research on the social impacts of GI development in urban areas has brought new perspectives on social equity in the distribution of this infrastructure and related services (Staddon et al., 2018; Wolch, Byrne, & Newell, 2014). GI projects lacking the forethought of their systemic impacts fail to reap their co-benefits and accrue resource distribution issues.

Very few studies have addressed the impact of neoliberal reforms on green space development in Indian cities. This chapter looks at the gating and 'enclavization' of urban green spaces, one aspect of neoliberal urban development. No study has analyzed the relationship between the development of gated enclaves and the fragmentation of urban green spaces in Indian cities. Evidence from landscape fragmentation studies clearly shows a link between rapid post-liberalization unplanned urbanization and urban green space fragmentation in Indian cities. Further, none of the studies has discussed the systemic linkages of gated and fragmented urban green space development on the resilience of cities to deal with environmental, climatic, and social stresses. This chapter aims to address this gap and inspect the missed opportunity of developing inclusive urban green spaces as a resilience-building tool. In addition, it also elaborates on the missed resilience-building opportunities owing to lost ecological and functional benefits from fragmentation and gating of urban green spaces. The chapter starts with building a narrative on how gated communities have driven the fragmentation of green spaces and made them exclusive with limited benefits. It further discusses case studies for better development of GIs in a private-enterprise-led development scenario. It draws recommendations and possible solutions using the lessons and the context of Indian cities. The following sections advance the understanding of relationships between green infrastructure, urban resilience, and the gating of urban green spaces. It further discusses the lost co-benefits and resilience-building opportunities due to enclaved green spaces within gated communities. The chapter reviews a case of Sector 78 in Noida to elaborate and suggest plausible design solutions for restructuring the green space within the gated communities. The chapter concludes by outlining the gaps in the neoliberal development of urban green spaces, their implications for urban resilience and the utilities of exclusionary urban green spaces, and the scope for further research.

3.2 Methodology

The principal realm of this chapter is the identification/formulation of a problem statement pertaining to the threats of neoliberal urban development to urban green space development and, thus, to urban resilience. Owing to the limited data availability, the methodology of this study relies primarily on existing literature, secondary data, and case studies. The chapter builds on a study of existing literature elaborating on developing gated green spaces in Indian cities. Inferences are drawn from this analysis to analyze the effect of neoliberal reforms and processes on the development of urban green space in Indian cities. These inferences and secondary data are used to evolve an analytical narrative to explain how a particular phenomenon of neoliberal development processes (the development of gated enclaves) affects the development of urban green spaces in Indian cities. The term 'analytic' here refers to constructing a narrative based on logical contestation arrived on by consideration of contextual discourses and derived inferences. This narrative further highlights how the fragmentation and exclusionary 'enclavization' of urban green spaces affects the resilience capacities of city residents. Case examples from existing empirical studies of the development and restructuring of green space in Indian cities are cited to support these arguments. The case study method is most suited to support this narrative as it presents concrete examples as evidence of the above-stated phenomenon.

Further, existing policies and guidelines are collated to portray the existing policy framework and associated institutions for urban green space development in India. The review of this policy framework and institutional capacities for developing and managing urban green spaces in India highlights the gaps in the same. The policy review and empirical analysis of the loss of urban green space and degradation in Indian cities are used to outline the gaps in the policy framework and institutional capacities for addressing the development of inclusive and interconnected urban green spaces. This analysis helps to formulate a theoretical framework, establishing a relationship between neoliberal urban development, gated enclaves, urban green spaces, and resilience.

The chapter further takes up a case example of Sector 78 in Noida (New Okhla Industrial Development Authority) for detailed discussion. This case example aids in elaborating on the shortcomings of enclaved urban green spaces through an on-ground example. A short analysis of the area of open and green spaces within the gated communities has been done to suggest two options for their restructuring. Although these suggestions are tailored for the specific case of Sector 78 and are only two among several plausible strategic interventions, they showcase a possibility for the design and development of better urban green spaces while respecting the residents' safety concerns of the gated communities.

3.3 Literature Review

The changes in land use and land cover in urban areas in the past decades have been studied by several authors for several Indian cities. Existing literature has already established a relationship between urban development patterns and the changes in urban green space. A review of these studies helps elucidate the relationship between neoliberal urban development in India, loss/degradation of urban green space, and urban resilience. The study further narrows the focus toward a specific neoliberal urban development phenomenon, that is, the development of gated communities and the impacts of creating gated urban green spaces within them. A review of policies and institutional arrangements for developing and managing urban green spaces also highlights the gaps in the policy framework and institutional capacities.

3.3.1 Neoliberal Development and Degradation of Existing Green Spaces

The previously existing green spaces within the city and on the urban periphery are an essential component of any city's green infrastructure. They are a substantial part of the natural ecosystem and carry out crucial ecological functions like maintaining healthy soils, hydrological functions (groundwater recharge, stormwater drainage, etc.), regulating the microclimate, and supporting biodiversity. Usually, these green spaces also serve essential provisioning (food and fodder) and cultural (religious, socio-cultural, and recreational activities) ecosystem services without any barriers to access. Appropriate planning for the conservation and management of these green spaces is crucial. Absence of suitable controls and regulation, as in the case of many rapidly growing cities following neoliberal urban development patterns. In such a scenario, green spaces fall prey to ill-suited degradation and removal, severely affecting the resilience capacity of such cities.

In the case of rapidly growing Indian cities, the process of degradation of urban green spaces starts right from the conception of the new urban habitats. Neoliberal reforms led to rapid urbanization and in-migration in Indian cities, causing the expropriation of natural green spaces (agricultural land, forest area, barren/ fallow land, etc.) to develop new housing and infrastructure to cater to the demands of the rising urban population. Additionally, the development of these privately acquired lands catering to the elite is usually in the form of gated enclaves, resulting in the exclusion of the low-income populations from accessing previously unrestricted green spaces and ecological resources. Several studies have analyzed the change in green cover in expanding Indian cities by monitoring the changes in land use/land cover (LULC) after economic liberalization. Table 3.1 lists a few examples of major Indian cities outlining the loss of open and green space and the stresses and threats the city faces as a result.

Table 3.1 Examples of degradation of open and green space in major Indian cities with associated stresses and threats to city's resilience

City	*Green space lost or degraded*	*Stresses or threats to the city's resilience*
Pune	During 1992--2001 18 km^2 of agricultural land and green spaces were lost for residential and infrastructure development, and a further 52.6 km^2 from 2001 to 2013 (Butsch et al., 2017)	Various environmental issues, encroachment of hill slopes and riverbeds (largely by informal settlements inhabited by a low-income population who can't afford formal housing), loss of biodiversity, water scarcity, urban heat islands (Imam & Banerjee, 2016)
Bengaluru	Productive agricultural land in Bengaluru Urban Agglomeration declined from 47% to 8% of the total area from 1981 to 2001 (Iyer, Kulkarni, & Raghavaswamy, 2007)	Degradation of biodiversity, urban flooding, land and water pollution, and air pollution (Ramchandra & Mujumdar, 2009; Mundoli, Manjunath, & Nagendra, 2014; Derkzen, van Teeffelen, Nagendra, & Verburg, 2017; Udvardi, 2014)
Delhi	The areas showing a significant decrease in vegetation cover coincide with the spatial pattern of urban development, especially in Gautam Buddha Nagar, Gurugram, and Faridabad, and are caused by the conversion of vegetated land to built-up. (Dutta, Rahman, Paul, & Kundu, 2021)	Burden on energy, land, and water resources, urban flooding, and urban heat islands (Imam & Banerjee, 2016)
Hyderabad	Green scrubland drastically declined from 46% to 2% of the total area from 1981 to 2001 (Iyer, Kulkarni, & Raghavaswamy, 2007), while residential land use in the fringe area increased from 8.69% to 12.66% during 1993–2000 (Chadchan & Shankar, 2012), implying a rise in the development of residential complexes	Urban flooding (Markandeya & Suryanarayana, 2009), water scarcity (Das & Skelton, 2019)

(*Continued*)

Table 3.1 (Continued)

City	*Green space lost or degraded*	*Stresses or threats to the city's resilience*
Gurugram	Absolute change in LULC during the period 1991–2018: • Agriculture and open lands: from 77.14% to 45.86% • Greenspaces: from 5.11% to 2.03% • Shrub and Aravalli ridge: from 13.94% to increase to 19.34% in 2009 but decline to 16.16% in 2018 The peri-urban expansion has been the primary type of built-up growth, causing the rapid transformation of open and greenspace into built-habitat.	Water scarcity, water pollution, air pollution, land degradation, urban floods, and adverse effects on residents' health due to pollution (Pramanik, Butsch, & Punia, 2021)

Source: Authors based on sources cited in the table.

Studies of LULC change in Pune showed that rapid urbanization and poorly controlled sprawl have resulted in the loss of agricultural and natural ecosystems in the fringe areas of Pune (Bhaskar, 2012; Butsch et al., 2017; Wagner, Kumar, & Schneider, 2013). As Pune developed into an industrial hub following the economic liberalization, the introduction of JnNURM in 2005 and the adoption of the Special Economic Zone policy by the Government of Maharashtra in 2006, the construction of residential buildings and gray infrastructure has taken place in the urban fringe (Bhaskar, 2012). After the economic liberalization, Gurugram also experienced rapid urbanization due to its location in the National Capital Region (NCR) Delhi and the emergence of a highly speculative real estate market due to poor land governance (Goldstein, 2016). This led to a decline in existing green spaces (Figure 3.1). The green spaces were converted into urban and sub-urban built-up areas, of which gated communities are a dominant fraction (Pramanik, Butsch, & Punia, 2021). The urban agglomerations of both Hyderabad and Bengaluru have experienced similar economic and demographic shifts and rapidly privatized urbanization post-liberalization (Biswas, 2019; Chadchan & Shankar, 2012). Both cities have experienced the conversion of existing green areas (productive agricultural land, green cover, eco-sensitive areas, and surface water bodies and wetlands in addition to green areas) to human habitats. The lost green area was predominantly agricultural land in the case of Bengaluru and scrubland in the case of Hyderabad (Iyer, Kulkarni, & Raghavaswamy, 2007). Delhi is one of the exemplary cities in India which have countered the loss of green spaces by greening measures. However, the

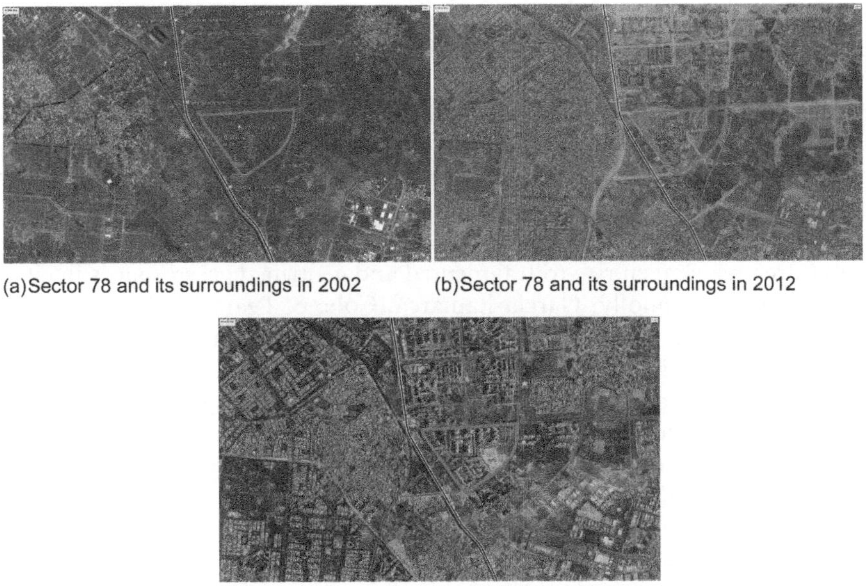

(a) Sector 78 and its surroundings in 2002 (b) Sector 78 and its surroundings in 2012

(c) Sector 78 and its surroundings in 2022

Figure 3.1 The change in the urban landscape of Noida's Sector 78 (boundaries in white) and its surroundings in the past two decades

Source: Authors' using Google Earth historical imagery.

loss of green spaces is still apparent in the peri-urban areas of NCR Delhi. This is attributed to the conversion of green spaces to built-up areas. This phenomenon of unplanned privatized urbanization in rapidly growing Indian cities has resulted in the encroachment/degradation of hill slopes, floodplains, and eco-sensitive areas and the loss of productive cropland and natural green spaces. This has resulted in various environmental issues and stresses in the urban systems (Table 3.1), thus affecting their resilience capacity.

3.3.2 *Gating of Urban Green Spaces*

Gated communities are residential areas with restricted and security-controlled access and a large subset of the enclaved urban spaces created by the processes of neoliberal urban development. The open spaces and amenities housed in these residential areas, which are otherwise public places, are privatized for the collective use of the residents. These areas are usually segregated by constructing designated perimeters (usually walls or fences) and controlling/regulating the entrances, preventing access by non-residents (Blakely & Snyder, 1997; Caldeira, 2000; Roitman, 2015). In India, gated communities are usually referred to by various names like colonies, townships, societies, complexes, and phases. Globalization and economic liberalization are the key factors resulting in the emergence of gated communities (Roitman, 2015). This is specifically true for India and several other South Asian cities (Chaudhuri & Jagadale, 2020). Liberalization of the real estate market and reduction of public housing brought about large-scale privatization and gentrification, leading to the segregation of the elite and exclusion of the poor from these private and semi-private spaces (Brosius, 2010; Chakravarthy & Riggs, 2021; Sridharan, 2011).

The spatial restructuring of cities and privatized development in the urban fringe area have given rise to fragmented and gentrified green spaces in cities (Anguelovski, Connolly, Garcia-Lamarca, Cole, & Pearsall, 2018; Heynen, 2013; Landry & Chakraborty, 2009). The semi-private open and green spaces within the gated communities are a subset of these fragmented urban green spaces (Yazar et al., 2019). The residents of these gated communities have high regard for privacy, security, and community association with individuals of a similar socio-economic background as them. This leads to the homogenization of the users of these green spaces and spatial stratification of the urban green spaces.

Figure 3.2 shows Sector 78 of Noida, which is a typical example of private-enterprise-led urban development in the form of gated communities. Noida is a planned city within the Delhi Metropolitan area and has received large

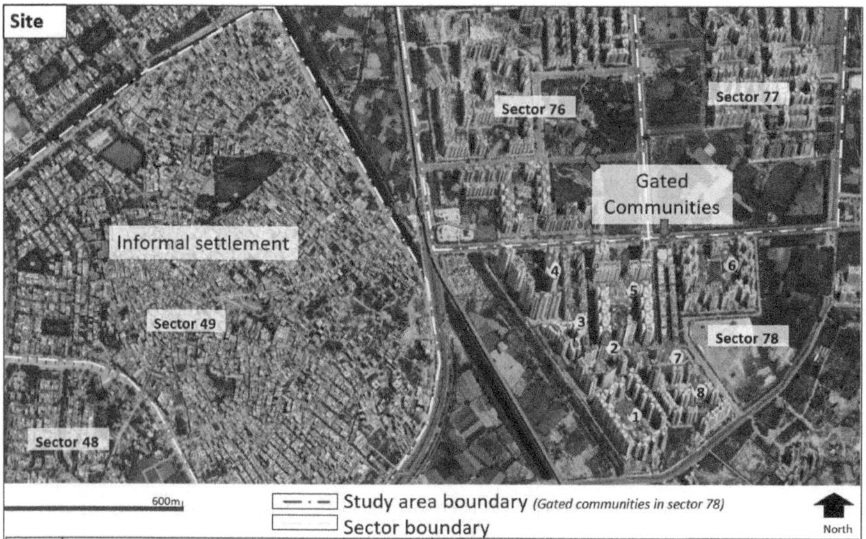

1	Antriksh Golf View 1	5	Mahagun Moderne
2	Sunshine Helios	6	The Hyde Park
3	Sikka Karmic Greens	7	Assotech Windsor Court
4	Mahagun Mezzaria	8	Antriksh Golf View 2

Figure 3.2 Selected area with eight gated communities selected for the study

Source: Authors using Google Earth.

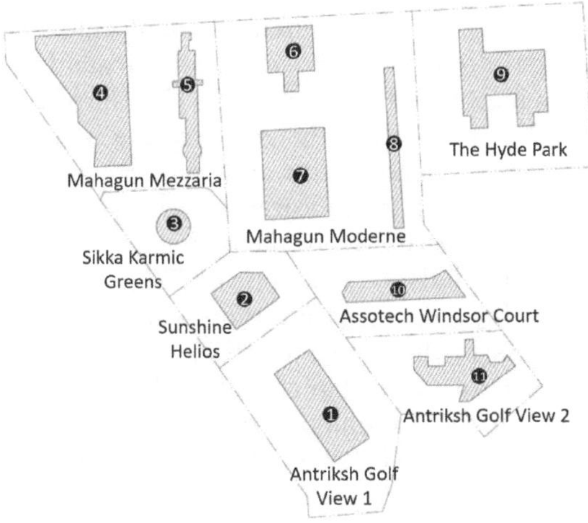

	Gated Community	Area of Green Spaces (sqm)	Area of Gated community	% of green space
1	Antriksh Golf View 1	9976	50893	20
2	Sunshine Helios	4955	21809	23
3	Sikka Karmic Greens	2075	19872	10
4	Mahagun Mezzaria	17660	65885	27
5		4900		7
6	Mahagun Moderne	5253	101277	5
7		12358		12
8		3405		3
9	The Hyde Park	12477	63587	20
10	Assotech Windsor Court	5197	30370	17
11	Antriksh Golf View 2	6073	28154	22
	Total Area	84329		

Figure 3.3 Existing placement of the central open and green spaces within each gated community

Source: Authors.

investments from largely private sources after liberalization (Shaw, 2013). In the past decades, the landscape of Noida has significantly changed as the city has urbanized with the aid of this private investment (see Figure 3.1). While infrastructure augmentation and improvements are made, many of these investments are in enclaved spaces, including office complexes, gated communities, and shopping centers (Schindler & Kishore, 2015). The sector houses eight gated communities with high-end residential buildings catering to high-income groups. An informal settlement is close to these gated communities and houses residents largely belonging to lower and middle-income groups. Figures 3.1 and 3.2 clearly show the landscape transformation in the past few decades. Productive agricultural land and publicly accessed open spaces have been replaced by a mix of unplanned informal settlements and planned residential and commercial enclaves. The informal settlements largely lack the provision of suitable open/green spaces catering to the residents. Although the planned gated communities have open and green spaces within their boundaries, these spaces are essentially fragmented (Figure 3.3) and consequently miss ecological and functional benefits. Additionally, they exclusively cater to the residents of the respective gated communities and bar both the residents of the informal settlements and the residents of other gated communities from using them.

3.3.3 Policy and Institutional Framework for Development and Management of Urban Green Spaces

While the case of Sector 78 points out the drawbacks in the structure and distribution of urban green spaces, these flaws don't necessarily occur due to a lack of plans and legislation for managing urban green spaces. Studies have already pointed toward the blatant ignorance of environmental guidelines and masterplan mandates by the development authorities and private developers in the case of rapidly developing cities (Butsch et al., 2017). Despite the existing legal framework (Table 3.2) mandating the conservation of forest lands and green spaces outside forests, degradation and removal of valuable ecological and biodiversity resources have repeatedly been observed in rapidly urbanizing cities. This is largely attributed to the political inclination toward developing these new urban habitats, lack of appropriate governance capacity and stewardship, and insufficient or missing representation of the needs and wishes of the landowners in these peri-urban areas. Peri-urban areas are governed mainly by Nagar or Gram Panchayats, which lack the institutional and financial capacity for decision-making regarding the conservation and planning of GI (Butsch et al., 2017). Studies for Bengaluru and Delhi highlight the role of institutions in conserving existing green spaces and appropriate planning for GI. A landscape fragmentation study of Bengaluru (Nagendra, Nagendran, Paul, & Pareeth, 2012) infers that large areas with existing green cover have been cleared for construction in the urban periphery resulting in the fragmentation of green spaces in the periphery.

On the other hand, while small neighborhood parks have been developed in the core of Bengaluru, their small size renders them inadequate for creating interconnected green infrastructure. Another study analyzing the landscape fragmentation in Delhi (Paul & Nagendra, 2015) inferred that the urban periphery consisted of the most fragmented green spaces. This indicates the existence of only small neighborhood parks and afforested patches in the transitional peri-urban areas in contrast to the better planned and conserved expanses of contiguous core forest and other semi-private and private green spaces in Lutyens' Delhi (city-core). The core areas of cities have functioning public institutions with suitable capacities that have effectively contributed to the conservation of green spaces in the city core, while poor capacities in the urban periphery have led to the loss of valuable GI (Paul & Nagendra, 2015; Nagendra, Nagendran, Paul, & Pareeth, 2012).

A critical factor in planning and managing green spaces in cities is the ambiguity in the roles and responsibilities for planning, developing, protecting, and managing urban green spaces. While guiding policies exist at the national level, the responsibility for executing and regulating these mandates lies with several agencies like local bodies, revenue and forest departments, etc. Also, from a legislative perspective, these urban green spaces are covered under various acts and rules like the Municipal acts, Indian Forests act, Land Revenue code, master plans, building bye-laws, etc. The actual functioning and details of urban GI also differ from state to state. Some states have enacted Tree Preservation acts and established statutory authorities like the 'Tree officer' to protect trees and other related incidental issues. However, in some states, these functions are carried out by Revenue and Municipal officers. In some other states, unique acts regarding the felling of trees in

Table 3.2 Policies and mandates for development and management of open and green spaces in urban India

Sr. no.	*Policy/guideline*	*Relevant mandates and guidelines*
1	The Forest (Conservation) Act, 1980	i Protection of forests ii Restriction on the de-reservation of forests or use of forest land for non-forest purposes
2	The Environment (Protection) Act and Rules, 1986	i Regulation of environmental pollution ii Power to the Central Government to make rules to protect and improve the Environment
3	The Biological Diversity Act, 2002 and Rules, 2004	i Conservation and promotion of biological resources ii Central Government to develop national strategies/ plans for conservation of biological diversity iii Mandates for biodiversity heritage sites iv Guideline for preparation of people's biodiversity registers
4	National Biodiversity Action Plan, 2008	i Guidelines for regulation of introduction of invasive alien species and their management ii Guidelines for assessment of vulnerability and adaptation to climate change and desertification
5	National Biodiversity Action Plan Addendum, 2014	i Addendum for documentation and protection of sacred groves
6	Handbook of landscape, 2013	i General guidelines for: a Planting for shelter, soil conservation, pollution control, environmental, economic, ecological, and aesthetic values, tackling urban heat island, etc. b Landscape design and selection of plant material
7	Urban Greening Guidelines, 2014	i Guidelines for strengthening policies for urban greens ii Guidelines for maintenance of plant material iii Guidelines for integration of urban green spaces into the city's development plan on various levels
8	National Mission for a Green India (One of 8 missions of NAPCC), 2015	i Increased forest/tree cover on 5 million hectares of forest/non-forest lands and improved quality of forest cover on another 5 million hectares (a total of 10 million hectares) is one of the mission's objectives. ii Ward level committees/ Resident Welfare Associations (RWAs) with support from Municipal organizations and the forest departments as responsible agencies in urban areas iii Sub-mission: Bringing urban/peri-urban lands under forest and tree cover (0.20 million hectares) a Securing of recorded or notified forest patches threatened by expanding urban/industrial development b Restoring representative ecosystems and plantation of diverse species mix to supplement natural regeneration c Open/green spaces like parks/woodlots on municipal land will be supported to enhance their biodiversity status d Financial support for diffused planting such as on avenues and in households e Institutional lands to be supported for taking up the planting of native species

(*Continued*)

Table 3.2 (Continued)

Sr. no.	*Policy/guideline*	*Relevant mandates and guidelines*
10	URDPFI Guidelines, 2014	i Green and forest cover to be a part of the development/Master plan and should be detailed further in the Zonal Development Plan ii Guidelines for green belts and green buffer zones iii Guidelines for various organized and unorganized greens iv Enhancing and expanding green cover based on local species
11	Draft National Forest Policy, 2018	i Managing and expanding green spaces in urban and peri-urban areas is one of the objectives ii Promotion of trees outside forests and urban greens to be taken up on a mission mode iii Management plans for urban greens to be prepared and implemented in consonance with the development plan of cities

Source: Authors based on listed policy documents.

non-forests and private lands are also applicable to urban areas. Thus, greater clarity and streamlining of roles and responsibilities are required to efficiently manage these green spaces.

An important consideration for building urban resilience is the appropriate planning for the distribution of open and green spaces within the city, ensuring equitable access to different population groups and providing maximum benefits and co-benefits. The existing techno-legal framework has placed very insignificant consideration toward the socio-economic dimension of green space development. The building bye-laws, Urban and Regional Development Plans Formulation and Implementation (URDPFI) guidelines, state's township policies, and Green India Mission all provide guidelines for the percentage of open or green areas to be achieved. However, none of these policies or mandates addresses the equitable distribution of the GI's benefits and access rights to the green spaces. Even the smart cities mission only propounds 'preserving and developing open spaces — parks, playgrounds, and recreational spaces'. in its mission objectives (MoHUA, 2021). The Climate Smart Cities Assessment Framework (CSCAF 2.0), developed by the Ministry of Housing and Urban Affairs (MoHUA) too, considers only factors like initiatives for conservation of open areas, the proportion of green cover in the city, initiatives for conservation and maintenance of biodiversity for the assessment, and overlooking the concept of equity (MoHUA, 2020). Greater consideration in policy planning is required for the equitable provisioning of the functions and co-benefits of urban green spaces to build the urban resilience of Indian cities.

3.4 Lost Opportunities due to Enclosed Green Spaces within Gated Communities

3.4.1 Possibility of Enhancing Urban Resilience through Green Infrastructure

Urban green spaces are an important part of any city's GI system. Efficient GI systems are strategically planned to form a network of interconnected green (and blue) spaces. The 'connectivity' of these spaces is crucial for connecting the system and enabling ecological processes (like stormwater runoff, groundwater recharge, air and water purification, biodiversity regulation, regulation of micro-climate, etc.) to function properly and maintain the resiliency of the system (Benedict & McMahon, 2002). Fragmentation of urban green spaces is a complex phenomenon, affected by several parameters. However, several studies of landscape fragmentation in Indian cities have indicated rapid settlement expansion and developmental activity to be the leading cause of fragmentation of urban green spaces in Indian cities (Gabril, Denis, Nath, Paul, & Kumar, 2019; Paul & Nagendra, 2015; Nagendra, Nagendran, Paul, & Pareeth, 2012). Due to poor planning and skewed development priorities, natural and planned green spaces become fragmented in rapidly urbanizing cities. This leads to the degradation in the quality and quantity of the green spaces and can even render them non-functional. The development of urban habitats in the form of gated communities and entry-restricted enclaves further intensifies the fragmentation of green infrastructure (Derkzen, van Teeffelen, Nagendra, & Verburg, 2017).

A comprehensive planning of the network of green spaces is crucial for GI to function efficiently. In addition to the physical fragmentation of the green spaces, fragmentation in GI's governance and stewardship also poses a significant challenge to the efficient development, management, and functioning of the GI system. The responsibility for developing and managing green spaces within gated communities lies with the Resident Welfare Associations (RWAs) or other private actors. Areas with highly fragmented and gated developments are governed and managed by various public and private actors with different territorial jurisdictions and widely varying and contradictory planning priorities. Several studies discuss the alignment of the goals for the design and planning of GI, and coordination for their implementation, operation, and maintenance becomes a daunting task in such cases (Vásquez, Devoto, Giannotti, & Velásquez, 2016; Nagendra, Nagendran, Paul, & Pareeth, 2012). The funding of GI in a fragmented development is yet another challenge. Often, the private developers and the RWAs are averse to investing funds in the development of GI as it is perceived as the responsibility of the local government. Due to the development of gated enclaves, the territorial jurisdiction and responsibilities of GI development and maintenance become muddled (Vásquez, Devoto, Giannotti, & Velásquez, 2016; Zuniga-Teran et al., 2019). Thus, forming a consensus on GI planning becomes even more difficult.

GI is an indispensable part of any healthy and resilient city. Appropriately planned GI can provide solutions to several climatic stresses, which can include

i. Management of urban floods through appropriate stormwater management;
ii. Reduction of urban heat stress by evapotranspiration and shading;
iii. Management of water scarcity through the infiltration of rainwater;
iv. Reduction of air and water pollution through natural purification processes;
v. Reduction of net emissions through carbon sequestration;
vi. Regulation of soil quality;
vii. Conservation and support of local biodiversity (Choi, Berry, & Smith, 2021; Staddon et al., 2018).

3.4.2 Tree Plantation and Biodiversity, Monocultures, and Exotic Species

Rapid urbanization and clearing of natural green spaces for the development of urban habitats have led to the depletion of local biodiversity. This loss could have been offset by developing artificial green spaces with diverse native species mimicking the natural landscape. However, several studies have instead noted the increasing use of exotic plant species and monoculture plant material instead of diverse native species in urbanizing cities (Butsch et al., 2017; Bhaskar, 2012; Nagendra, Nagendran, Paul, & Pareeth, 2012). The aesthetics of neoliberal urban developments is often a priority for private developers. The 'beautification through plantation' approach is followed to promote the perception of 'green' space to their clientele, focusing on the quantity and aesthetics of green spaces instead of their quality. Thus, privatized urbanization has led to the increased plantation of fast-growing and aesthetically pleasing exotic plant species and the loss of native flora and fauna (Bhaskar, 2012). A study analyzing the tree diversity of urban parks in Bengaluru (Nagendra & Gopal, 2010) inferred that a considerable proportion (77%) of the trees in urban parks in Bengaluru were comprised of exotic species. The study also inferred that the newly developed urban parks had a greater proportion of exotic species compared to the older parks in the city. This trend of changing urban plant diversity is alarming as large proportions of exotic plant species can have severe detrimental effects on the local biodiversity, health of local ecosystems, and hydrological processes (for example, depletion of surface and groundwater resources by water-intensive exotic species).

Another inference from the study of the historical evolution of tree species diversity in Bengaluru revealed that urban parks were slowly phasing out the trees with larger canopies. These parks were instead opting for medium-sized trees or narrow canopies for easier maintenance, which doesn't provide the same ecological benefits as the larger tree species. It has not been indicated in the study, but the fragmentation of green spaces and reduction in their size can also prompt a similar selection of plant species. Several shortcomings often restrain smaller sites for tree plantation. These may include low stocks of 'plantable space', inhospitable urban fabric in the vicinity (e.g., high-rises, electric wires, hard paving, etc.), physical confinement, and absence of other physiological constraints required for a healthy tree growth (Jim, van den Bosch, & Chen, 2018). Thus, the fragmentation of green spaces limits the variety of larger plant materials in the city's GI system.

The type of vegetation and biodiversity are essential constraints in determining the quality of green spaces. GI with diverse and native flora and fauna form healthy ecosystems which can sustain themselves. GI consisting of native plant materials is robust as they are suitable for the local climatic and hydrological conditions. Their suitability to the local area enables them to perform ecological processes and support the resilience of the urban system.

3.4.3 Variety of Functions

Green spaces are an indispensable part of any healthy and resilient city. However, in addition to the vital services, a tactfully planned and suitably maintained network of green spaces can also provide several co-benefits which can add to the social resilience of the city and the quality of life of its inhabitants. These co-benefits can include

i. Improvement of the physical well-being of the residents by reduction of diseases caused by environmental pollution and inviting outdoor space for physical activity;
ii. Improvement of the mental well-being of the residents by providing a natural landscape for residents seeking peace and tranquility;
iii. Extended interconnected networks of urban green spaces also provide the opportunity to develop cycling and walking tracks;
iv. Use as recreational spaces or as a space for conducting socio-cultural activities, thus promoting social cohesion among the residents;
v. Opportunities for education and awareness of the importance of urban green spaces and resilience-building practices (Choi, Berry, & Smith, 2021; Staddon et al., 2018).

All these benefits and co-benefits of green spaces can help build urban resilience by ensuring the functioning of critical socio-ecological systems. However, due to the rapid privatized urbanization following the economic reforms and the development of gated communities, Indian cities are deprived of several of these benefits and co-benefits of GI systems. Poor planning before the development of gated communities can result in the loss of natural ecosystems and fragmentation of green spaces, making the green spaces lose their functionality.

3.4.4 Social Integrity

Well-planned GI networks can promote social cohesion and can even create economic value. However, poorly planned and exclusionary green spaces can have the opposite effects and create severe socio-economic problems in a city. As socio-economic systems are an integral part of any urban system, urban resilience depends as much on the socio-economic phenomenon as the physical constraints. Therefore, ensuring social inclusion of different socio-economic groups and equity in access and use of the resources and services provided by the GI is pivotal in the planning and development of GI networks (Staddon et al., 2018).

With the advent of private investment-led economic and urban growth in Indian cities, the development of highly exclusionary spaces has become mainstream in rapidly growing cities. Gated communities form a considerable part of these exclusive enclaves that cater to the higher-income groups. The development of these gated communities has contributed significantly to the eviction of marginalized populations (occupying these spaces in the form of informal settlements) and expropriation of productive cropland from farmers (many a time despite their unwillingness) (CSE, 2011; Mahadevia, 2016; Das, 2015; Sood, 2015; Shaban & Sattar, 2016; Bose, 2013). The development of gated and restricted green spaces in these residential complexes remains largely inaccessible or unusable to the lower-income population. Instead, such polished and exclusive landscapes only raise the real estate prices of the surrounding area, further pushing away the urban poor. The loss of their homes to insensitive eviction and the inability to afford homes in the gentrified neighborhoods often forces these populations to relocate to exceedingly vulnerable areas (like flood-prone or low-lying areas of the city).

In addition, the urban greening policies and programs are severely lacking in ensuring an inclusive pathway for their planning and implementation. Contrary to their goals, these initiatives often act as 'tools for displacing the urban poor' (Mahadevia, 2016). The plight for removal of encroachments from the green belt in Delhi Master Plan 2021, while stringently disregarding all appeals of the slum population for exemption and resettlement, is an example of the same systemic exclusion (Dupont & Ramanathan, 2008; Mahadevia, 2016). Several studies have outlined the disregard for the needs of the urban poor and the marginalized in a neoliberal India (Menon, 2013; Mahadevia, 2016; Das, 2015; Bhagat, 2017; Patel, Sliuzas, & Mathur, 2015). These studies have discussed the stark inequalities in the distribution of public amenities due to exclusionary development paradigms, focusing largely on housing needs and the need for basic amenities like water supply, sanitation, and solid waste management for the urban poor. The studies specifically analyzing the exclusionary conduct for provisioning environmental and ecological services due to neoliberal planning practices in Indian cities are very few and require greater attention. One example is the creation of systemic barriers for the urban poor in accessing urban parks and green spaces. A study on the access to urban parks and the benefits of green spaces in Hyderabad (Basu & Nagendra, 2021) demonstrated the same. The study inferred that the parks almost exclusively provided recreational services (primarily targeted toward the upper-income groups) and restricted all access to provisioning services like food and fodder (primarily targeted toward the lower-income groups and the urban poor). The study also discovered that the parks in wealthy neighborhoods had visitors almost exclusively belonging to the middle- and upper-income groups. The underlying causes for the highly skewed proportions of visitors in these parks were inferred to be the barriers of gentrification and entry fees. However, secondary to the provisioning of basic amenities, the provisioning of environmental and ecological services to the urban poor is essential for resilience building in an equitable manner.

3.5. Possible Strategies for Better Green Spaces in Gated Communities

Evidence in the above sections points out the limitations in the current planning of gated communities and the green spaces within. However, a possibility lies in rearranging the greenspaces to form a long-connected stretch that can accommodate a variety of functions. Moreover, with the outward-oriented placement of green infrastructure, the nearby residents from informal settlements can also access the green spaces. For redressal of security concerns of the residents, boundary walls require replacement at the inner edge of GI away from roads. The above scenario is explained by rearranging the green spaces in the example shown in Figure 3.4.

This example suggests an alternative design of the open and green spaces within a gated community. The site area selected for this study (Figure 3.2) is in Sector 78 in Noida, Uttar Pradesh. The selected area houses eight gated communities listed in Table 3.3. All these gated communities have small and fragmented open and green spaces within their sites, which are in a central area in almost all cases (Figure 3.3). The vegetation in these spaces primarily consists of manicured lawns and small, sparsely planted trees with small canopies. Due to gating and entry restrictions, these spaces serve very limited functions and are largely inaccessible to non-residents of the gated community.

Alternative design strategies (scenarios 1 and 2) for these spaces are suggested in Figure 3.4 to reduce fragmentation and promote access to these green spaces. Instead of placing these green spaces in a central area of the gated community, the places can be shifted to the periphery of the site by removing walled restrictions of the gated community to allow access for non-residents. These options, while allowing access to both the residents and non-residents, also address the safety concerns of the gated community

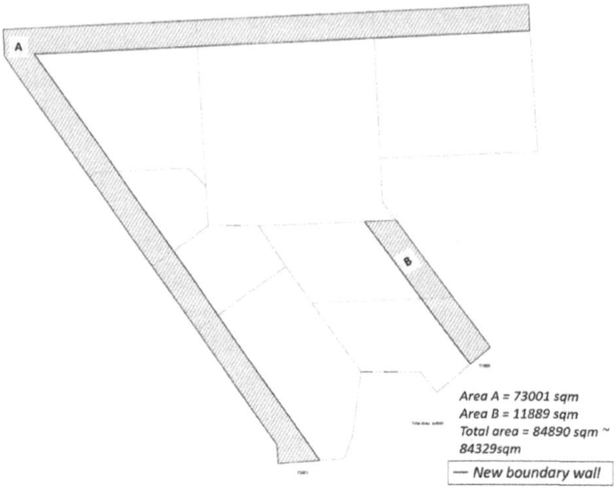

Scenario 1

Scenario 2

Figure 3.4 Two different scenarios for restructuring open and green spaces

Source: Authors

residents, as it only allows access to the green space, not to the residences. The design takes into consideration the area of actual space allotted for open and green space in each gated community. It ensures minimum deviation in the final green area allocated from each gated community's site. Planning the restructuring of the green space in this way allows the residents of the gated communities to access larger and more functional green spaces with multiple co-benefits, promoting their resilience capacity.

The development of suitable building bye-laws for green space in newly developed areas and gated communities can be an alternative option as a

Table 3.3 Area schedule of the open and green spaces in the gated communities before and after restructuring

Name of the gated Community	*Total area of the gated community (m2)*	*Existing green area (m2)*	*Percentage of the total area*	*Area of restructured greens (m2)*	*Percentages after restructuring*
Antriksh Golf View 1	50,893	9,976	19.60	9,995	19.64
Sunshine Helios	21,809	4,955	22.72	5,095	23.36
Sikka Karmic Greens	19,872	2,075	10.44	2,067	10.40
Mahagun Mezzaria	65,885	17,660	34.24	22,617	34.33
Mahagun Moderne	101,277	4,900 5,253 12,358 ,405	20.75	20,702	20.44%
The Hyde Park	63,587	12,477	19.62	13,520	21.26
Assotech Windsor Court	30,370	5,197	17.11	5,330	17.55
Antriksh Golf View 2	28,154	6,073	21.57	6,219	22.09

Source: Authors.

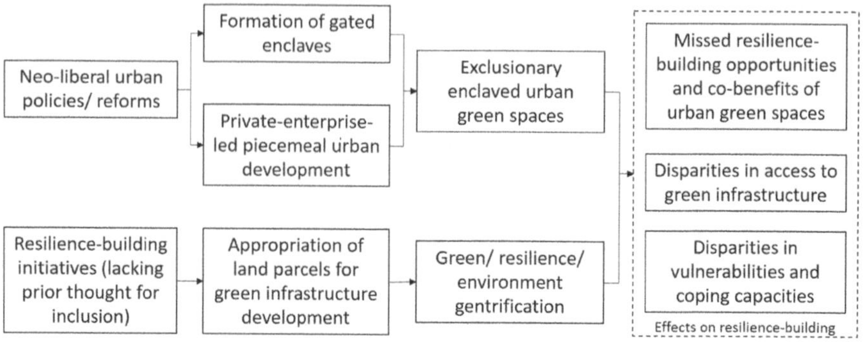

Figure 3.5 Preliminary theoretical framework elaborating the relationship between neo-liberal urban development, gated enclaves, urban green spaces, and resilience

Source: Authors

suitable tool for ensuring the development of functional and equitable green spaces in newly developed gated communities. Options for retrofitting or improving the green spaces within existing gated communities can also be explored.

3.6 Conclusion

This chapter attempts to establish a relationship between the effects of neo-liberal urban development in the form of gated/enclaved spaces on urban green space development and urban resilience. A basic theoretical framework may evolve from the results of this study (Figure 3.5).

The rapid growth and transformation of Indian cities after the neoliberal reforms have created socio-economic inequalities among city residents. Economic liberalization, deregulation, and foreign direct investment have diverted large quantities of urban and peri-urban land for developing townships and gated communities without properly considering environmental or socio-economic impacts. Urban development through gated and enclaved urban spaces has contributed to the rise of fragmented, enclosed, and restrictive urban green spaces. This change in access to green spaces from public to private/semi-private is pushing the urban poor toward greater vulnerability, employing systemic exclusion from accessing the benefits of GI. Even for the elite having access to these fragmented urban green spaces, the functionality and co-benefits are minimal compared to what an otherwise larger and interconnected system of urban green spaces can provide. Thus, gating and fragmentation of urban green spaces limit the opportunities for resilience building not only for the urban poor but for all the residents of the city.

Building resilient cities has become a priority for cities and nations worldwide with changing climate and increasing stresses on the urban systems. GI, capable of providing multiple socio-economic and ecological benefits, is an excellent tool for developing resilience-building solutions. Urban green spaces are among the primary avenues for implementing these solutions. However, resilience-building tools and programs must alter their approach to include the equity dimension. The execution of the resilience-building schemes needs to be developed with forethought to ensure the inclusion of the needs of different socio-economic groups. The urban sustainability agenda requires reframing to weed out exclusionary policies. Especially with the conflicting objectives of the neoliberal development agenda, greater thought, and consideration into the aspects of social injustice and systemic inequalities are required to build resilient cities. Noida's Sector 78 presents evidence of the fragmented and exclusionary development of urban green spaces in present-day Indian cities, which are rapidly developing and driven by neoliberal policies. Management of urban green spaces in most Indian cities is done based on very basic environment management legislation. This legislative and institutional framework struggles to manage the needs of rapidly growing cities and keep pace with the conflicting development goals. Thus, this framework fails to create biodiverse, interconnected, functional, and equitable urban green spaces. The design solutions for Sector 78, discussed in the chapter, show the possibility of creating more functional and inclusive green spaces without compromising the needs of the residents of the gated communities. It presents one among many pathways that can reinforce the resilience capacity of urban residents by harnessing greater socio-economic and ecological benefits of urban green spaces.

This chapter presents an unexplored perspective on the neoliberal development of urban green spaces and its complex effects on cities' resilience. While the chapter limits itself to the specific discussion of gated urban development in detail, it opens the scope for further academic discourse on the effect of various neoliberal development phenomena on a city's resilience. It also sets the stage for further research and development of solutions for developing more connected, functional, and equitable urban green spaces in rapidly expanding and developing cities.

References

Alves, A., Gersonius, B., Kapelan, Z., Vojinovic, Z., & Sanchez, A. (2019). Assessing the co-benefits of green-blue-grey infrastructure for sustainable urban flood risk management. *Journal of Environmental Management, 239*, 244–254. https://doi.org/10.1016/j.jenvman.2019.03.036

Anguelovski, I., Connolly, J. J., Garcia-Lamarca, M., Cole, H., & Pearsall, H. (2018). New scholarly pathways on green gentrification: What does the urban 'green turn' mean and where is it going?. *Progress in Human Geography*, 1064–1086. https://doi.org/10.1177/0309132518803799

Anguelovski, I., Shi, L., Chu, E., Gallagher, D., Goh, K., Lamb, Z., . . . Teicher, H. (2016). Equity impacts of urban land use planning for climate adaptation: Critical perspectives from the global North and South. *Journal of Planning Education and Research, 36*(3), 333–348. https://doi.org/10.1177/0739456X16645166

Basu, S., & Nagendra, H. (2021). Perceptions of park visitors on access to urban parks and benefits of green spaces. *Urban Forestry & Urban Greening, 57*. https://doi.org/10.1016/J.UFUG.2020.126959

Benedict, M. A., & McMahon, E. T. (2002). Green infrastructure: Smart conservation for the 21st century. *Renewable Resources Journal, 20*(3), 12–17. Retrieved September 15, 2021, from https://www.merseyforest.org.uk/files/documents/1365/2002+Green+Infrastructure+Smart+Conservation+for+the+21st+Century..pdf

Bhagat, R. B. (2017). Migration, gender and right to the city: The Indian context. *Economic & Political Weekly, LII*(32), 35–40. Retrieved October 26, 2021, from http://dspace.stellamariscollege.edu.in:8080/xmlui/bitstream/handle/123456789/8630/migration.pdf?sequence=1&isAllowed=y

Bhaskar, P. (2012). Urbanisation and changing green spaces in Indian cities (Case study- City of Pune). *International Journal of Geology, Earth and Environmental Sciences, 2*(2), 148–156. Retrieved October 7, 2021, from http://www.cibtech.org/jgee.htm

Biswas, A. (2019). Why Indian cities are so chaotic? Decoding from the urban development efforts of Chandigarh. *Smart and Sustainable Built Environment*, 438–456. https://doi.org/10.1108/SASBE-05-2018-0023

Blakely, E. J., & Snyder, M. G. (1997). *Fortress America – Gated communities in the United States*. Snyder, Mary Gail. Retrieved September 10, 2021, from https://www.google.co.in/books/edition/Fortress_America/v2EjE0RrpdcC?hl=en&gbpv=1&pg=PA7&printsec=frontcover

Bose, P. S. (2013). Bourgeois environmentalism, leftist development and neoliberal urbanism in the City of Joy. In T. Samara, S. He, & G. Chen (Eds.), *Locating right to the city in the Global South* (pp. 139–163). Routledge. https://doi.org/10.4324/9780203091104-13

Brosius, C. (2010). *India's middle class: New forms of urban leisure, consumption and prosperity*. Routledge India.

Butsch, C., Kumar, S., Wagner, P. D., Kroll, M., Kantakumar, L. N., Bharucha, E., . . . Kraas, F. (2017). Growing 'smart'? Urbanisation processes in the Pune Urban agglomeration. *Sustainability, 9*(12). https://doi.org/10.3390/SU9122335

Caldeira, T. P. (2000). *City of walls*. University of California Press. https://doi.org/10.1525/9780520341593/HTML

Chadchan, J., & Shankar, R. (2012). An analysis of urban growth trends in the post-economic reforms period in India. *International Journal of Sustainable Built Environment, 1*(1), 36–49. https://doi.org/10.1016/J.IJSBE.2012.05.001

Chakravarthy, S., & Riggs, E. P. (2021). Post-independence homescapes in Delhi: Mohan Rakesh's Andhere Band Kamre and a nouveau middle-class amidst persistent inequality. *South Asian History and Culture*. https://doi.org/10.1080/19472498.2021.1956118

Chaudhuri, H. R., & Jagadale, S. R. (2020, September 14). Normalised heterotopia as a market failure in a spatial marketing system: The case of gated communities in India. *Journal of Macromarketing, 41*(2), 297–314. https://doi.org/10.1177/0276146720957382

Choi, C., Berry, P., & Smith, A. (2021). The climate benefits, co-benefits, and trade-offs of green infrastructure: A systematic literature review. *Journal of Environmental Management, 291*. https://doi.org/10.1016/J.JENVMAN.2021.112583

CSE. (2011). *Resource (In)efficient townships*. Centre for Science and Environment.

Das, D. (2015). Making of high-tech Hyderabad: Mapping neoliberal networks and splintering effects. *Singapore Journal of Tropical Geography, 36*(2), 231–248. https://doi.org/10.1111/SJTG.12112

Das, D., & Skelton, T. (2019). Hydrating Hyderabad: Rapid urbanisation, water scarcity and the difficulties and possibilities of human flourishing. *Urban Studies*, 1553–1569. https://doi.org/10.1177/0042098019838481

Derickson, K. D. (2016). Resilience is not enough. *City*, 161–166. https://doi.org/10.1080/13604813.2015.1125713

Derkzen, M. L., van Teeffelen, A. J., Nagendra, H., & Verburg, P. H. (2017). Shifting roles of urban green space in the context of urban development and global change. *Current Opinion in Environmental Sustainability, 29*, 32–39. https://doi.org/10.1016/j.cosust.2017.10.001

Dupont, V., & Ramanathan, U. (2008). The courts and the squatter settlements in Delhi-Or the intervention of the judiciary in urban "governance". In I. Baud & J. de Wit (Eds.), *New forms of urban governance in India. Shifts, models, networks, and contestations* (pp. 312–343). Sage Publications.

Dutta, D., Rahman, A., Paul, S. K., & Kundu, A. (2021). Spatial and temporal trends of urban green spaces: An assessment using hyper-temporal NDVI datasets. *Geocarto International*, 1–18. https://doi.org/10.1080/10106049.2021.1989499

Ellis, J. (2013). Sustainable surface water management and green infrastructure in UK urban catchment planning. *Journal of Environmental Planning and Management, 51*(1), 24–41. https://doi.org/10.1080/09640568.2011.648752

Foster, J., Lowe, A., & Winkelman, S. (2011). *The value of green infrastructure for urban climate adaptation*. The Center for Clean Air Policy (CCAP). Retrieved April 15, 2021, from http://www.ggi.dcp.ufl.edu/_library/reference/The%20value%20of%20green%20infrastructure%20for%20urban%20climate%20adaptation.pdf

Gabril, E. M., Denis, D. M., Nath, S., Paul, A., & Kumar, M. (2019). Quantifying LULC change and landscape fragmentation in Prayagraj district, India using geospatial techniques. *The Pharma Innovation Journal, 8*(5), 670–675. Retrieved October 24, 2021, from http://www.thepharmajournal.com/

Goldstein, S. R. (2016). Planning the millennium city: The politics of place-making in Gurgaon, India. *International Area Studies Review, 19*(1), 12–27. https://doi.org/10.1177/2233865916628798

Gould, K. A., & Lewis, T. L. (2018). From green gentrification to resilience gentrification: An example from Brooklyn. *City & Community, 17*(1), 12–15. https://doi.org/10.1111/CICO.12283

Heynen, N. (2013). Urban political ecology I: The urban century. *Progress in Human Geography, 38*(4), 598–604. https://doi.org/10.1177/0309132513500443

Imam, A. U., & Banerjee, U. K. (2016). Urbanisation and greening of Indian cities: Problems, practices, and policies. *Ambio, 45*(4), 442. https://doi.org/10.1007/S13280-015-0763-4

Iyer, N. K., Kulkarni, S., & Raghavaswamy, V. (2007). Economy, population and urban sprawl: A comparative study of urban agglomerations of Bangalore and Hyderabad, India using remote sensing and GIS techniques. *PRIPODE workshop on Urban Population, Development and Environment Dynamics in Developing Countries*. CICRED. Retrieved October 23, 2021, from http://cicred.org/Eng/Seminars/Details/Seminars/PDE2007/Papers/IYER_Neelakantan_paperNairobi2007-project.pdf

Jim, C. Y., van den Bosch, C. K., & Chen, W. Y. (2018). Acute challenges and solutions for urban forestry in compact and densifying cities. *Journal of Urban Planning and Development, 144*(3). https://doi.org/10.1061/(ASCE)UP.1943-5444.0000466

Kearns, A., Saward, R., Houlston, A., & Rayner, J. (2014). Building urban resilience through green infrastructure pathways. *Resilient Sustainable Cities*, 64–77. https://doi.org/10.4324/9780203593066-14

Landry, S. M., & Chakraborty, J. (2009). Street trees and equity: Evaluating the spatial distribution of an urban amenity. *Environment and Planning A: Economy and Space, 41*(11), 2651–2670. https://doi.org/10.1068/A41236

Leitner, H., Sheppard, E., Webber, S., & Colven, E. (2018). Globalising urban resilience. *Urban Geography*, 1276–1284. https://doi.org/10.1080/02723638.2018.1446870

Liao, K.-H., Deng, S., & Tan, P. Y. (2017). Blue-Green infrastructure: New frontier for sustainable urban stormwater management. In P. Tan & C. Jim (Eds.), *Greening cities. Advances in 21st century human settlements* (pp. 203–226). Springer. https://doi.org/10.1007/978-981-10-4113-6_10

Mahadevia, D. (2016). Segmentation and enclavization in urban development. In I. Vojnovic (Ed.), *Building sustainable communities: A global urban context* (pp. 199–226). Michigan State University Press. https://doi.org/10.13140/RG.2.1.3074.4081

Markandeya, K., & Suryanarayana, G. (2009). Urban floods: Case study of Hyderabad. *NIDM Journal Disaster & Development*, 121–138. Retrieved October 23, 2021, from https://nidm.gov.in/PDF/Journal/Journal20092.pdf#page=130

Meerow, S., & Newell, J. P. (2016). Urban resilience for whom, what, when, where, and why? *Urban Geography, 40*(3), 309–329. https://doi.org/10.1080/02723638.2016.1206395

Meerow, S., & Newell, J. P. (2017). Spatial planning for multi-functional green infrastructure: Growing resilience in Detroit. *Landscape and Urban Planning, 159*, 62–75. https://doi.org/10.1016/j.landurbplan.2016.10.005

Mell, I. C. (2017). Greening Ahmedabad—creating a resilient Indian city using a green infrastructure approach to investment. *Landscape Research*, 289–314. https://doi.org/10.1080/01426397.2017.1314452

Menon, G. A. (2013). Citizens and 'squatters': The contested subject of public policy in neoliberal Mumbai. *Ethics and Social Welfare, 7*(2), 155–169. https://doi.org/10.1080/17496535.2013.779007

MoHUA. (2020). *Climatesmart Cities assessment framework 2.0*. https://www.niua.org/csc/assets/pdf/CSCAF_2_Booklet.pdf

MoHUA. (2021). *About smart cities | Mission objectives | Smart city features*. smartcities.gov.in.: https://smartcities.gov.in/about-scm

Mundoli, S., Manjunath, B., & Nagendra, H. (2014). Effects of urbanisation on the use of lakes as commons in the peri-urban interface of Bengaluru, India. *International Journal of Urban Sustainable Development*, 89–108. https://doi.org/10.1080/19463138.2014.982124

Nagendra, H., & Gopal, D. (2010). Tree diversity, distribution, history and change in urban parks: Studies in Bangalore, India. *Urban Ecosystems, 14*(2), 211–223. https://doi.org/10.1007/S11252-010-0148-1

Nagendra, H., Nagendran, S., Paul, S., & Pareeth, S. (2012). Graying, greening and fragmentation in the rapidly expanding Indian city of Bangalore. *Pareeth, Sajid, 105*(4), 100–106. https://doi.org/10.1016/J.LANDURBPLAN.2012.01.014

Patel, S., Sliuzas, R., & Mathur, N. (2015). The risk of impoverishment in urban development-induced displacement and resettlement in Ahmedabad. *Environment and Urbanisation, 27*(1), 231–256. https://doi.org/10.1177/0956247815569128

Paul, S., & Nagendra, H. (2015). Vegetation change and fragmentation in the mega city of Delhi: Mapping 25 years of change. *Applied Geography, 58*, 153–166. https://doi.org/10.1016/J.APGEOG.2015.02.001

Pramanik, S., Butsch, C., & Punia, M. (2021). Post-liberal urban dynamics in India – The case of Gurugram, the 'Millennium City'. *Remote Sensing Applications: Society and Environment*. https://doi.org/10.1016/J.RSASE.2021.100504

Ramchandra, T. V., & Mujumdar, P. P. (2009). Urban floods: Case study of Bangalore. *Disaster & Development: Journal of the National Institute of Disaster Management, 3*(2), Special Issue: Urban Floods- II, 1–97. Retrieved October 16, 2021, from https://nidm.gov.in/PDF/Journal/Journal20092.pdf#page=10

Reid, J. (2013). Interrogating the neoliberal biopolitics of the sustainable development-Resilience nexus. *International Political Sociology*, 353–367. https://doi.org/10.1111/IPS.12028

Roitman, S. (2015). Gated communities: Definitions, causes and consequences. *Proceedings of the Institution of Civil Engineers – Urban Design and Planning* (pp. 31–38). https://doi.org/10.1680/UDAP.2010.163.1.31

Sankhe, S., Vittal, I., Dobbs, R., Mohan, A., Gulati, A., Ablett, J., . . . Sethy, G. (2010). *India's urban awakening: Building inclusive cities, sustaining economic growth*. McKinsey Global Institute. Retrieved September 30, 2021, from https://tnl-uploads.s3.ap-southeast-1.amazonaws.com/production/36a6706c-6cb1-4f71-a761-94747c8a5ecd.pdf

Schindler, S., & Kishore, B. (2015). Why Delhi cannot plan its 'new towns': The case of solid waste management in Noida. *Geoforum, 60*, 33–42. https://doi.org/10.1016/J.GEOFORUM.2015.01.008

Shaban, A., & Sattar, S. (2016). Critical reflection on contemporary urbanization in India. *Shelter, 17*(1), 31–39. Retrieved September 28, 2021, from www.hudco.org

Sharma, R. N., & Shaban, A. (2006). Metropolitisation of Indian economy: Lessons In urban development. *The IUP Journal of Governance and Public Policy, I*(2), 17–35. Retrieved September 28, 2021, from https://ideas.repec.org/a/icf/icfjgp/v01y2006i2p17-35.html

Shaw, A. (2013). Metropolitan city growth and management in post-liberalized India. *Eurasian Geography and Economics*, 44–62. https://doi.org/10.2747/1539-7216.53.1.44

Sood, A. (2015). Industrial townships and the policy facilitation of corporate urbanisation in India. *Urban Studies, 52*(8), 1359–1378. https://doi.org/10.1177/0042098014562318

Sridharan, N. (2011). Spatial inequality and the politics of urban expansion. *Environment and Urbanization Asia, 2*(2), 187–204. https://doi.org/10.1177/097542531100200204

Staddon, C., Ward, S., De Vito, L., Zuniga-Teran, A., Gerlak, A. K., Schoeman, Y., . . . Booth, G. (2018). Contributions of green infrastructure to enhancing urban resilience. *Environment Systems and Decisions, 38*(3), 330–338. https://doi.org/10.1007/S10669-018-9702-9

Tierney, K. (2015). Resilience and the neoliberal project: Discourses, critiques, practices—And Katrina. *American Behavioral Scientist*, 1327–1342. https://doi.org/10.1177/0002764215591187

Tripathi, S. (2018, May 8). *Do economic reforms promote urbanization in India?* Retrieved September 28, 2021, from Munich Personal RePEc Archive (MPRA): https://mpra.ub.uni-muenchen.de/86591/

Udvardi, M. (2014). Bangalore: Urban development and environmental injustice. *Thesis*. Wellesley College. Retrieved October 16, 2021, from https://repository.wellesley.edu/islandora/object/ir%3A489/

Vásquez, A., Devoto, C., Giannotti, E., & Velásquez, P. (2016). Green infrastructure systems facing fragmented cities in Latin America – Case of Santiago, Chile. *Procedia Engineering, 161*, 1410–1416. https://doi.org/10.1016/J.PROENG.2016.08.602

Vives-Miró, S. (2011). Producing a "successful city": Neoliberal urbanism and gentrification in the tourist city – The case of Palma (Majorca). *Urban Studies Research*, 13. https://doi.org/10.1155/2011/989676

Wagner, P. D., Kumar, S., & Schneider, K. (2013). An assessment of land use change impacts on the water resources of the Mula and Mutha Rivers catchment upstream of Pune, India. *Hydrology and Earth System Sciences, 17*(6), 2233–2246. https://doi.org/10.5194/hess-17-2233-2013

Wilson, D., & Jonas, A. E. (2018). Urban resilience: An urban political movement. *Urban Geography, 39*(8), 1265–1267. https://doi.org/10.1080/02723638.2018.1452873

Wolch, J. R., Byrne, J., & Newell, J. P. (2014). Urban green space, public health, and environmental justice: The challenge of making cities 'just green enough'. *Landscape and Urban Planning, 125*, 234–244. https://doi.org/10.1016/j.landurbplan.2014.01.017

Wright, H. (2011). Understanding green infrastructure: The development of a contested concept in England. *The International Journal of Justice and Sustainability, 16*(10), 1003–1019. https://doi.org/10.1080/13549839.2011.631993

Yazar, M., Hestad, D., Mangalagiu, D., Saysel, A. K., Ma, Y., & Thornton, T. F. (2019). From urban sustainability transformations to green gentrification: Urban renewal in Gaziosmanpaşa, Istanbul. *Climatic Change, 160*(4), 637–653. https://doi.org/10.1007/S10584-019-02509-3

Ziervogel, G., Pelling, M., Cartwright, A., Chu, E., Deshpande, T., Harris, L., . . . Zweig, P. (2017). Inserting rights and justice into urban resilience: A focus on everyday risk. *Environment and Urbanisation, 29*(1), 123–138. https://doi.org/10.1177/0956247816686905

Zuniga-Teran, A. A., Staddon, C., Vito, L. D., Gerlak, A. K., Ward, S., Schoeman, Y., . . . Booth, G. (2019). Challenges of mainstreaming green infrastructure in built environment professions. *Journal of Environmental Planning and Management, 63*(4), 710–732. https://doi.org/10.1080/09640568.2019.1605890

4 Mapping Migration as the Metaphor for Regional Inequalities

Vanitha Putta and Arindam Biswas

4.1 Introduction

In the past two decades, India has seen the movement of people in mass numbers due to various reasons, from distress migration to mass migration. With advancements in innovation and technology, India has witnessed a shift in the socio-economic ladder, which has implied significant transformations in spatial elements. The spatial diversity in India concerning opportunities and development has induced interest and preference for people to move internally within the country. In addition to the technical advancements in communication and means of transport, the rise in awareness of growth opportunities and challenges of migration have catalyzed the scale, complexity, and choice of a particular destination for internal migration in India (IOM, 2013). Recent studies show a paradigm shift from considering migration as a sign of crisis to a common and adaptive element of society (Birx, 2010).

According to the global migration report, international migrants constitute about 250 million persons, and more than 750 million are internal migrants (World Bank Group, 2017). The migration of people is the second most important reason for urbanization after a natural increase in population. The Constitution of India guarantees freedom of movement for all citizens and prohibits discrimination and denial of access to public job opportunities based on place of birth or residence.

The diverse characteristics of states and regions in India, in terms of geographical location, topography, and natural resources, have contributed to the heterogeneous nature and regional disparities. Of the several dimensions of inequalities spanning the demography and geography of India, the chapter chooses to examine the interlink between migration and inequalities through migrant data and relevant socio-economic aspects. The chapter aims to investigate the genesis of internal migration patterns as a response to arising inequalities in the source and destination of migrants. This chapter studies the interrelation between regional disparities and internal migration patterns. The objectives of this chapter are

DOI: 10.4324/9781003280866-4

i. to comprehend the scope and complexity of state-level internal migration in India;
ii. to examine the various measures of inequality and its dimensions in the context of migration; and
iii. to investigate the dynamics of migration in correlation with various inequality attributes.

The book chapter consists of seven sections beginning with an introduction to the subject, followed by a brief review of the existing discourses on inequalities and the intersectionality between migration and inequalities. The following section discusses the conventional and emerging forms of inequalities and methods of measuring in the context of migration. It attempts to broaden the understanding of the emerging forms of inequalities at the regional level against the backdrop of migration patterns and processes. The chapter elaborates on the research methodology, data sources, and analysis methods used and presents a list of variables used to assess migration patterns and regional disparities and their interrelation. The following section discusses the magnitude and complexities of internal migration in India, followed by an analysis of state-level data to establish internal migration and rising inequalities. The chapter concludes by discussing how regional inequalities are a metaphor for internal migration patterns and demonstrating the need for a micro-level investigation.

4.1.1 Migration and Inequalities: Intersection

India has been a host of complex disparities across regions, and the processes of globalization and urbanization have further contributed to the widening inequalities at various territorial levels within the country. Inequality, typically classified based on economic and social aspects, overlaps in terms of its different attributes and has a causal relationship. Although income and wealth inequality are widely considered determinants to measure inequalities in a region, the aspects such as location and agglomeration externalities reflecting the concentration or congestion of economic activity are highlighted in recent studies on spatial and regional inequalities (Kanbur & Venables, 2005). Inequality is usually measured between or within regions at the macro- or micro-scales. It is also essential to consider inequality between a group of individuals or communities in a location. In addition, social inequality has multiple aspects, such as gender, caste, ethnicity, religion, access to resources and services, etc. (Drishti, 2019). Besides, the rise in the private sector and changing role of government have contributed to emerging forms of inequality in India (Pandey & Gautam, 2020).

According to the World Inequality Report 2022 (Chancel et al., 2022), the top 10% and top 1% of Indian citizens possess 57% and 21% of the country's total income, respectively, and the bottom 50% share has decreased to 13%, suggesting a high degree of inequality at the national level. The report also states the deterioration of inequality data released by the government and consequent difficulties in measuring the inequality status of the country. The intersection between migration and inequality is interrelated through manifold aspects. The existing or perceived inequalities often result in people's voluntary or involuntary movement in anticipation of better opportunities. However, migration can itself result in additional imbalances. Migrants struggle with and manifest different forms of inequality at their destinations (Collins et al., 2020).

Migrant groups and individuals are frequently stratified based on Census data. The streams of migration, reasons for migration, duration of stay, gender, age, caste, educational level, and employment are often the basis of stratification between and within migrants in migration research in India. India's demographic and geographic heterogeneity has contributed to emerging inequalities among non-migrants and migrants.

Furthermore, migration flows reflect a complex interconnected pattern with multiple origins and destinations of migrants in India, consisting of 28 states and 8 union territories. Mapping migration patterns and processes regarding socio-economic dimensions at macro- and micro-levels is challenging. Thus, the various discourses on migration studies in India have been limited to significant migration streams in the country – inter- and intra-state migration and inter- and intra-district migration. The lack of data availability on interconnected flows within the country, states, and districts is a vital drawback in the dearth of momentum in migration research. Although there are recent developments in the emphasis given to the collection of migration data at the global and national levels, India is at a nascent stage in this course.

The Sustainable Development Goals (SDGs) 2030 agenda targets to reduce inequalities in Goal 10. 'Migrants and urban poor' is listed as one of the 14 vulnerable population groups identified for focused initiative and progress monitoring of SDGs (NITI Aayog, 2021). The global indicators framework has targets and indicators related to migrants under goals 8, 10, and 17. However, the national indicator framework has not listed indicators related to migrants against these goals and targets. The indicators for achieving reduced inequality are limited to women and minority groups (Table 4.1).

Collaboration between the International Organization for Migration India (IOM India), India Center for Migration (ICM), and the Global Migration Data Analysis Centre (GMDAC), funded by the IOM Development Fund, is one recent creation in India toward the development of efficient migration policy (IOM – UN Migration, 2022). IOM India aims to improve migration data collection and develop migrant-centered policies and programs through this initiative. By implementing the global compact for safe, orderly, and regular migration, the project does, however, predominantly address international migration to accomplish target 10.7 of the SDGs 2030 Agenda. As per World Migration Report 2022 (McAuliffe et al., 2022), with around 18 million of the total population living abroad, India is the largest source of the migrant population worldwide. Although international migration

Table 4.1 Migration-related goals and targets in the Sustainable Development Goals 2030 Agenda (UNSD, 2020)

SDG No.	*Goal*	*Target*	*Indicator*
8	Promote sustained, inclusive, and sustainable economic growth, full and productive employment, and decent work for all	8.8 Protect labour rights and promote safe and secure working environments for all workers, including migrant workers, in particular, women migrants, and those in precarious employment	8.8.1 Frequency rates of fatal and non-fatal occupational injuries, by sex and migrant status 8.8.2 Increase in national compliance of labour rights (freedom of association and collective bargaining) based on International Labour Organization (ILO) textual sources and national legislation, by sex and migrant status
10	Reduce inequality within and among countries	10.7 Facilitate orderly, safe, regular and responsible migration and mobility of people, including through the implementation of planned and well-managed migration policies	10.7.1 Recruitment cost borne by employee as a proportion of yearly income earned in country of destination 10.7.2 Number of countries that have implemented well-managed migration policies
		10.c By 2030, reduce to less than 3 per cent the transaction costs of migrant remittances and eliminate remittance corridors with costs higher than 5 per cent	10.c.1 Remittance costs as a proportion of the amount remitted
17	Strengthen the means of implementation and revitalize the Global Partnership for Sustainable Development	*Data, monitoring and accountability* 17.18 By 2020, enhance capacity-building support to developing countries, including for least developed countries and small island developing States, to increase significantly the availability of high-quality, timely and reliable data disaggregated by income, gender, age, race, ethnicity, migratory status, disability, geographic location and other characteristics relevant in national contexts	

needs attention for better policy integration, concurrently, it is imperative to improve data collection and data management of internal migrants and facilitate them.

4.1.2 Measuring Migrant Inequalities

Measuring migrant inequalities includes multiple and overlapping links between migrant and non-migrant populations and between, amongst, and within migrant populations (Collins et al., 2020). A comparative analysis of the net migration rate, in-migration rate, and out-migration rate of origin and destination regions and their development indicators like per capita income and gross domestic product forms the basis of conventional methods for measuring regional disparities and migrant inequalities. The simple implication of these numbers is associating high and low migration movements with the region's development. Even if economic factors are crucial for studies on inequality, it is clear that inequality has multiple facets, including economic, social, political, and environmental aspects. At the national level, differences based on class, color, ethnicity, age, gender, or citizenship status are considered frequently. Although these are complex and interwoven, income inequality is known to be the fundamental cause of inequalities (Collins et al., 2020). The purpose and choice of space for measuring inequality are essential, along with the appropriateness of such inequality measures and their relativeness to the context. Andrew McKay (McKay, 2002) refers to a few inequality measures such as dividing the population into quintile groups, Lorenz Curves, Gini Coefficients, and Theil Index. However, the data availability limitations in India restrict the comprehensive understanding of inequality between groups or communities. Table 4.2 lists some adopted approaches to measuring inequalities.

Determinants at both the macro- and micro-levels influence the migration phenomenon. The macro-level approach emphasizes migration due to national or global factors. The micro-level approach is the factors affecting the decision to move at an individual or household level. Interconnections between the macro- and micro-levels are apparent in a complete migration model (De Jong & Fawcett, 1981). Migration models have seen compelling advancements in discourses on the attractiveness of a destination and migration decision-making, which extended beyond the conventional pull and push factors. The pull factors of a location are the indicators for the high attractiveness of any place to be the preferred choice for migration. At the global or regional level, push factors for the migration of people or communities can be political, economic, social, and environmental. At a micro-level, the push factors for the migration of individuals or households can be employment, education, marriage, health, business, etc.

Table 4.2 List of studies showing adopted approaches to measure inequalities

Inequality studies	*Measures*	*Elaboration*
Regional inequality (Okun & Richardson, 1961)	Migration flows between low-stagnant regions, low- growing regions, high-stagnant regions, and high- growing regions	Per capita income, migration rate by nativity, and race
Regional Inequality (Kundu & Gupta, 1996)	Pattern of internal migration in India, state-level comparison	Demographic variables, variation in male migrants, growth rates of migration across all migration streams, out-migrants and in-migrants percentage
Regional inequality index for State Domestic Product and its components (Barua & Chakraborty, 2010)	Income, agriculture, primary sector, manufacturing services, agriculture and the primary sector, and infrastructure	Using non-linearity trends in the Theil Index of Inequality Assessing openness for trade
State-wise divergence analysis (Stewart & Moslares, 2012)	State domestic product, per capita average growth rate, Gini coefficient, and literacy rate	
Manual on Inequality in India (Sinha, 2015)	Economic dimension, gender, access to essential services, access to land, access to justice	
Inequality-adjusted Human Development Index (Suryanarayana et al., 2016)	Income Education Health	Gross National Income per capita Estimate of school life expectancy Life expectancy
Five dimensions of migrant inequality (Friesen, 2020)	Group Classification	Birth country/ethnicity etc.
	Types of inequality	Income
	Migration temporality	Different phases in the migration process (pre-migration, post-migration)
	Intersectionality	Gender, age, education level and types of inequality, temporality, and spatiality
	Spatiality	Spatial clustering

(*Continued*)

Table 4.2 (*Continued*)

Inequality studies	*Measures*	*Elaboration*
Dimensions of Migrant Deprivation (study conducted to investigate inequality amongst young migrants) (Lewycka et al., 2020)	Socio-economic inequalities	Household deprivation, neighborhood deprivation, school decile level
	Access	Citizenship or permanent residency after ten years or more, unable to access healthcare
	Social connectedness	Like school, people at school care a lot, sense of belonging at school, feel settled
	Discrimination	Bullied at school, the experience of racial discrimination
	Health	Weekly smoking, overweight or obese, symptoms of depression
Regional Inequality in India (Pandey & Gautam, 2020)	Livelihood inequality	Household-level physical capital, wealth quintile-wise distribution of assets, human capital index, natural capital
	Education inequality	Enrolment in educational institutions (income and caste-wise)
	Health inequality	Workforce participation, wage gap, sex ratio, literacy rate, violence against women, Women Empowerment Index
	Gender inequality	Health expenditure as a percentage of total state expenditure, per capita health expenditure, health expenditure as a percentage of Gross State Domestic Product (GSDP), health personnel
Regional Disparity in Patterns of Out-migration (Banerjee and Das, 2021)	Demographic variables	Population density, percentage share of the urban population, literacy rate, percentage share of workers in the agricultural and non-agricultural sector
	Migration variables	Out-migration, in-migration, net-migration rate
	Socio-economic variables	Human Development Index, Gross State Domestic Product (GSDP), and Net State Domestic Product (NSDP) per capita, poverty rate

4.1.3 Methodology

Migration as a process has relative benefits and drawbacks concerning the development attributes of a region. Migration can contribute to economic development or can have negative repercussions. At the same time, the relationship between the economic progress of a region and migration levels may

Table 4.3 Variables considered for statistical analysis

Migration	*Social-economic variables*
Net migration rate	Level of Urbanization
In-migration	Urban population
Out-migration	Per capita income
Age	Gross State Domestic Product
Gender	Net State Domestic Product
Duration of stay	Rural Unemployment
Reasons of migration	Urban Employment
Economic activity	Infant Mortality rate/Birth rate
Streams of migration	Death Rate
	Poverty Rate
	Minimum Wage per day

or may not be causal. The determinants used for assessing the intersectionality between migration flows and spatial inequalities in India are considered in the context of internal migration processes in India and derived from the literature study, which reflects the motivation for movement or relative attractiveness of opportunities of a destination. The analysis consists of two segments. In the first segment, we look at the migration patterns in India's states and union territories, and in the second, we find a relationship between the migration rate and socio-economic factors. Under the two segments, Table 4.3 lists the variables considered for the analysis.

The first segment of the analysis shows a state-level comparison concerning net-migration rate, out-migration, and in-migration rate, which displays the states most chosen and least chosen for migration. Also, a further examination of the duration of stay, reasons for migration, the economic activity of migrants, and the educational level of migrants is analyzed through the lens of gender and age groups. Heat maps are used to represent the analysis, which gives an insight into the gender inequality dimension and migration behavior based on age groups of migrants. The second segment of the analysis comprehends the association between the migration rate of states and socio-economic variables through Pearson's Correlation Coefficient and Linear Regression Analysis methods. The sources for data for the first segment are Migration Tables from Census data for the 2011 year and the second segment from statistical reports of the Reserve Bank of India.

4.1.4 *Internal Migration in India: Scale and Complexities*

Over 98 million people in India migrated within and outside the country during the 1990s. However, migration began slowing down in the 1970s. Over the decade since 1951, the number of migrants climbed by around 22% between 1991 and 2001. According to the census of India, migration rose from 28% in 1991 to 38% in 2011, and intra-state migrants constitute 87%. Migrants constitute more than one-third of the entire population, with about

70% female migrants (Census of India, 2011). Internal migration in India includes about 455 million persons who move between and within states and union territories of the country.

The migration data in India is collected by the Census and the National Sample Survey Organization (NSSO). The Census data identifies migrants by Place of Birth (PoB) and Place of Last Residence (PoLR), whereas NSSO identifies migrants by Place of Last Residence. However, since NSSO data is based on a sample survey, only Census data is considered for the study. The differences and similarities of migration data estimates based on PoB and PoLR have been extensively discussed and debated. Comparing both estimates reveals that PoLR is considered over PoB since it gives a higher estimate of internal migration (Bhagat, 2005). de Jong and Fawcett provide a summary of the factors that determine how migration typologies are classified, including time (permanent, temporary), distance (short, long), boundaries crossed (internal, external), areal units involved (communities, countries, states, etc.), and the numbers involved (individuals, groups) (de Jong & Fawcett, 1981). Migration in India is examined based on the following classification: (a) place of origin and destination defined by political or administrative boundaries, (b) duration of stay of the migrant, (c) movement of people, (d) push and pull factors, and (e) migration influenced by globalization aspects. The sub-categories are listed in Table 4.4.

Table 4.4 Classification of migrants (Derived from various literature studies)

	Categories	*Sub-categories*	
a	**Place of origin and destination**	Internal migration	Rural-urban, urban-urban, urban-rural, rural-rural Inter-state, intra-state, inter-district, intra-district
		External migration or international migration	Immigration, emigration, legal, and illegal, refugees
b	**Duration of stay**	Permanent migration, temporary migration, seasonal migration	
c	**Movement of people**	Step migration, circular migration, chain migration	
d	**Push and pull factors**	Voluntary migration	
		Involuntary migration	Internally displaced people, refugees
e	**Factors influenced by globalization**	Transmigrants, brain drain, middlemen, diaspora	

Although all the categories and sub-categories of migration seem distinct but are usually intertwined, the various causes or reasons to decide to move from a particular geographic location remain the motivation for migration.

4.1.4.1 Demographic Factors

Of the total internal migrants in India, people moving inter-state and intra-state are around 12% and 87%, respectively. As per the Census 2011, the share of migrants to total migrants of the country is highest in Maharashtra and Uttar Pradesh, followed by Andhra Pradesh, West Bengal, Tamil Nadu, Bihar, Gujarat, Karnataka, and Madhya Pradesh. In addition, Maharashtra and Uttar Pradesh are cumulatively populated by about 24% of the total migrant population. The popular destinations for these migrants are Maharashtra and Delhi, with the highest in-migrants of 17% and 12%, respectively, followed by Uttar Pradesh, Gujarat, Haryana, Karnataka, and Madhya Pradesh. Uttar Pradesh, with 23% of out-migrants, is the origin of the most significant out-migration followed by Bihar with 14% of out-migrants (Table 4.5).

The net migration rate (NMR) of various states is used to determine the variation amongst different regions to obtain an overview of state-level imbalance in terms of pushing and pulling people to multiple destinations from different origins. The NMR is the change in the population of people in-migrating and out-migrating from or within a location or region. NMR is calculated by dividing net in-migrants by a state's total population in a year. A deduction between the volume of in-migrants and the volume of out-migrants in a state in a specific year gives the value of net in-migrants. A higher in-migration rate implies a high attractive index of the state and vice versa, and a higher out-migration rate implies a low attractive index of the state and vice versa. However, NMR interpretations can be misleading as the levels of migration rate can be driven by either low mobility of people or high counterbalanced in and outflows.

Streams of migration: The four types of classification are based on the movement of people between and within states and between and within districts namely: inter-state migrants, intra-state migrants, inter-district migrants, and intra-district migrants. Further, the four streams of migration include migrants moving between rural and urban areas, e.g., rural to rural migration, rural to urban migration, urban to rural migration, and urban to urban migration. India has around 87% of intra-state migration, while inter-state migration is about 12%, implying people prefer moving within the state over moving to another state. Inter-state migration is highest in Chandigarh, with about 93% of migrants arriving from other states, followed by Delhi with 88 %. Intra-state migration is highest in Manipur (97%), Andhra Pradesh (95%), Kerala (95%), Odisha (94%), Bihar (94%), Assam (94%), Jammu and Kashmir (93%), and Uttar Pradesh (92%). Further, the intra-district

Table 4.5 State-wise comparison of migration data

State/country	*Migrants of the total population (%)*	*Migrant percentage of total migrants (%)*	*In-migrants (%)*	*Out-migrants (%)*	*Net migration rate (%)*
India	37.6	100.0			
Jammu and Kashmir	22.4	0.62	0.29	0.61	-13.9
Himachal Pradesh	38.6	0.58	0.73	0.99	-20.4
Punjab	49.5	3.01	4.59	3.21	26.9
Chandigarh	64.3	0.15	1.17	0.49	349.0
Uttarakhand	42.8	0.95	2.30	1.83	25.5
Haryana	41.8	2.32	6.68	4.27	51.7
NCT Of Delhi	43.0	1.59	**11.67**	2.87	284.4
Rajasthan	32.2	4.84	4.80	6.92	-16.8
Uttar Pradesh	28.3	12.39	7.49	**22.70**	-41.3
Bihar	26.2	5.98	2.05	**13.74**	-60.9
Sikkim	40.5	0.05	0.11	0.04	65.0
Arunachal Pradesh	45.6	0.14	0.25	0.07	71.3
Nagaland	27.8	0.12	0.20	0.08	31.5
Manipur	24.1	0.15	0.04	0.14	-19.5
Mizoram	35.3	0.08	0.08	0.06	10.0
Tripura	35.4	0.29	0.16	0.16	0.4
Meghalaya	25.6	0.17	0.20	0.13	12.7
Assam	34.1	2.34	0.91	1.22	-5.3
West Bengal	36.6	7.34	4.39	4.43	-0.3
Jharkhand	29.3	2.12	4.05	3.14	14.9
Odisha	36.7	3.38	1.58	2.34	-9.9
Chhattisgarh	34.8	1.95	2.34	1.28	22.5
Madhya Pradesh	34.1	5.43	5.06	5.49	-3.2
Gujarat	44.5	5.90	7.22	2.90	38.8
Daman and Diu	61.1	0.03	0.23	0.03	434.2
Dadra and Nagar Haveli	54.7	0.04	0.25	0.03	346.1
Maharashtra	51.1	12.59	**16.75**	5.65	53.6
Andhra Pradesh	45.4	8.42	2.93	3.74	-5.2
Karnataka	43.3	5.81	5.98	4.61	12.2
Goa	78.2	0.25	0.50	0.20	112.1
Lakshadweep	31.6	0.00	0.01	0.03	-148.9
Kerala	53.5	3.92	1.21	2.38	-19.1
Tamil Nadu	43.3	6.86	3.04	3.66	-4.6
Puducherry	57.1	0.16	0.63	0.53	41.0
Andaman and Nicobar Islands	56.8	0.05	0.15	0.04	159.1

movement of migrants is higher than the inter-district movement (Census of India, 2011) (Figure 4.1).

Migration between rural and urban areas indicates a higher migration between rural-to-rural areas and high out-migration from rural areas. According to the 2011 Census, over 47% of all migrants in India travel from rural to rural areas, compared to 64% of migrants who leave rural areas and

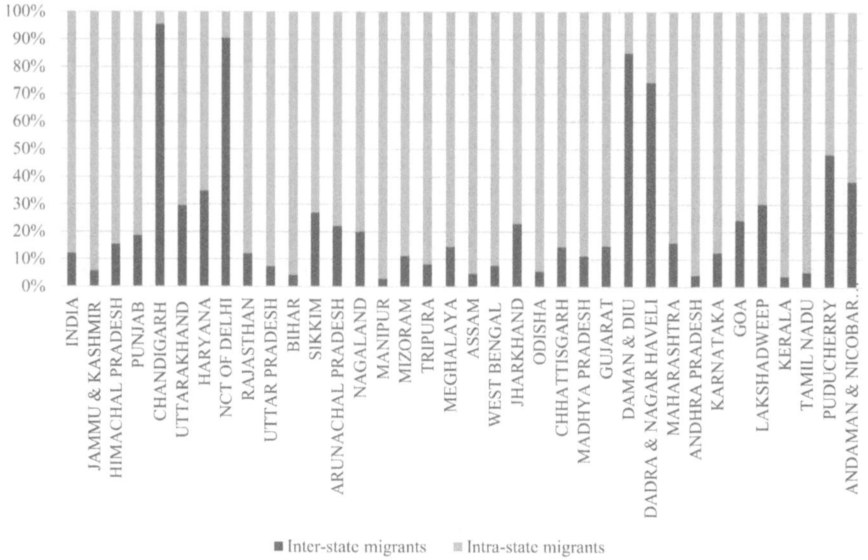

Figure 4.1 State-wise share of inter-state and intra-state migrants

23% who move to urban areas. Substantially high in-migration is indicative in rural areas than urban areas. A state-wise comparison indicates the highest out-migration from rural areas in the states of Bihar (81%) and Himachal Pradesh (81%), followed by Jharkhand (79%), Chhattisgarh (78%), Rajasthan (75%), and Daman & Diu (75%). Urban to urban migration is high in the state of Puducherry (41%), Chandigarh (39%), Delhi (34%), and Tamil Nadu (31%) (Census of India, 2011) (Figure 4.2).

Variation by gender: State-wise variation based on gender is essential to understand how movements of men and women vary between states. Female migrants constitute more than two-thirds of total migrants. The highest female migration percentage is observed in the state of Bihar with about 86%, followed by 80% and 79% of female migrants in Uttar Pradesh and Rajasthan. Almost all the states have more than 60% share of female migrants, excluding Chandigarh, NCT Delhi, Nagaland, Mizoram, Meghalaya, Sikkim, Arunachal Pradesh, Lakshadweep, Andaman and Nicobar Islands, Puducherry, Maharashtra, Kerala, and Tamil Nadu. Daman and Diu has the highest share of male migrants. The comparative data implies that states in the country's northeast region have a proportional share of migrants in terms of gender. However, it is observed that female migrants' movements depend on the migration of male members or families (Figure 4.3).

Variation by age: Age is the most fundamental socio-economic characteristic influencing the relative frequency of migration (Cris Lewis, 1977). Based on the summary of major motives related to migration (de Jong & Fawcett,

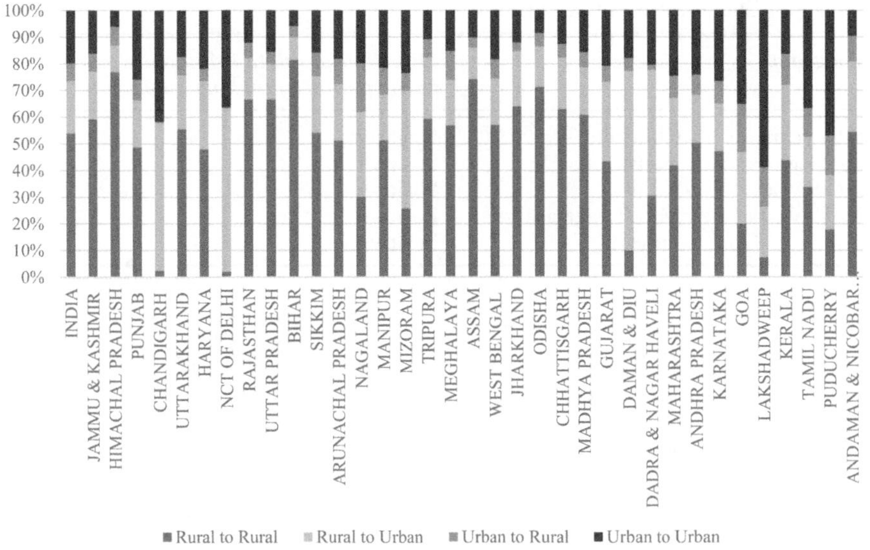

Figure 4.2 State-wise streams of migration

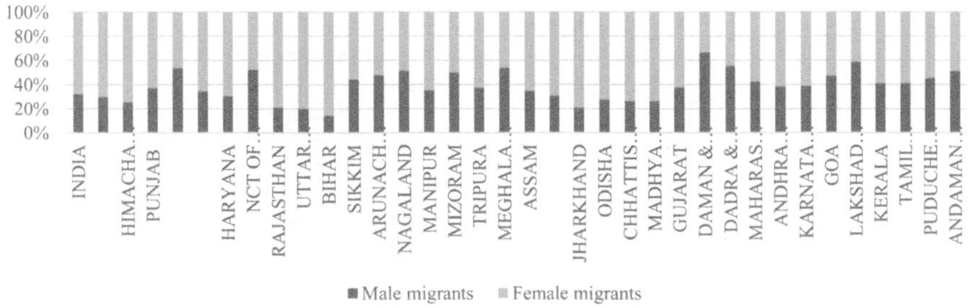

Figure 4.3 State-wise variation of the percentage of migrants based on gender

1981) and the widely studied relationship between age and migration rate (Cris Lewis, 1977), a classification of age groups is derived to show the direction of the relationship with the decision to move (Table 4.6). Migration variation based on gender, when examined along with age groups, displays a wide disparity between the movements of men and women of different states.

Figure 4.4 shows the heat mapping of state-wise variation in percentages of male and female migrants based on the above five age group categories. The proportion of female migrants is higher in the age brackets 25—39 and 40–59 years. A higher share of female migrants is observed in Bihar state, with 33% in the age group 25–39 years, followed by Uttar Pradesh, Jharkhand, Rajasthan, and Punjab. Across all states, a significant proportion of male

Table 4.6 Classification of age groups

Age group	*Category*	*Direction of relationship with participation in making a decision to move*
0–14 years	Children	Negative
15–24 years	Youth	Positive
25–39 years	Adults	Positive
40–59 years	Middle-age adults	Positive
60+	Elderly	Positive

Figure 4.4 State-wise variation of the percentage of migrants based on gender and age

migration is less than 10%, excluding northeastern states, Union territories, Gujarat, Karnataka, Maharashtra, and Tamil Nadu. Simultaneously female migration share is higher across all states in age brackets 25–39 and 40–59 years. Although the mapping seems to reflect more female migration, it is notable that, in India, 15–24 years and 25–39 years are the age ranges when women get married. Thus, it is unknown to what extent women in a household are involved in deciding on migration. However, the mapping shows an evident spatial inequality between male and female migrants amongst different age groups.

Variation by education level: Census data collect migrants' educational levels in five categories apart from a migrant's literate or illiterate status. The five levels of education include: (i) literate but below matric/secondary, (ii) matric/secondary but below graduate, (iii) technical diploma or certificate not equal to a degree, (iv) graduate and above other than a technical degree, and (v) Technical degree or diploma equal to degree or post-graduate degree. As per Census 2011, around 61% of migrants are literate, of which one-third is of education level below matric/secondary. About half of literate migrants are below graduate level, and only 8.5% of literate migrants have a technical diploma and above education level (Figure 4.5).

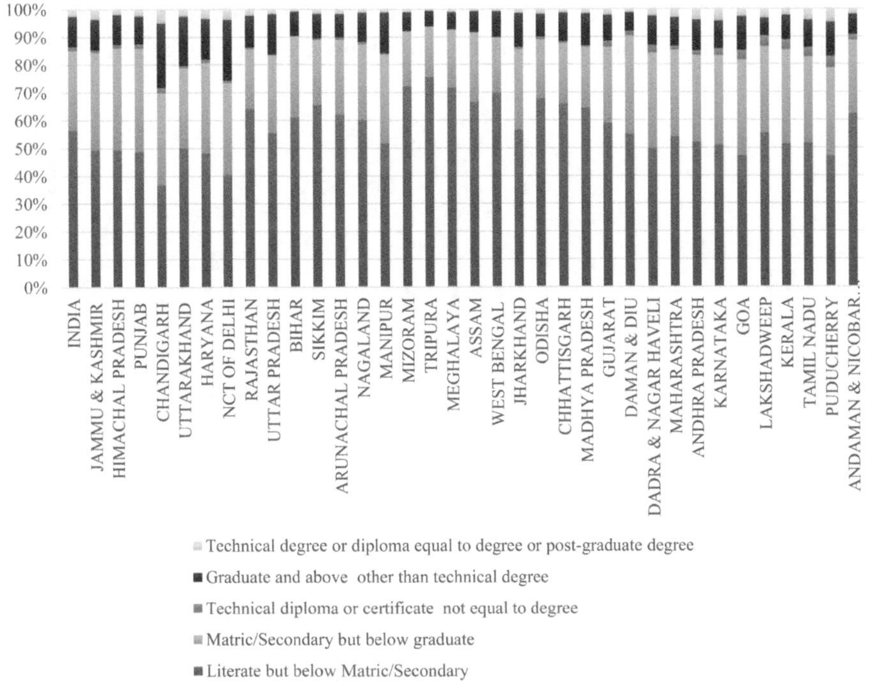

Figure 4.5 Percentage of state-wise migrants based on the education level

Variation based on the duration of stay: Data on migrants are gathered by the Census of India based on how long they have lived in the area enumerated since leaving their previous domicile. The duration of stay is classified into four categories – people who stay in the place of enumeration for less than one year, from one to four years, four to nine years, and for ten years and above. Through this information, the temporary and permanent migrants can be determined. However, the data do not provide information on seasonal and circular migration. As per the Census 2011, around 53% of migrants have stayed in their destination location for ten years and above. People who have migrated for less than one year are about 4%. Around one-third of the total migrant's stay in their destination states is less than nine years. A comparison of the state-wise share of migrants based on the duration of stay indicates a higher percentage of migration for ten years and above (Figure 4.6).

Examining the duration of stay in relation to age groups indicates the decision-making power of migrants and their preferences. A mapping of the duration of stay of migrants across states of India based on age groups in Figure 4.7 indicates migrants in the age bracket 25–59 years have preferred to stay for a longer duration in the destination states, followed by the age group of migrants above 60 years.

Variation by economic activity: Census of India classifies workers as main and marginal workers based on their work. People who worked for 183 days or more during the course of the year are referred to as main workers, whereas those who worked for fewer than 183 days are referred to as marginal workers. The term 'non-workers' refers to those who are not engaged in any type

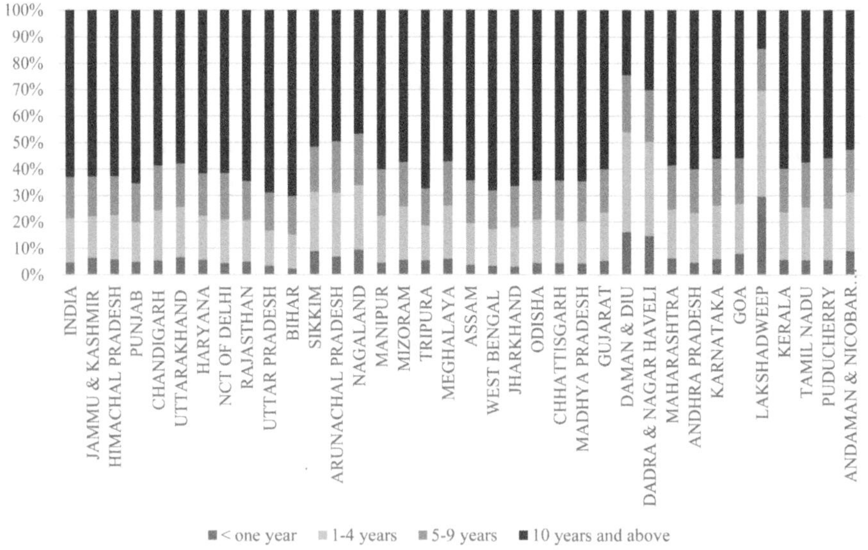

Figure 4.6 State-wise percentage of migrants based on duration of stay

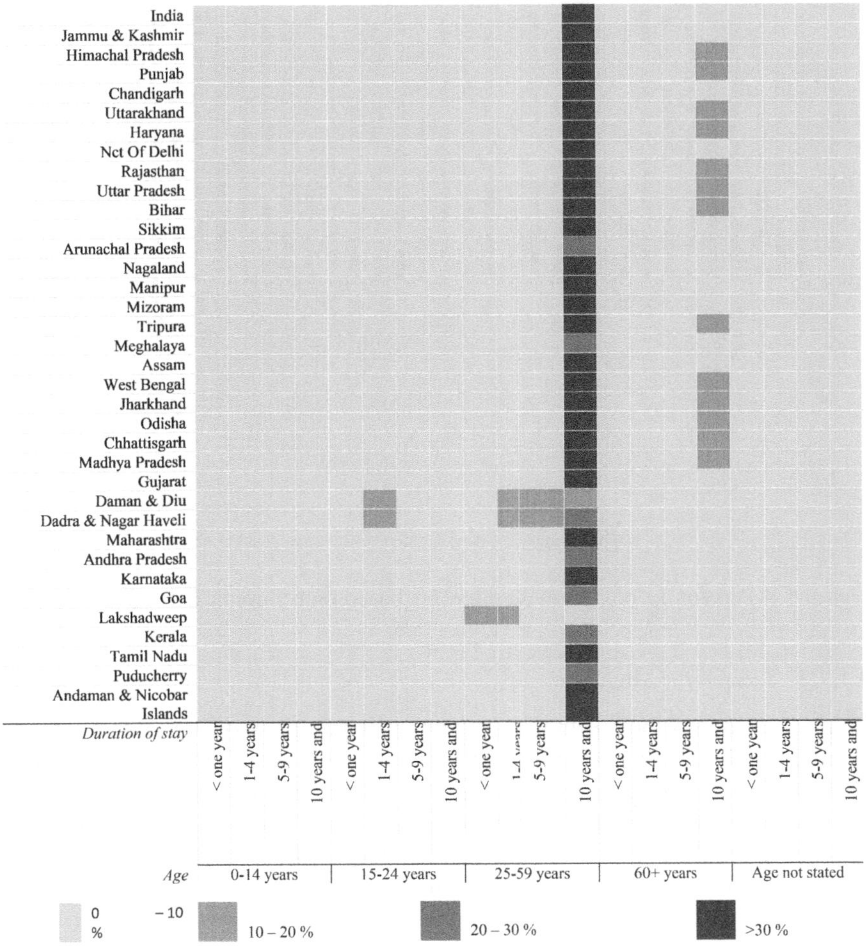

Figure 4.7 State-wise variation of the percentage of the duration of stay of migrants based on age groups

of economic activity. The Census 2011 reports that main and marginal workers account for 30% and 12%, respectively, of the total migrants in India. Concurrently, more than half of the migrant population (i.e., 57%) is classified as non-workers. The highest percentage of non-working migrants are in Kerala (70%) and Punjab (69%), followed by Uttar Pradesh (67%), West Bengal (66%), Puducherry (66%), Haryana (64.7%), and Bihar (64.3%) (Figure 4.8).

Economic activity seen in relation to age groups reflects an effective depiction. Non-workers are more prevalent in the 0–14 and over 60 age groups. However, the percentage of non-working migrants is high in the age brackets of 15–24 years and 25–39 years across all states, indicating a high unemployment rate for migrants looking for work (Figure 4.9).

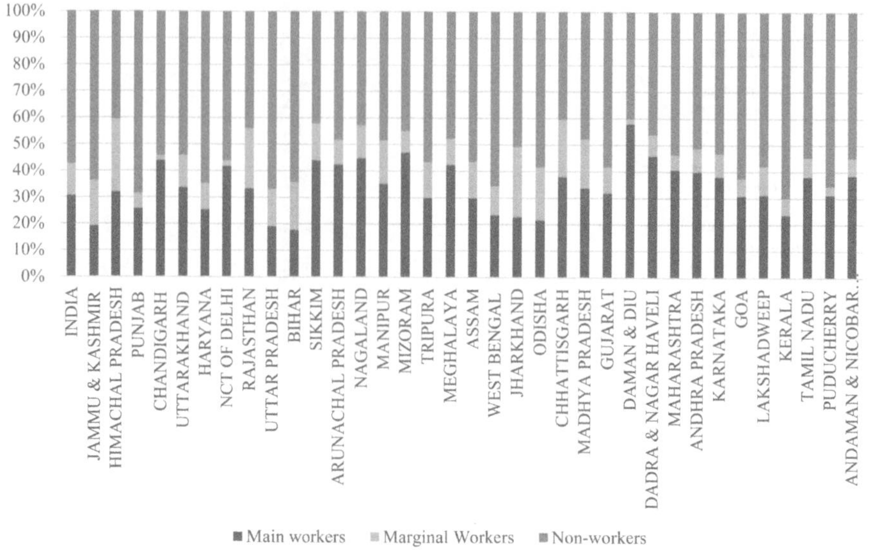

Figure 4.8 Percentage of state-wise migrants based on economic activity

4.1.4.2 *Reason for Migration*

Reasons for migration are vital in understanding the spatial inequalities between origin and destination locations. They reflect the motivation behind migration and indicate the availability or lack of aspects anticipated by people moving to their origin or destination place. According to the 2011 Census, there are seven reasons stated for people to migrate, including work or employment, business, education, marriage, moving after giving birth, moving with a household, and other reasons. As per the Census of 2011, marriage is the primary driver of female migration in India, accounting for over 45% of all female migrants. The states where female migration is high due to the reason for marriage are Bihar (73%), Jharkhand (64%), Uttar Pradesh (64%), and Rajasthan (63%). Other states with more than 50% of female migration due to the reason of marriage are Himachal Pradesh (57%), Madhya Pradesh (56%), Chhattisgarh (56%), Odisha (52%), and Jammu & Kashmir (50%). The most prominent reason for high male migration is work or employment observed in NCT Delhi (26%) and all Union Territories of India and northeastern states (Figure 4.10).

4.1.5 *State-Level Analysis*

The following section presents a regression analysis between migration rate and socio-economic and development variables to understand inequalities better. The Sustainable Development Goals Index 2020–2021 (NITI Aayog, 2021) report has listed the states of Meghalaya and Chandigarh as the top

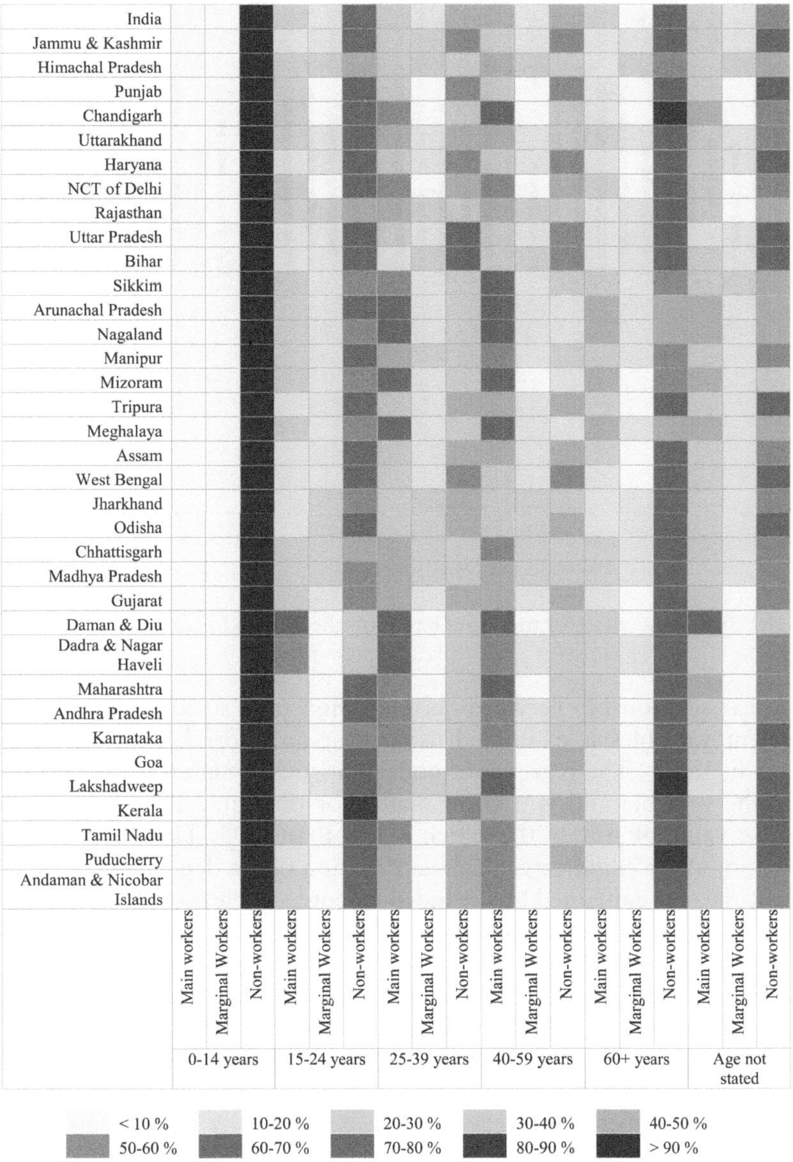

Figure 4.9 State-wise variation of the percentage of economic activity amongst migrants based on age group

performers under the reduced inequality goal. The report also states that in 'SDG 10: Reduced Inequality', the country's score has increased from 64 to 67 from 2019 to 2020, thus changing India's category from the Performer to the Front Runner.

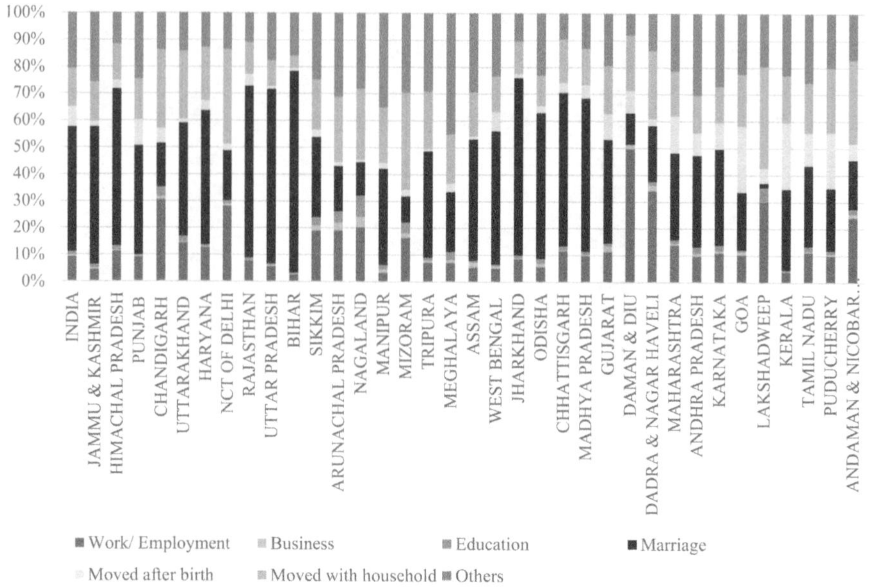

Figure 4.10 State-wise share of migrants based on the reason for migration

The linear relationship between net migration rate, socio-economic, and development variables is examined using Pearson's correlation and linear regression methods. The regression model statistically significantly predicts the outcome variable and is a good match for the data, as shown by the significance value of p (0.000), which is less than 0.05. The coefficient of determination (0.887) indicates that the variation of the dependent variables around the mean is explained by the independent variable, i.e., the net migration rate. The correlation coefficient (Multiple R) is 0.942, showing a strong linear relationship (Table 4.7).

The Pearson correlation coefficients indicate a negative relation with poverty, birth, death, infant mortality, employment, NSDP, and GSDP. A strong association is shown with variables of urban population, urbanization level, per capita income, minimum wages, and per capita Net State Domestic Product.

4.2 Conclusion

The intersectionality between migration and inequalities is a vast subject with multiple layers. The variation in in-migration and out-migration rates of the states indicates high attractiveness as destinations for people who choose to migrate. It also implies that these states have relatively better opportunities and resources. The scale and complexities of internal migration in India are evident through the complex interconnected movements between and within

Table 4.7 Correlation analysis between migration rate and socio-economic variables (Census of India, 2011; RBI, 2021b, 2021a)

	Pearson's correlation	*P-value*	*Coefficients*	*Standard error*	*t Stat*
Urban population	0.586012316	0.001648013	0.228082332	0.061068	3.73492
Level of urbanization AEGR	0.458242965	0.786080357	0.159154774	0.577216	0.275728
Poverty rate (based on MRP consumption) 2011–2012	−0.024359396	0.023158195	0.2288376	0.091699	2.49554
Birth rate	−0.079682413	0.566171712	−0.204021179	0.348699	−0.58509
Death rate	−0.5143583	0.162130276	−1.490210734	1.019679	−1.46145
Infant mortality rate	−0.302224238	0.030292411	0.266384452	0.11272	2.363238
Per capita income at constant (2011–2012) prices	0.676235912	0.91174587	−0.049625311	0.44112	−0.1125
Per capita NSDP (Rs.) current prices BASE: 2011–2012	0.676233832	0.911573189	0.049722554	0.441117	0.11272
GSDP Current Prices (Rs. in lakh) BASE: 2011–2012	−0.165089894	0.700038061	4.5309E−07	1.16E−06	0.391849
Net State Domestic Product (Current Prices) (₹ Lakh) BASE: 2011–12	−0.165876527	0.700838887	−5.09168E−07	1.3E−06	−0.39075
Rural unemployment rate	−0.051190862	0.320154266	−0.045764751	0.044689	−1.02407
Urban unemployment rate	−0.170779537	0.245257575	0.040914588	0.033995	1.203546
Minimum wages per day (Rs.)	0.478537335	0.360451657	0.025635002	0.027275	0.939863

states. The chapter highlights migration patterns concerning gender and age groups. A state-level analysis approach has highlighted how people's movements vary when examined through the lens of gender and age variation. The analysis also reflects a strong inclination toward migrant movements in states with higher urban populations and urbanization, e.g., Maharashtra and Delhi. Also, a preference for movement within the states is higher than migration to other states. A high rural out-migration (64%) indicates a dearth of opportunities or resources. However, movement between rural to rural areas is higher than the preference to migrate to urban areas. Examining migrant movements based on gender indicates a balanced share of migrants in the country's northeast region.

High female migration constitutes amongst the age group 25–59 years. The correlation analysis through Pearson's coefficient and linear regression methods shows a strong association between migration rate and urban population, level of urbanization, per capita income, minimum wages, and Net State Domestic Product. Cumulatively, a macro-level analysis has emphasized the existence of spatial inequality amongst the states, but assessing them at the micro-level can expand the research on migrant inequalities. For instance, the association between socio-economic variables and migration rate may be further expanded to identify the destination attractiveness index of a location. Consequently, a micro-level investigation can reveal the motivations and stages in the migrant decision-making process. Although the analysis implies gender inequality amongst migrants across all states, a further micro-analysis at the individual level can give a fair picture of micro-aspects of gender inequality and the quantum of participation of women in the process of decision-making – whether to migrate or not and preference of destination location. The data mapping of migrant movement patterns between the states interlinking the inequality attributes at a regional scale delves into exposing a new perspective and an addition to the migration studies.

References

Banerjee, P., & Das, B. (2021). Regional disparity in patterns of out-migration from West Bengal: Evidences from census data. *Demography India*, *50*(2), 131–151.

Barua, A., & Chakraborty, P. (2010). Does openness affect regional inequality? A case study for India. *Review of Development Economics*, *14*(3), 447–465. https://doi.org/10.1111/j.1467-9361.2010.00564.x

Bhagat, R. B. (2005). Conceptual issues in measurement of internal migration in India. *XXVth IUSSP International Conference Held in Tours, France*, 18–23.

Birx, J. H. (2010). *21st century anthropology: A reference handbook, volume 1*. Mexico: SAGE Publications.

Census of India. (2011). *Migration tables*. Census 2011. https://censusindia.gov.in/census.website/data/census-tables

Chancel, L., Piketty, T., Saez, E., Zucman, G.et al. ;World Inequality Report 2022, World Inequality Lab wir2022.wid.world

Collins, F. L., Simon-Kumar, R., & Friesen, W. (2020). Introduction: The intersections of inequality, migration and diversification. In *Intersections of inequality, migration and diversification* (pp. 1–15). Springer International Publishing. https://doi.org/10.1007/978-3-030-19099-6_1

Cris Lewis, W. (1977). The role of age in the decision to migrate. *The Annals of Regional Science*, *11*(3), 51–60. https://doi.org/10.1007/BF01287768

de Jong, G. F., & Fawcett, J. T. (1981). Motivations for migration: An assessment and a value-expectancy research model. In *Migration decision making* (pp. 13–58). Elsevier. https://doi.org/10.1016/B978-0-08-026305-2.50008-5

Drishti. (2019). *Inequality in India.* [Online] https://www.drishtiias.com/to-the-points/Paper2/inequality-in-india

Friesen, W. (2020). Quantifying and qualifying inequality among migrants. In *Intersections of inequality, migration and diversification* (pp. 17–42). Springer International Publishing. https://doi.org/10.1007/978-3-030-19099-6_2

IOM. (2013). *Internation organization for migration.* [Online] http://publications.iom.int/

IOM - UN Migration. (2022, May 31). *Improving data collection — How India is using data to create opportunities for migrants.* Medium. https://medium.com/@UNmigration/improving-data-collection-how-india-is-using-data-to-create-opportunities-for-migrants-b975ae79da9a

Kanbur, R., & Venables, A. J. (2005). *Spatial inequality and development.* Oxford: Oxford University Press.

Kundu, A., & Gupta, S. (1996). Migration, urbanisation and regional inequality. *Eonomic and Political Weekly*, *31*(52), 3391–3398.

Lewycka, S., Peiris-John, R., & Simon-Kumar, R. (2020). Inequality and adolescent migrants: Results from youth 2000 survey. In *Intersections of inequality, migration and diversification* (pp. 109–129). Springer International Publishing. https://doi.org/10.1007/978-3-030-19099-6_6

McAuliffe, M., Lee, T., & Abel, G. (2022). Migration and migrants: A global overview. In M. McAuliffe & A. Triandafyllidou (Eds.), *World migration report 2022* (pp. 21–57). International Organization for Migration.

McKay, A. (2002). Defining and Measuring Inequality. *Inequality Briefing*(1), pp. 1-6.

NITI Aayog. (2021). *SDG India Index & dashboard 2020-21 partnerships in the decade of action.* https://wir2022.wid.world/www-site/uploads/2022/03/0098-21_WIL_RIM_RAPPORT_A4.pdf

Okun, B., & Richardson, W. R. (1961). Regional income inequality and internal population migration. *Economic Development and Cultural Change*, *9*(2), 128–143.

Pandey, A., & Gautam, R. (2020). Regional inequality in India: A state level analysis. *Journal of Community Positive Practices*, *20*(4), 56–85. https://doi.org/10.35782/JCPP.2020.4.04

RBI. (2021a). *Handbook of statistics on Indian economy.* https://rbi.org.in/scripts/annualpublications.aspx?head=handbook%20of%20statistics%20on%20indian%20economy

RBI. (2021b). *Handbook of statistics on Indian states.* https://rbi.org.in/scripts/AnnualPublications.aspx?head=Handbook%20of%20Statistics%20on%20Indian%20States

Sinha, A. (2015). *Manu,al on inequality in India – Major dimensions and policy concerns, ;Centre for Budget and Governance Accountability, ;= New Delhi. ;*

Stewart, R., & Moslares, C. (2012). *Income inequality and economic growth : The case of Indian states 1980-2009-10* (No. 31; 57).

Suryanarayana, M. H., Agrawal, A., & Prabhu, K. S. (2016). Inequality-adjusted human development index: States in India. *Indian Journal of Human Development*, *10*(2), 157–175. https://doi.org/10.1177/0973703016675793

UNSD. (2020). *Global indicator framework for the Sustainable Development Goals and targets of the 2030 Agenda for Sustainable Development*. United Nations Statistics Division. https://unstats.un.org/sdgs/indicators/Global%20Indicator%20Framework%20after%202022%20refinement_Eng.pdf

World Bank Group. (2017). *World Bank*. [Online] http://pubdocs.worldbank.org/en/992371492706371662/MigrationandDevelopmentBrief27.pdf

5 Regional Disparities and Five-Year National Development Plans in Emerging Asian Economies

A Case of Thailand

Fumihiko Seta

5.1 Introduction

5.1.1 Asian Economic Growth and Fixing Regional Disparities

The East and Southeast Asian countries have gradually promoted industrialization and economic growth since the 1970s and have achieved remarkable economic success continuously. In the 1970s and 1980s, South Korea, Taiwan, Singapore, and Hong Kong became known as Newly Industrialized Economies (NIEs). From the latter half of the 1980s, some ASEAN (Association of Southeast Asian Nations) countries, such as Thailand, Malaysia, and Indonesia, showed rapid economic growth by introducing manufacturing industries, including those invested by foreign capitals. This trend continued until the 1998 Asian economic crisis when many countries experienced a sudden economic stagnation. Post-economic crisis, the economies recovered moderately. After half a century, the economic status of these countries has risen dramatically to developed or middle-income countries (Eichengreen et al., 2013). In the process of such economic growth, urbanization has progressed rapidly. It creates an extreme concentration of population and economic activities in metropolitan areas. Since the industrial revolution, all Western countries have experienced intense urbanization in the modernization process. Still, the urbanization and the concentration of metropolitan areas in East and Southeast Asian countries are generally more rapid and haphazard.

It is well known that the main source of economic growth in an economy is industrial activities. The necessary conditions for industrial locations are proximity to various functions, i.e., substantial basic physical infrastructures (ports, airports, roads, industrial complexes, etc.), important organizations such as the government and headquarters of major companies, and population agglomeration as a source of an abundant labor force. They are usually located only in specific metropolitan areas such as capital cities. Typically, industries seek human resources with higher education who could contribute to operations and management rather than simple workers who could be obtained anywhere in their national territory. Such knowledgeable human resources tend to be concentrated in specific metropolitan areas with a well-developed educational environment and sophisticated living infrastructures. The growth of these

DOI: 10.4324/9781003280866-5

metropolitan areas has widened the gap with rural areas, and the trend continues to this day. In the 21st century, this contextuality of industrialization, economic growth, and workforce agglomeration is more obvious in practice and people's consciousness. In countries that have achieved economic growth, the problem of poverty has been addressed to a large extent, even in rural areas. Even the inequality issues seem less threatening than they used to be. However, rural areas and small cities have become more aware of the spatial inequality between metropolitan and non-metropolitan areas (rural areas and small cities). People living in metropolitan areas become oblivion of the situation of the rural areas and regard rural development as relatively insignificant.

The global perception of urban expansion has also been steadily changing. The economic development and accompanying industrialization brought about the problems of enlarging megacities. Every country has formulated a national plan to curb agglomerations and promote economic development in peripheral cities and rural areas. Official Development Assistance (ODA) from developed countries generally prioritized rural development to prevent people from flowing into metropolitan areas where the capacity of infrastructures is too limited to support a more incoming population. The consequences of large-scale rural-urban migration threaten the urban living environment and are a major cause of breeding slums in urban areas.

As many countries are now orienting toward neoliberal economies, the competition between countries is intensifying. Thus, it is difficult for these countries to initiate policies to curb agglomeration in metropolitan areas. In the past, most infrastructure development projects used to be funded by loans from ODAs of developed countries. However, many such development is now endowed by public-private partnerships (PPPs), which require significant demand to recover vast investment funds for infrastructure and generate profits for private stakeholders. Only metropolitan areas with plenty of population and economic activities fulfill this condition for PPP investments. In addition, sustainable development goals (SDGs), the basic blueprint for achieving an improved and more sustainable future for all, came into effect in 2015. The 11th SDG (Sustainable Cities and Communities) suggests a balanced growth of rural and urban areas as a response to various problems caused by urbanization. It is generally understood that a consensus is reached to allow urbanization and population influx and to seek solutions for the city itself rather than suppressing inflow to metropolitan areas and the development of rural areas. It might be incorrect to claim that the era of promoting rural areas has gone, and the national spatial structures worldwide have started to develop on urban growth.

5.1.2 Regional Disparity and Division of the People between Rural and Urban Areas in Thailand

Many researchers have studied Thailand as a prominent and typical example of the issues related to regional disparity. Bangkok, the capital of Thailand, is the biggest urban region of the country and is at the center of the overwhelming inequality discussion in the literature. The gap between Bangkok and the lower-order cities, e.g., Chiang Mai in the north and Nakhon Ratchasima in the northeast, is one of the largest in the world. The phenomenon is similar to South Korea, where the concentration in Seoul and Gyeonggi Province is remarkable. Since the 1960s, the Thai economy has been gradually industrialized and urbanized. During this phase, Thailand was also promoting import substitution industrialization. From the latter half of the 1980s, investment in the manufacturing industry, including the introduction of foreign capital, progressed sharply, and a huge metropolitan area centered around Bangkok emerged. Despite the Asian economic crisis in the latter half of the 1990s and the repeated political changes since the 2000s, the trends in the national economy, industrial location, territorial structure, and regional disparities in Thailand have not changed significantly.

The central management functions of the public and private sectors are concentrated in the center and sub-centers of the capital Bangkok. In addition, various growing industries centered around the manufacturing industry are extended from the Bangkok Metropolitan Region (BMR). The BMR consists of Bangkok and neighboring five provinces – three eastern provinces (Chachoengsao, Chonburi, and Rayong provinces, called ESB) and Ayutthaya province in the north. These provinces are located around 100–200 km from the center of Bangkok, with decent accessibility. However, the expansion of the metropolitan area has been stopped owing to a large regional disparity between the extended BMA and the rural areas in Thailand. Interestingly, the reduction of nominal disparity in the absolute poverty rate between rural and urban areas complicates the argument. According to government statistics, the long-term absolute poverty rate in rural areas has steadily declined while considering data over several decades. The Gini coefficient, indicating the regional disparity between rural and urban areas, is also declining in the long run. Even after achieving decent economic growth, people's perception of regional disparities is becoming stronger in Thailand. Thailand's national public opinion has been politically divided since the early 2000s when it tried to rebuild the country after the Asian economic crisis. The situation where both powers wore red and yellow shirts and demonstrated and supported each other continued for more than ten years. As of 2022, the incumbent government is expected to continue after the national election to hold power, even after the national elections. Many people believe that they are not correctly representing the citizen. With various political decisions still mixed, one of the biggest issues is to resolve the division between rural and urban areas and the resulting regional disparities.

Japan continues to have a great influence on Thailand's national spatial structure and regional disparities. The economic growth of East and Southeast Asia is partly achieved by imitating Japan's promotion of heavy industry and the development of processing trade and partly by incorporating the advancement of the Japanese manufacturing industry in surrounding

Asian countries. This phenomenon is typically referred to as an example of 'flying geese economy' (flying geese morphological economic development). The appreciation of the Japanese yen in the latter half of the 1980s, especially due to the Plaza Accord in 1985, encouraged many Japanese manufacturing companies to expand overseas. Bangkok and its neighboring provinces became one of its prominent investment regions. Additionally, the Japanese government extended ODA to Thailand not only in improving rural areas but also in developing infrastructures in the expanded metropolitan area of Bangkok, especially in the Eastern Seaboard Development (ESB). Japan continued to contend with China and other countries and invested in many infrastructure development projects in Thailand even after the infrastructure development framework shifted from ODAs to PPPs. Most of the emergent PPP investment ventures were within the metropolitan area.

5.1.3 Chapter Summary

The regional disparity in Thailand is a consequence of continuing economic growth benefiting from globalization. Like many other emerging and developing countries, Thailand formulates its National Plans every five years. Its five-year plans constantly mention regional disparities and advocate corrections. In reality, it has formed an extended metropolitan area surrounding Bangkok and made it the center of economic growth, intensifying private and public investment. Economic growth in Thailand and some other Southast Asian countries progressed with the global expansion of multinational companies within its territories. Such expansions emerged from the developed economies, including Japan. This expansion in developing economies started in the latter half of the 1980s when liberalization was promoted worldwide. The sudden growth stagnation during the 1997 Asian economic crisis is closely related to neo-liberalized policies, which allowed global capital backflow. The growth of the Bangkok metropolitan region accelerated during this period, and the regional disparities with the other provincial areas widened due to economic growth. The disparities emerged as a political issue, especially in the 21st century, after the emergence of the Thaksin administration in the early 2000s. Since then, the disparity of people between rural and urban areas has continued. One may argue that the context of inequality is similar to that of developed countries. In the United Kingdom, the result of Brexit's referendum was largely divided between urban and rural areas. In the USA, white workers in declining regions strongly support former president Donald Trump, who was often controversial due to many discriminatory remarks. These phenomena contribute to further segregation of people because of regional disparities. The awareness of regional disparities among the people is more serious, as they are related to the deterioration of the actual rural and urban disparity problems. However, it does not necessarily have a strong correlation with recent trends.

In this chapter, the author first reviews how the Thai government has dealt with the regional disparities through National Plans from a long-term perspective. Further, the chapter reviews the temporal changes in the regional disparity between rural and urban areas through economic indicators. The chapter refers to the spatial accumulation of industrial locations as an attribute of widespread rural-urban disparity. Finally, the chapter discusses the recent spatial strategies in Thailand aiming for further growth with 'Thailand 4.0' while responding to the 'trap of middle-income countries'.

5.2 Thailand's National Plans and Its Transition

5.2.1 Decentralization and Development of Rural Provinces by National Plans in the Latter Half of the 20 century

The Thai government's response to regional disparities on a national scale has been reflected through national plans enacted by the National Economic and Social Development Board (NESDB) since 1961. The country is undergoing the 13th Five-year National Plan (NESDP: National Economic and Social Development Plan). It has set goals for national economic growth and social development and supportive policies and investment allocations, alleviating regional disparities at national and regional scales. Since the 1990s, it has also considered relations with neighboring countries, including CLMV countries (Cambodia, Laos, Myanmar, and Vietnam), that share land borders with the rural provinces (Figure 5.1).

Thailand's third National Economic and Social Development Plan (1971–1976) focused on decentralization to address regional disparities. Early industrialization started to progress during this period, with a significant population concentration in Bangkok. It was from the 1980s when urbanization progressed in neighboring provinces. The development centers were set up in the central cities of the regions to promote the decentralization of industrial agglomerations from the fifth plan (1981–1986) to the seventh plan (1991–1996). One of the main policies of these five-year plans is that the Board of Investment (BOI) set zones to selectively provide preferential treatment, such as tax exemption and removal of foreign capital restrictions for investment in provincial regions. Three types of zones were set to apply generous treatment in rural provinces in Zone 3 than in provinces located in the metropolitan area in Zone 1 (Figure 5.2). The minimum wage policy also promoted the decentralization of labor-intensive industries by creating a regional gap in the minimum wages of day laborers. Furthermore, the development of infrastructures, such as the construction of roads, ports, and airports, and the establishment of industrial complexes were carried out to promote industrial agglomeration in major areas nationwide.

Investment in infrastructure and development of three provinces of ESB toward the east of Bangkok focused on constructing highways, deep ports, logistics railways, industrial complexes, etc. At that time, these three

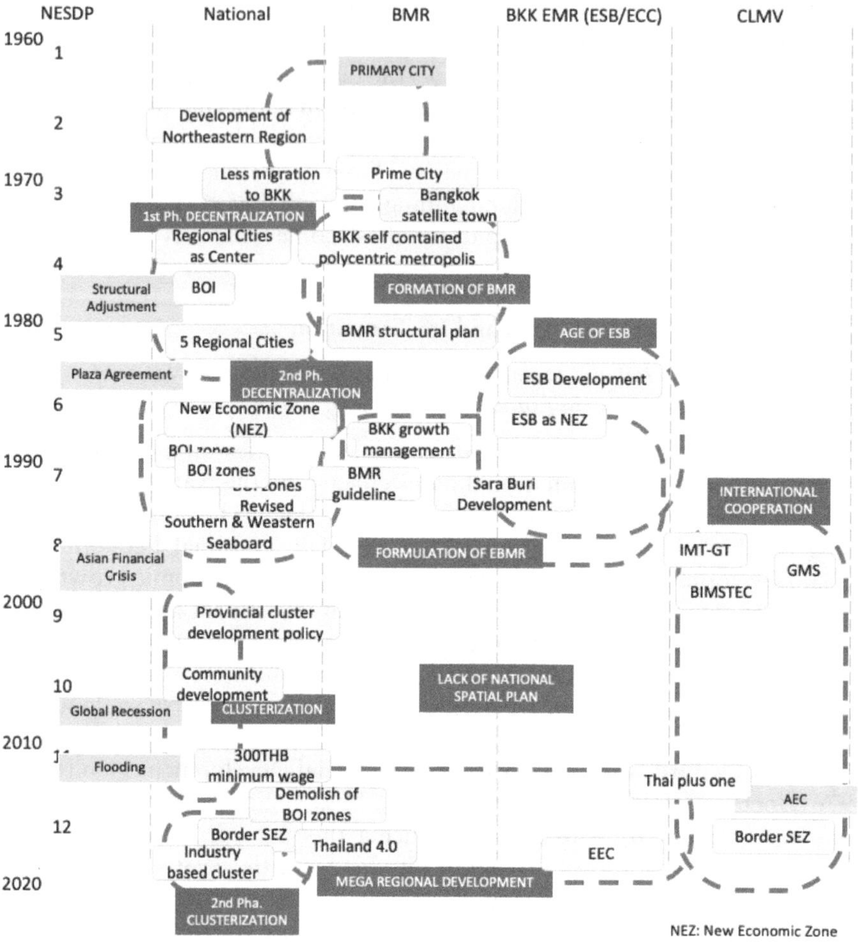

Figure 5.1 Transitions of national plans and related policies and strategies in Thailand (*Source:* Miyamoto (2021))

provinces were regarded as areas far enough from the capital of Bangkok and as targets of regional decentralization. Now, BMR and these eastern provinces are virtually connected with an extended metropolitan area.

5.2.2 *Transformation after the Asian Economic Crisis*

In July 1997, the Asian economic crisis broke out, triggered by sharp currency depreciation. Thailand was most strongly affected by this crisis, forcing changes in national land policy. Under the guidance of the International Monetary Fund (IMF), the Thai government has relaxed or abolished various

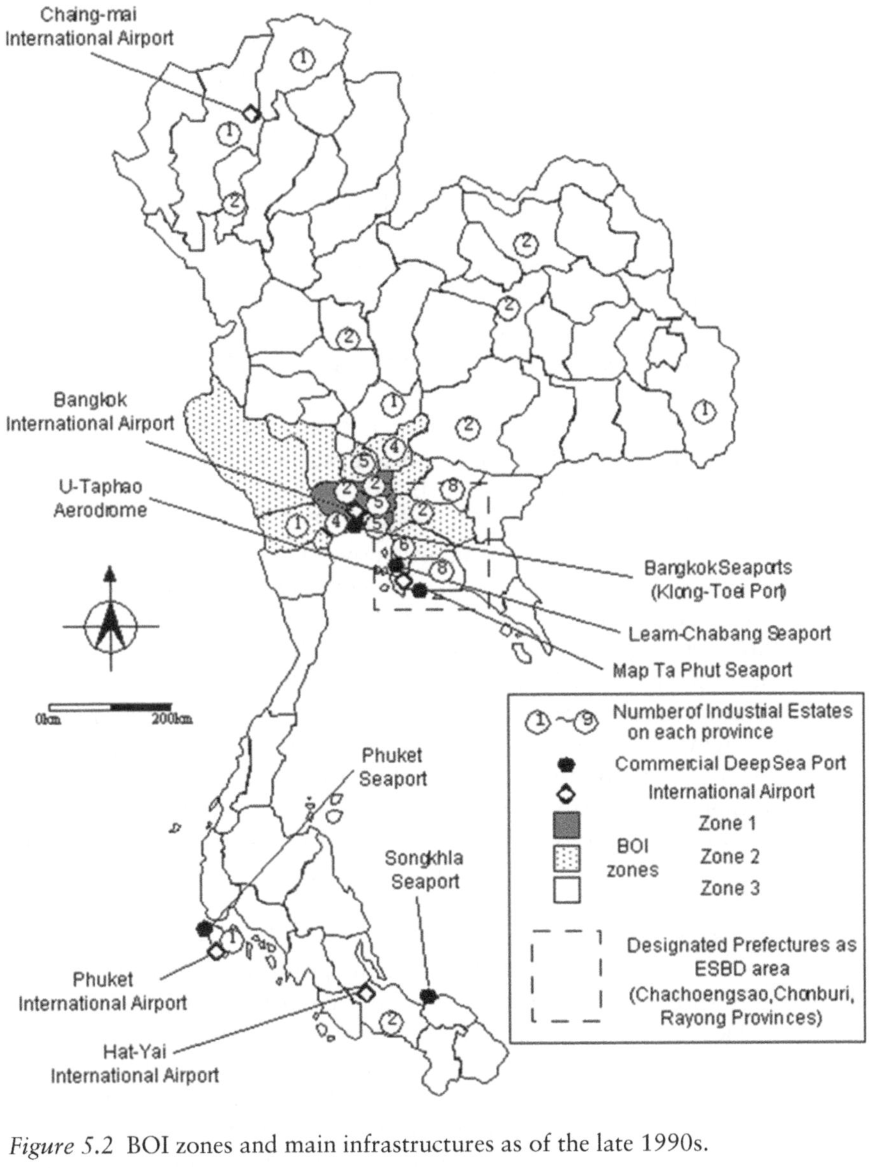

Figure 5.2 BOI zones and main infrastructures as of the late 1990s.
(*Source:* Seta (1998))

restrictions on foreign capital to protect and nurture domestic industries and curb the foreign capital outflow. Before the relaxation, the entry of foreign companies (foreign capital of 50% or more) into the manufacturing industry with an export ratio of less than 50% was not permitted except in provincial provinces (BOI's Zone 3). After the economic crisis, industrial sectors established or invested by foreign companies with due approval from BOI have been expanded. In 1999, the Foreign Business Law was also amended, reducing bottlenecks of entry restrictions on industrial sectors. In the year 2000, BOI's investment incentives were also renewed. Investment in the manufacturing industry up to a foreign capital ratio of 100%, regardless of location or export ratio, was permitted. The BOI's zonal policy emphasized 18 provinces in Zone 3, which were considered underdeveloped in the year 2000 as 'special districts'. The zonal code of the other two provinces of Rayong and Phuket changed to Zone 2 from Zone 3 due to their affluence. During this period, infrastructure improved both in metropolitan and rural regions. Some of the notable development projects are the extension of Laem Chabang Port, the opening of the entire outer ring road in 1998, the Bangkok-Chonburi Road in 1998, , and the new Bangkok (Suvarnabhumi) International Airport in 2006.

The National Economic and Social Development Plan (NESDP) continued its policy of rectifying Bangkok's overconcentration and targeted decentralization. The policy continued even during the drastic change of administration's policy after the Asian economic crisis in 1997. Since 2001, the Thaksin regime also focused on measures against poverty in rural areas. However, it was not by the conventional regional development by industry (manufacturing industry, agricultural processing industry, etc.) but through the policies benefiting citizens directly in rural areas, such as the 'One Village, One Product' movement or 30 baht (approximately US$ 0.85) medical care. A large population in rural areas strongly supported the Thaksin regime. At the same time, many metropolitan region residents were concerned and suspicious about the powerful political methods of the regime's private businesses (insider trading, profit provision to family and relatives, etc.). As a result, the country's public opinion was divided and represented by the so-called 'yellow shirt' and 'red shirt' groups, representing the opinions of rural and metropolitan areas.

The method of decentralization by regional development, carried out by the national plans, was incompatible with the political method of Thaksin. The NESDB authority, responsible for national plans, was overlooked in its due decision-making rights. In 2006, the Thaksin regime collapsed in a coup d'état. Change of regime always creates conflict between the old and new. After the coup, the era of policy uncertainty continued as the respective powers took control alternately and crushed the policies promoted by each other. After the economic crisis, Thailand's manufacturing industry location policy did not fundamentally alter the policies of regional disparities. There were some isolated efforts, such as prioritizing locations in rural provinces. However, many restrictions in metropolitan areas were weakened, and infrastructures were improved as deemed by the foreign capital policies. The original spatial preferences of industries were more easily reflected in their actual locations, which means agglomeration to the metropolitan area was further strengthened.

5.2.3 New National Plans in the Late 2010s

Prime Minister Prayut (initially the provisional prime minister), who took the regime in 2014 and is still the prime minister as of June 2022, abolished the BOI zone system in 2015. Instead, he launched a new investment incentive policy to benefit high-value-added industries that promote the growth of Thai domestic companies on a project-by-project basis. After overcoming the Asian economic crisis, Thailand has become a middle-income country. However, the new policy promotes domestic and foreign investment that contributes to continuous economic growth to strengthen the industry's competitiveness and break away from the 'middle-income trap' rather than relying solely on cheap labor. In 2016, it formulated a new national industrial strategy, 'Thailand 4.0', which emulated Germany's Industry 4.0 and declared economic sophistication. This Eastern Economic Corridor (EEC) strategy proposed by NESDB was implemented in three ESB provinces. These areas have already been integrated with the Bangkok metropolitan area through industrial agglomeration and are becoming a continuous metropolitan area. They are planned to be connected with the central part of Bangkok and two international airports by high-speed railways. The strategy aims to develop a wide region along the Gulf of Thailand and promote high-value-added industries recommended by the new national strategy.

The 12th National Economic and Social Development Plan, which is a five-year plan from 2017, is the first national plan based on the ultra-long-term strategy ('The 20-year National Strategy' (2018–2037)). Since the Prayut regime continued until now, the plan will have a sufficient impact on other government policies. Like the previous NESDPs, the plan emphasizes the problems of the overconcentration of Bangkok and the necessity of developing rural areas. Specifically, it describes 'Strategy for Regional, Urban, and Economic Zone Development' as the ninth of the ten basic strategies. National Economic and Social Development Council (NESDC), the reorganized authority of NESDB, considers this strategy to be the ideal way of promoting development in the northern, northeastern, central, and southern regions. In addition, this plan also aims to correct regional disparities by using the concept of clusters and corridors, aiming for development not only in the central part where industrial agglomeration is already progressing but also in the other three regions simultaneously.

However, the degree of weighing in the plan seems to be different between the central region and others. The government plans to enact a new special law on developing the EEC and promote industrial locations and urban development by designated special zones. However, specific regional promotion measures in rural areas are limited to promotion in the agriculture, forestry, and fisheries-related industrial sectors, which lack specificity. It can be understood from the plan emphasizing the development of the whole country, especially the national economy, which has become a middle-income country and faces new challenges. Correction of regional disparities is also mentioned as an issue, but the intention to alleviate and eliminate the fixed disparities is considered weaker than ever.

5.3 Regional Disparities and Recognition of the Citizen

In Thailand, the income disparity of the people has always been a serious policy consideration. The Gini Coefficient, which indicates income disparity, is in the middle. In recent years, it has been reported that 1% of the people occupy about 70% of the wealth, which is worse than in India and Russia[1] . However, making a simple international comparison is difficult because of the differences in data collection methods and acquisition time[2] . According to a report from the Thai government statistics (Economic Statistics Office, 2020), the Gini coefficient has been on a long-term declining trend since the 1990s with some fluctuations. The Gini coefficient of Gross Provincial Products (GPP) per capita clearly shows regional disparities and has been on a long-term upward trend from the 1980s to the mid-2000s (Limpanonda, Suphannada, 2012). However, in recent studies, the Gini coefficient at the regional level (seven regions) peaked in the early 1990s and has decreased since the mid-2000s (Kenji Nozaki, 2018).

Bangkok is included in the six provinces of BMR among seven regions, while the three provinces of ESB are included in the eastern Region. The study suggests that the development of Eastern Seaboard Development contributed to alleviating regional disparities. Egawa (Egawa, 2018, 2019) describes that the disparity during the Prayut regime has not widened much, considering the evaluation of economic indicators. However, the public has become aware of disparities and is dissatisfied with economic policies not benefiting rural areas and low-income populations. He argues that the reason for such a situation is the falling price of rice, Thailand's main agricultural product. There are criticisms of excessive preferential treatment toward the manufacturing industry and the high value-added service industry based on 'Thailand 4.0'.

Studies on industrial locations, especially manufacturing locations, as a major cause of regional disparities at the national level indicate similar findings. In each province where the agriculture, forestry, and fisheries industry produces most of the total regional production, there is a strong correlation between the increase in factory workers with the relocated industries and the increase in total regional production and per capita income. In recent years, the ratio of various service sectors has grown steadily in Bangkok's metropolitan region, including core cities in rural regions. The impacts of the service sector's growth on the provincial gross domestic product cannot be ignored. Many service sectors are responsible for consumption correlated with the agglomeration of the population.

5.4 Transition and Fixation of Industrial Location

Firstly, the transition in gross domestic product per capita by country and region is studied to observe the regional disparities in Thailand. The regional disparity was originally large between BMR and other regions. However, as industrial agglomeration progressed from the 1990s, especially in the ESB area, the growth of the three provinces surpassed the BMR. During the first half of the 2000s, the disparity became even larger. The growth rate became relatively moderate after experiencing a temporary recession due to the Lehman shock in 2008. The disparity continues to grow during this period and remains in the system (Figure 5.3). In the industrial composition of the three ESB provinces, the second industry's contribution has always exceeded 60% since the 1990s. It differs from the BMR, which depends on the service industry and other provinces, where agriculture, forestry, and fisheries contribute the bulk of the product output. In ESB, manufacturing industries became core industries through the agglomeration of factories to achieve continuous growth.

Researchers use several statistical and data analysis methods for analyzing industrial location choices. In this chapter, the locational data of major manufacturing industries and their offices are taken from open-source data published by a private organization. The organization continuously collects information on industrial locations, which is analyzed and interpreted, while referring to relevant research. Until the 1960s, most industries were situated in Bangkok, and Samut Prakan and Pathum Thani provinces are located North and South of Bangkok, respectively. The trend was similar till the early 1980s. However, in the latter half of the 1980s, agglomeration increased sharply in Ayutthaya Province, located further North, and in Chonburi and Rayong Provinces in the East. This trend has not changed since the 2000s, even after the political turmoil, including the coup d'état, the Asian economic crisis, and the failure of the decentralization policy. Some existing research (Apisek Pansuwan, 2018) (Fan & Wu, 2017) also shows similar findings.

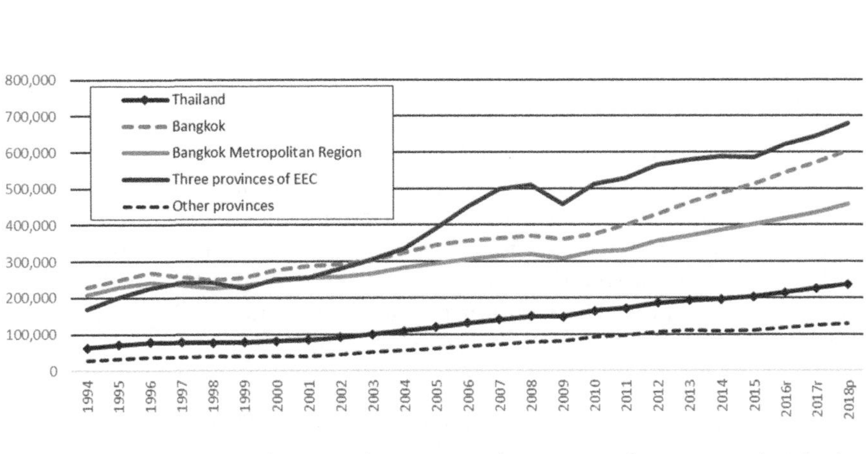

Figure 5.3 Transition in the gross domestic product (nominal) per capita by Thailand and region (unit: 1 million baht)

(*Source:* Edited by the author from the website of the Office of the National Economic and Social Development (NESDC))

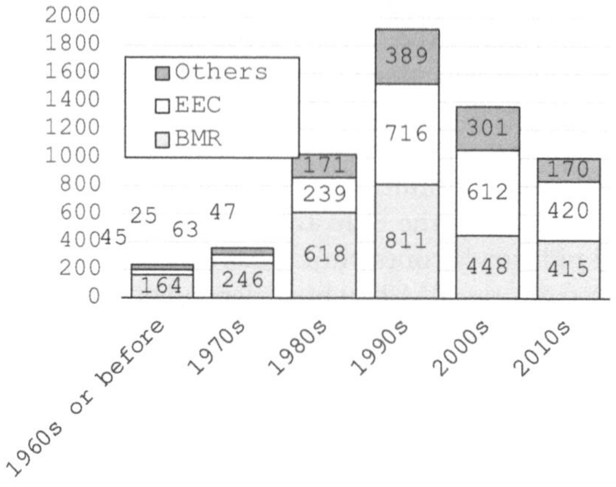

Figure 5.4 Changes in the number of factory locations by region by period.

Source: Miyamoto (2021) (The author edited).

An increase in the percentage of industrial locations in the EEC since the 2000s is observed from the analysis of Thai industrial location choices. On the other hand, the location in rural provinces, which occupy most of the land, has not progressed since the 1960s. The only exception is the Northern Region Industrial Estate (NRIE), built and operated by the Industrial Estate Authority of Thailand (IEAT) in 1983 near the second largest city, Chiang Mai, located approximately 1,000 km north of Bangkok. Electrical and electronic industries have primarily occupied this complex, forming an industrial cluster involving processing and assembling using cheap labor. However, in recent years, the expansion of industrial agglomeration in such rural provinces has not progressed due to the relative rise in labor costs compared to neighboring countries. The agglomeration is limited within the industrial zone and is not extended beyond its boundaries (Figure 5.4). The establishment of cores based on the national economic and social development plan, the development of industrial zones, and the granting of benefits by the investment committee have limited effects on the regional decentralization of manufacturing industries' locations. The trend of industrial locations around BMR and several surrounding provinces in the east and the north has not changed significantly. The location gradually expands to the northeastern part, but such expansion is becoming less dynamic.

5.5 Conclusion: The Future of Thailand's Regional Disparity

This chapter introduced Thailand as an example of regional disparities in emerging Asian economies and the government's response to them. The chapter discusses the principal policies based on the National Plans, which try alleviating regional disparities. The chapter also discusses the changes in the manufacturing industry's location trends. The regional disparities and setting corrections as the primary goal of the national land plan have continued in Thailand for about half a century since the beginning of urbanization. However, the content and specific direction have changed during that time. The management of the three provinces of ESB continues to have a special meaning in planning and analyzing regional disparities. Initially, these three provinces were also the target areas for correcting disparities with the Bangkok metropolitan area and the decentralization of industrial locations. However, due to the designation as the ESB development program and the intensive infrastructure development, the industrial locations have advanced, and the economic disparity with Bangkok has narrowed. At the same time, ESB has been substantially integrated with the existing Bangkok metropolitan area, and the regional disparity with rural areas has widened.

The 12th national plan that includes BMR and the three provinces in the same region follows the originally planned regional division by the central government. However, the scope of capturing spatial disparities has changed compared to the earlier national plans and regional decentralization policies, which were divisive in nature. The government's policy to promote development around the Eastern Economic Corridor in these three provinces encourages regional disparities by agglomerating value-added industries, a priority for the Thai economy. The realized industrial location helps to expand the existing metropolitan area. However, there is a limit to its growth as it agglomerates within a certain range and results in a widening gap between metropolitan and rural areas. Such a trend of spatial polarization in Thailand continues even after many national plans and repeated regime changes. The Thai government is promoting the Eastern Economic Corridor to enhance the future national economy and take advantage of the expansion by deepening the industrial agglomeration in the three target provinces.

The author argues that it is unlikely that the regional disparities in Thailand may be alleviated in the short to medium term. In provincial cities and rural areas, the declining workforce and aging population problems have become a new cause for concern. It may potentially widen the regional disparities further at the national level. Many immigrant laborers from neighboring countries have gathered around the border and in the metropolitan area, grabbing hard jobs that Thais no longer want to do. The government needs to develop industrial agglomerations in rural areas using a mechanism different from that used in the metropolitan region to alleviate regional disparities in Thailand. A renewed approach may become fruitful rather than introducing policies to channel existing industries located in the metropolitan region to rural areas.

Notes

1 For example, the Bangkok Post 'Report: Thailand most unequal country in 2018' was reported on December 6, 2018. https://www.bangkokpost.com/business/1588786/report-thailand-most-unequal-country-in-2018

2 For example, according to the World Bank's open data website, 'GINI index (World Bank estimate)' (viewed on January 20, 2020), Thailand's Gini coefficient was 0.365 (36.5%) in 2017. It stands at the 90th position among 164 countries (viewed on January 20, 2020). https://data.worldbank.org/indicator/SI.POV.GINI

References

Egawa, A. (2018). Reconsidering the income disparity problem: Talking with theory and data. *Thailand Information (Taikoku Joho)*, 52(4), 45–56-. (in Japanese)

Egawa, A. (2019). Where does the "worsening feeling" of disparity in Thailand come from? "Instututional Bulletin (*Shoho*)". *Japanese Chamber of Commerce in Bangkok*, *685*, 33–41. (in Japanese)

Pansuwan, A. (2018). Industrial location patterns based on foreign direct investment in Thailand after trade liberalization. *Humanities, Arts and Social Sciences Studies, 18*(2), 511–534.

Fan, B.-n., & Wu, X.-y. (2017). *Influences factors between THAI FDI Policy and Regional Distribution of FDI - Based on 77 Provinces During 1985-2016 Panel Data.* 2017 2nd International Conference on Computer, Network Security and Communication Engineering (CNSCE 2017), pp. 286–291.

Eichengreen, B.,, Park, D., & Shin, K. (2013). *Growth slowdowns redux: New evidence on the middle-income trap.* NBER Working Paper Series 18673. National Bureau of Economic Research.

Economic Statistics Office . (2020). *Thailand's Key Macroeconomic January 2020*, ;Bank of Thailand

Limpanonda, S. (2012). *Provincial disparities in Thailand: Convergence, agglomeration economies and effects on poverty, 1988–2008* [PhD thesis]. SOAS, University of London.

Miyamoto, R. (2021). *A study of manufacturing-based urbanization process in the "global southeast": A case study of Thailand* [Tthe master's thesis in the Department of Urban Engineering, Graduate School of Engineering]. The University of Tokyo.

Nozaki, K. (2018). Recent decrease of regional disparity within Thailand. *Business and Management Studies*, *4*(2). https://doi.org/10.11114/bms.v4i2.3020

Seta, F., & Matsuyuki, M. (2000). Appropriate geographical structure for metropolitan areas- trial to decentralise industrial locations and activities in case of Thailand. In O. G. Ling, Urban Redevelopment Authority (Eds.), *Model .cities -Urban best practices*, (pp. 174–185). The Institute of Policy Studies.

6 Appraising the Spatial Polarization in Indian Urbanization in a Neoliberal Era

A Case Study of the Hyderabad Metropolitan Region

Shraddha Pandit and Arindam Biswas

6.1 Introduction

The introduction of the New Economic Policy in 1991 benefitted India from the opportunities of a globalized world. However, these benefits got concentrated in specific economic sectors favoring only a small section of people. While industries like information technology (IT) and information technology-enabled services (ITES) flourished due to their high-value addition property and their potential to augment global competitiveness (Jadhav & Baragade, 2019), other sectors have significantly fallen short of receiving such prominence. This economic sectoral concentration has further aggravated the difference between different geographic locations and skill types (Venables, 2018). The cities and towns that have been able to capitalize on the benefits of such tradable sectors are emerging as new regions of development while others are falling back. In the urban literature, this process of deepening hierarchical structure (Matlovic, Klamar, Kozon, Ivanová, & Machilko, 2018) and the growing gap between 'geographic locations' (Wulff & Reynolds, 2010) is often termed 'spatial polarization'.

The literature shows that this spatial concentration of economic growth in a neoliberal economy results in social polarization within globalized cities as they attract both high-skilled and low-skilled workers from the surroundings at the cost of declining middle-skilled workers (Zwiers, Kleinhans, & Ham, 2015; Sassen, The Global City: New York, London, Tokyo, 2001). This social polarization often manifests itself in the spatial concentration of the affluent and poor at different locations within the city, giving rise to a process of spatial polarization (Sassen, The Global City: New York, London, Tokyo, 1991; Sassen, The Global City: New York, London, Tokyo, 2001; Sassen, The Global City: Introducing a Concept, 2005). That means spatial polarization has different connotations at different spatial scales. While at a national or subnational scale, it signifies a growing gap between geographic locations due to differences in the concentration of economic growth, at a city/neighborhood scale, it is depicted through an increasing gap between socio-economic conditions of parts of urban areas due to the concentration of affluent and poor. Polarization has a stronger spatial manifestation at the

DOI: 10.4324/9781003280866-6

urban scale since economic and political players modify the built environment to build a new social structure (Osolen, 2010)

Following the neoliberal reforms, India followed a concentration strategy and emphasized the agglomeration economies that led to a massive concentration of service activities in a few inland cities in India (Mohan, 2007). While metropolitan cities like Delhi, Mumbai, Chennai, Bangalore, and Hyderabad experienced a thriving economy due to the concentration of the economic mass and a growing IT-based economy, other regions lagged, thereby making spatial polarization an inevitable phenomenon at a national scale. However, in an Indian context, it is still unclear how this metropolitan polarization and the growing influence of neoliberal policy initiatives have impacted the city's spatial structure and how these changes manifest spatial polarization at the city scale. Since 1991, Indian cities have experienced extensive changes in their growth patterns. Increasing reliance on the market economy has turned these cities into market-driven polycentric towns mostly recognized by leapfrog development and fractured and divided urban space. However, whether they depict spatial polarization is still a poignant research question. This chapter attempts to address the spatial changes caused by the changing economic conditions of an Indian city in the post-liberal era and its relation to spatial polarization.

The chapter contains six sections. Following the Introduction section, the second section describes the study area and explains the research methodology used. The third section unfolds the growth trajectory of Hyderabad in the neoliberal era and the changing role of its policy initiatives to induce spatial restructuring in the City. The fourth section explores the gradual impact of this spatial restructuring on the polarization of urban geography. The fifth section provides an analytical discourse on some case study areas in Hyderabad to provide empirical evidence of the growing polarization trend. Lastly, the sixth section presents the overall conclusion.

6.2 Study Area and Research Methodology

The research contextualizes its study area in Hyderabad (Figure 6.1), India's fourth-most populous city and the sixth-most populous metropolitan region (Kamraju & Vani, 2018). The city was previously the capital of Andhra Pradesh state in India. In 2014, Andhra Pradesh was bifurcated to form two separate states – Telangana and Andhra Pradesh. Since then, Hyderabad has served as the capital of Telangana. The city covers almost 650 km^2 (Das & Lam, High-tech utopianism: Chinese and Indian science parks in the neo-liberal turn, 2016) and its metropolitan area extends to 7257 km^2 (Hyderabad Metropolitan Development Authority, 2018). Hyderabad has been selected as the study area for this study for several reasons. Firstly, Hyderabad's extensive change in economic growth following the neoliberal reforms. According to the Global Metro Monitor Report, 2010, the annual percentage growth in income within Hyderabad was 5.4% during 1993–2007,

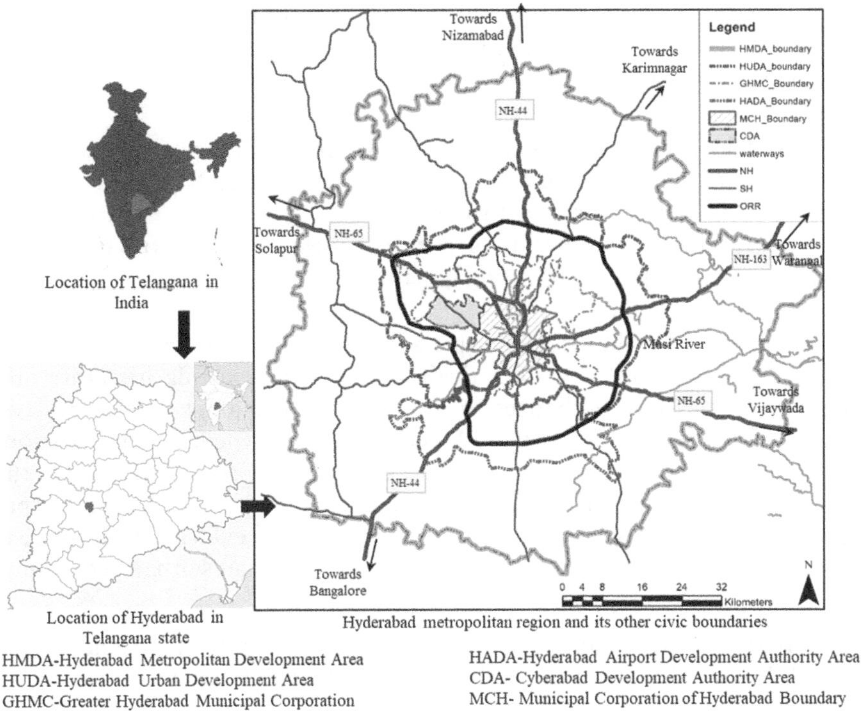

Figure 6.1 Location of the study area

which was the second highest among all Indian cities (Metropolitan Policy Program, Brookings Institution; LSE Cities, London School of Economics and Political Science; Deutsche Bank Research, 2010). Secondly, the rapid population growth in Hyderabad in the post-1991 period comprised both the slum population and rising millennials, thereby signifying a growing social polarization in the city's urban landscape. Hyderabad experienced a 76.71% rise in its population during 1991–2011, including a surge in its slum population. According to the Census reports in 2001, the percentage of the slum population to the city's total population was 17.2%, which increased to 32.7% by 2011. The city also experienced a 78% growth in 'High-Net-Worth Individuals' (HNWI) during 2012–2022 (Henley & Partners, 2023), which indeed reflects a growing social polarization in the city.

Thirdly, the city's spatial restructuring and extensive spatial growth due to neoliberal reforms made it a predominant site for spatial changes. After 1991, the city expanded rapidly, and by 2007, the erstwhile Municipal Corporation of Hyderabad (MCH) boundary was increased from 170 km^2 to 650 km^2 to form the Greater Hyderabad Municipal Corporation (GHMC) (Greater Hyderabad Municipal Corporation, 2021). Therefore, Hyderabad is one of the relevant study areas for our research.

The chapter aims to understand how neo-liberalization has influenced the spatial polarization in Hyderabad. To achieve this aim, the research has formulated two objectives:

i. To explore Hyderabad's growth trajectory in the post-liberalization period and to investigate the shifting policy trends that influenced Hyderabad's spatial restructuring;
ii. To comprehend the escalating effect of these spatial restructurings on driving spatial polarization in Hyderabad.

The research undertakes a qualitative approach to achieve these objectives. For the first objective, it systematically reviews the existing literature and records the consecutive changes in Hyderabad's economy. It also reviews the major policies in the post-1991 period to acknowledge their contribution toward spatial restructuring of the city. For the second objective, the research attempts to interlink the role of spatial changes in increasing the spatial polarization in Hyderabad. It also presents visual evidence of some case study areas to depict the polarization trend in Hyderabad's urban geography.

6.3 Hyderabad's Development Trajectory under Neoliberalism and Its Spatial Restructuring with Changing Policy Paradigms

The growth history of Hyderabad has a long and glorious past. It has observed multiple economic transitions since its inception, but neo-liberalism has given its economy an altogether new dimension. After independence, like other Indian cities, Hyderabad struggled with acute poverty, and no single private sector economy existed in the city. The limited job opportunities compelled the ambitious locals to outmigrate from Hyderabad. According to Rees and Harvey (2020), in 1991, the per capita GDP of Andhra Pradesh was only 75% of the national average, and it continued to be so from 1980 to 1997. Being the capital, Hyderabad also experienced the same staggering economy, but the downfall became more severe in Hyderabad due to the religious riots (Rees & Harvey, 2020). However, after 1991, as the neoliberal policies started trickling down to the regional level, Hyderabad's economic experience changed manifold, affecting the city's urban morphology. This section details out Hyderabad's major developmental changes and spatial restructuring due to neoliberal policy initiatives.

6.3.1 Hyderabad's Development Trajectory in the Neoliberal Period and the Growth of Specialized Enclaves

States of India started reforming their state economy post-liberalization in the 1990s. The erstwhile Andhra Pradesh state was a forerunner in utilizing this advantage of neoliberalism. The state and its erstwhile capital, Hyderabad, followed the structural reforms suggested by the World Bank

(Das, 2015a) and received attention for their constant efforts toward establishing an IT-based economy (Shaw, 1999). From 1995 to 2004, the Andhra Pradesh government implemented a slew of policy measures and neoliberal reforms that transformed the city from a historical city to a burgeoning IT center. In this changing development paradigm of Hyderabad, the most prominent feature was the growth of specialized knowledge enclaves around the city's peripheries that nurtured an environment suitable to the growing IT communities.

The inspiration for constructing these specialized enclaves was taken from Malaysia's Multimedia Super Corridor (MSC) and Silicon Valley of the USA (Das, 2015a). In the late 1990s and the early 2000s, three major knowledge enclaves were constructed outside the MCH Boundary. These included the Hyderabad Information Technology and Engineering Consultancy City (HITEC City) and the Cyberabad area in the Northwestern part of Hyderabad, the Hyderabad Airport Development Authority Area (HADA) in the southern periphery of the city, and the Genome Valley in the Northern side of Hyderabad. Among all these specialized enclaves, the growth of HITEC city and the subsequent development of the Cyberabad area played the most significant role in the economic growth of Hyderabad.

The 1.4 million sq. ft. of IT space of HITEC City was created through a Public-Private Partnership (PPP) involving a private firm and Andhra Pradesh Industrial Infrastructure Corporation (APIIC). The first phase of this knowledge enclave commenced in 1998 with the construction of an intelligent building called '"Cyber Towers", after which it started attracting many international companies to set up their offices in Hyderabad' (Das, 2015a). As a result, multinational companies like Oracle Corporation, GE Capital, Google, Amazon, Facebook, Deloitte, Tech Mahindra, Tata Consultancy Service, IBM, and other IT parks started mushrooming along the HITEC city (Figure 6.2), thereby intensifying a private sector-led growth along the western parts of the City (Anarock Property Consultants Pvt. Ltd., 2018).

Following the construction of HITEC city, the Cyberabad Development Area (CDA) (Figure 6.2) was created to develop a large, modern enclave around the IT parks (Kennedy & Zérah, 2008) to facilitate the growth of more knowledge-based industries (Das, 2015b). The state government consciously put an effort to generate an agglomeration economy effect that can place Hyderabad parallel to other world-class cities (Das, 2015b). However, the development of Cyberabad took place at the cost of the eviction of people from 17 villages located along the western peripheries of Hyderabad.

The second specialized enclave was at the Hyderabad airport region developed along the city's southwestern periphery. With the growth of MNCs, there was a growing need to develop an international airport. Therefore, the state government gave 458 km^2 of the area around Shamshabad to the Hyderabad Airport Development Authority to develop a privately managed international airport and a logistics hub (Das, 2015b), which can enable the ease of doing business of these newly grown IT parks.

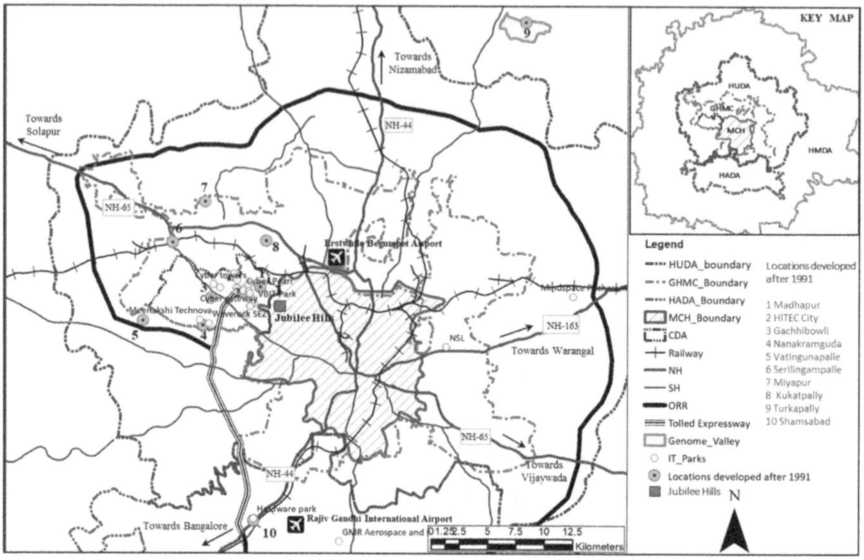

Figure 6.2 IT parks and major locations developed after 1991 in urban peripheries of Hyderabad

(*Source:* Google Earth images)

The third specialized knowledge enclave around Hyderabad was the 'Genome Valley', which was constructed as a part of the 'Biotech Policy', 2001. 'Genome Valley' was developed within an area of approximately 600 km^2 in the northern part of Hyderabad city, covering the mandals of Shamirpet, Medchal, Keesra, and Uppal in Ranga Reddy District (Department of Industries and Commerce, Government of Andhra Pradesh, India, 2001) to facilitate a specialized environment for the biotech sector. The aim to develop all these knowledge enclaves was to facilitate an investment-friendly climate in the state and its capital, Hyderabad. The new policies were also developed to support a specialized environment for the emerging tradable sectors, elaborated in the following section.

6.3.2 *Major Policy Drifts after 1991 and Their Contribution to the Spatial Restructuring of Hyderabad*

The neoliberal policy initiatives and the governance system in the post-1991 period have considerably played a vital role in the growth of knowledge enclaves and in promoting a new spatial structure of Hyderabad. In this period, the Andhra Pradesh government majorly adopted several capacity-building and incentive tools focusing on the IT and ITES sector (Figure 6.3) that not only emphasized the growth of individual IT parks and specialized enclaves but also favored placing them in the urban peripheries of the city.

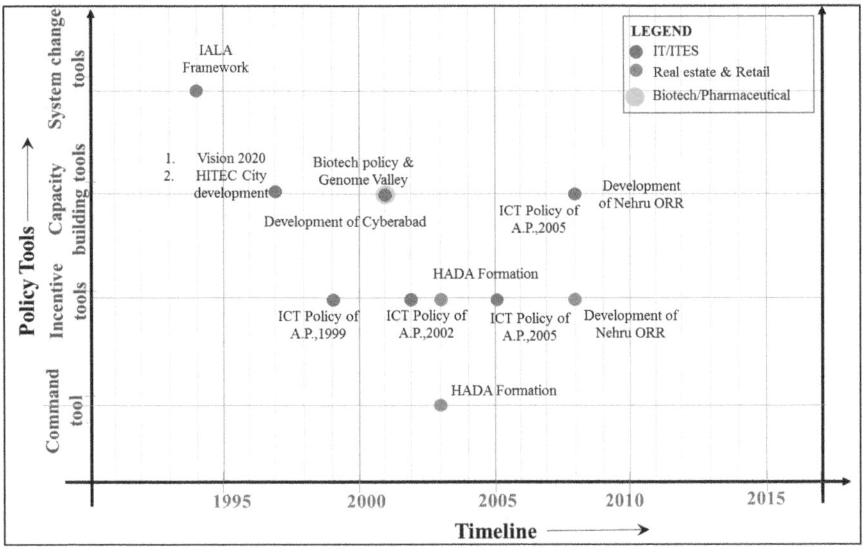

Figure 6.3 Timeline-wise policy tools and their application to related industries/sectors

(*Source:* Compiled by authors from the related policy documents)

These initiatives primarily include the Industrial Area Local Authority (IALA) framework, the Vision 2020 policy, the Information and Communication Technology (ICT) policies of Hyderabad, and several others.

The IALA framework was introduced in the Panchayati Raj Act and Municipalities Act of Andhra Pradesh in 1994 to emphasize the privatized management of selected industrial spaces (Kennedy & Sood, 2019). The framework delegated the management of industrial enclaves from the MCH to the IALAs, which are ad hoc entities operated by the Andhra Pradesh Infrastructure Development Corporation (APIIC/TSIIC) (Kennedy & Sood, 2019). The IALAs were given the authority to collect taxes and develop premium roads and infrastructures within their respective zones (Sood, 2016). IALAs are needed to remit 35–50% of the property tax to their respective municipalities (Telangana State Industrial Infrastructure Corporation Limited, 2020). This increased self-reliance prioritized the growth of more IALAs within the city that can individually support an IT-based environment (Figure 6.4).

Following the IALA framework, in 1999, the state government framed the Vision 2020 policy that emphasized the growth of the service sector, biotechnology, and related services (Kennedy & Zérah, 2008), and thereby, it called for investments in premium urban infrastructures (Das, 2015a). Vision 2020 policy further accomplished its objectives through the ICT policies that played a significant role in the urban restructuring of Hyderabad. In 1999,

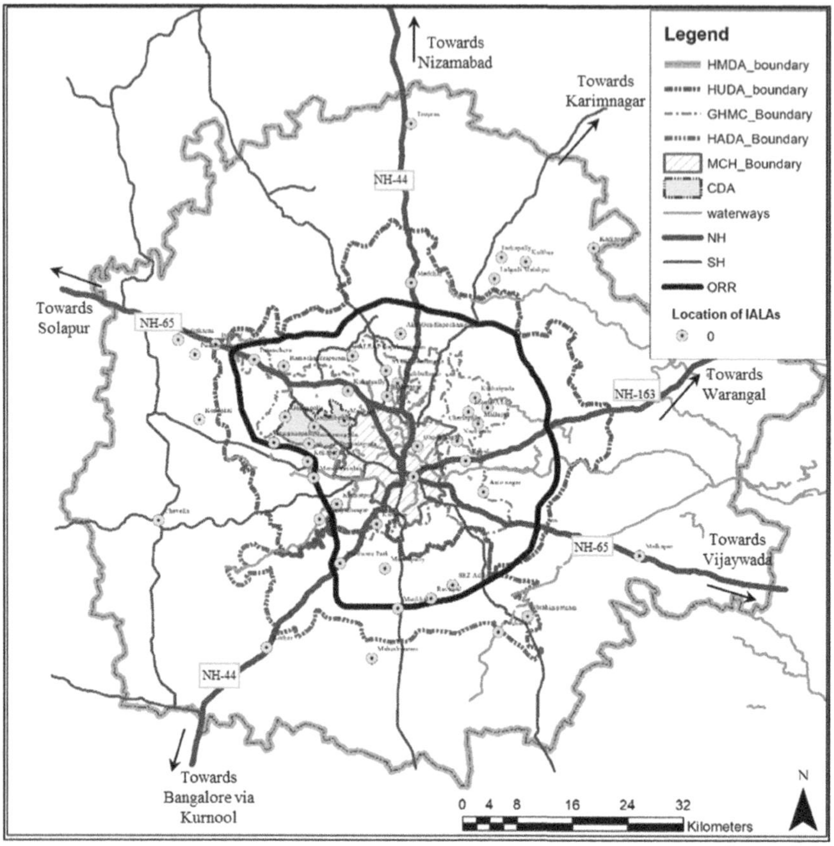

Figure 6.4 Location of IALAs in Hyderabad Metropolitan Region

(*Source:* Telangana State Industrial Infrastructure Corporation Limited, 2018)

the state government formulated its first ICT policy that provided a 50% exemption on FAR for IT parks, establishing facilities outside the municipal limit. The policy reinforced the development of IT parks and their related residential activities in the urban peripheries of Hyderabad, especially around the HITEC city, where they could incur the benefits of agglomeration economies. With the development of the CDA area in 2001, the growth of world-class infrastructures was further emphasized in and around the HITEC city area to ensure a specific type of urban development (Kennedy, 2006).

The state government revised the ICT policy in 2002 to exempt the IT parks from zoning regulations and facilitate them with a discount on land costs. The policy is applied explicitly on government lands in the city's western periphery (Kennedy, 2006). In 2005, the policy was again revised to remove the restriction on FSI norms for IT parks having separate campuses subject to a prescribed fee (Information Technology and Communications Department, Government of Andhra Pradesh, 2005). The ICT policies thus ensured better incentives for the IT parks and encouraged the growth of their separate campuses in the urban fringes.

Apart from these policy initiatives, the development of HADA and the construction of the Outer Ring Road (ORR) also contributed to the spatial restructuring of Hyderabad. By replacing the erstwhile Begumpet airport, the government strategically located the international airport and the HADA area along the city's southern periphery to strengthen the global connectivity of HITEC city and enhance its connection with Bangalore. A tolled expressway was also added to establish a direct link between HITEC city and the airport (Das, 2015a). These initiatives deliberately emphasized the growth of real estate activities along the western peripheries of the city. Wide growth corridors on both sides of ORR reinforced the growth of construction and real estate activities along the urban fringes (Parthasharathy, 2016). However, these initiatives failed to be beneficial for the qualitative improvement of the inner-city area residents.

The review of the post-1991 major policies of Hyderabad thus portrays that the changing policy paradigms primarily restructured the city in two ways:

i. Creation of a specialized IT-based environment in the urban peripheries without making it a substantial part of the inner city areas;
ii. Putting more focus on the growth of individual enclaved IT industries and their related amenities that could function independently.

These transitions have also contributed to the concentration of the two socio-economic extremes at different locations in the city, thereby aggravating spatial polarization in its urban geography. This aligns with our main argument of the paper and has been discussed in detail in the following section.

6.4 The Role of the Spatial Restructurings in Inducing Spatial Polarization of Hyderabad

Hyderabad's peri-urban areas provided a living laboratory for infrastructure-led growth strategies and implementing global growth sectors (Kennedy, 2006). As a result, the city exhibited a mushrooming of institutional and residential enclaves across its peripheries (Chadchan & Shankar, 2009). However, the growth of these specialized enclaves primarily benefitted the high-skilled people over the locals, creating a splintered urban space (Das, 2015b). These enclaves often act as infused islands within the city's spatial fabric. Providing high-tech infrastructures connects them to more distant areas. Still, it disconnects them from their surroundings (He & Wang, 2019), thereby contributing to increased spatial inconsistencies in the city that eventually induce spatial polarization in the cityscape. This section further explores the role of neoliberal spatial restructurings' in the spatial polarization of Hyderabad.

6.4.1 Emerging Trends of Spatial Polarization in Hyderabad

Following the neoliberal reform, Hyderabad observed extensive suburban growth due to its thriving IT and ITES sectors and an increase in the city's nodal communities. The city, however, experienced most of its development along its western and northwestern parts due to the government's preferential treatment (Haynes, 2020). The development was designed to attract the elite sections, comprising the digerati communities, the returning NRIs, and other high-skilled people. The idea behind developing HITEC city was to create a global space for hi-tech industrial agglomeration. Therefore, the government employed spatial mechanisms like constructing large office complexes with futuristic architectural styles to make it an exclusive area separate from all the outside elements (Sam, 2012). Even during the development of the Cyberabad, the primary objective was to attract the NRIs, so there was due consideration toward developing upscale housing and gated communities to accommodate the returning NRIs (Chacko, 2007). Cyberabad was developed by displacing local farmers from 17 villages (Parthasharathy, 2016; Das, 2015a). High-quality infrastructure within it encourages more gated developments (Das, 2015b). Gradually, it emerged as a self-reliant techno township that could provide working and living conditions that the higher-income groups could only aspire to (Kennedy, 2006). Cyberabad, therefore, primarily attracted the relatively affluent people of coastal Andhra Pradesh or those involved in the IT sector (Markandey & Alam, 2020b; Anilkumar, et al., 2022), leading to a concentration of the upper class of the city and the emerging middle class that prefers a clean and healthy environment (Markandey, 2011).

In this development, the authorities deliberately ignored the rural migrants migrating to the city for economic opportunities. With the increasing profit-ridden formal land market along the Cyberabad area, the lower-income people were left behind from this globalized environment. They mostly flocked around the previously undeveloped territory or the vacant patches of the erstwhile MCH boundary (Ramakrishnaiah, Ramamoorthy, & Kumar , 2020). Before 1991, the slums were majorly located within the MCH boundary of Hyderabad. After 1991, the slums continued to concentrate within the MCH core. The data indicates that from 2001 to 2011, the slum population increased by 264% in GHMC, and 66% of this slum concentration happened within the erstwhile MCH boundary (Greater Hyderabad Municipal Corporation, 2013). Thus, Hyderabad is experiencing a city-scale spatial polarization between its wealthy suburbs and the increasingly informal and decaying city core.

The spatial restructuring also contributes to another kind of polarization in its spatial fabric. The increased dereliction of authority and the policy changes mostly contributed toward the growth of poverty patches beside the globally networked premium enclaves. Such polarization does not essentially portray a city-scale phenomenon but rather a spatial reflection of the social polarization happening at a very micro-scale in the city. The existing IALA framework and the ICT policies are the major drivers of this change. Due to the IALA framework, municipalities lose tax revenues from a considerable land parcel while they remain responsible for providing services to these areas (Kennedy & Sood, 2019). This territorial conflict eventually affects the municipal service delivery of areas that are part of the municipality but fall beyond the IALA boundary. The lacunae affect the land market, and these areas become the possible habitats of those who cannot afford to participate in the non-affordable privatized spaces of the IALAs. Therefore, the jurisdictional difference between the GHMC and the IALAs is a major driver in creating spaces for poverty patches beside the premium enclaves.

A study in 2005 revealed that the most recent slums started growing abutting the residential and industrial enclaves of the western and northwestern peripheries of Hyderabad city (Markandey, 2020). There is a growing concentration of non-notified slums in relatively new areas like Serilingampally and Kukatpally (Markandey, 2020a; Markandey & Alam, 2020b), located in the city's western periphery. However, their growth is more sporadic and does not follow any specific pattern. Therefore, the social polarization in Hyderabad is now spatially manifesting itself in the polarization between neighborhoods of two socio-economic extremes, situated close to each other. It makes the city landscape more fragmented. The following section highlights some case studies across Hyderabad portraying this emerging trend of spatial polarization.

6.5 Polarization in Hyderabad: Evidence from Case Studies

We conducted empirical studies (Figure 6.4) in June 2022 in some locations of Hyderabad that predominantly emerged after 1991 to validate our argument on spatial polarization. These areas include Masthan Nagar near Road 46 of the Jubilee Hills, Srirama Colony near Madhapur Police Station, the informal settlements (Ragpickers' Colony and Artsans' Colony) opposite the HITEC city, and Widia Colony near Miyapur Patel Cheruvu (Figure 6.5).

The first case study area is Masthan Nagar, where we found an array of temporary shelters for the rural migrants of Andhra Pradesh and Telangana, lying in juxtaposition to the luxurious plotted developments of the Jubilee Hills area (Figure 6.6). The migrants stay there for over ten years but hardly receive any basic amenities. They primarily engage as construction labor in the nearby construction sites.

The second case study area is the Srirama Colony. In this locality, we found semi-permanent houses (Figure 6.7) of the low-yield service workers in contrast to the high-rise residential and commercial enclaves. The interviews with some residents revealed that they are either locals or migrants from different parts of Telangana who migrated to this place after the growth of the HITEC city area. The people in the locality face severe infrastructural issues

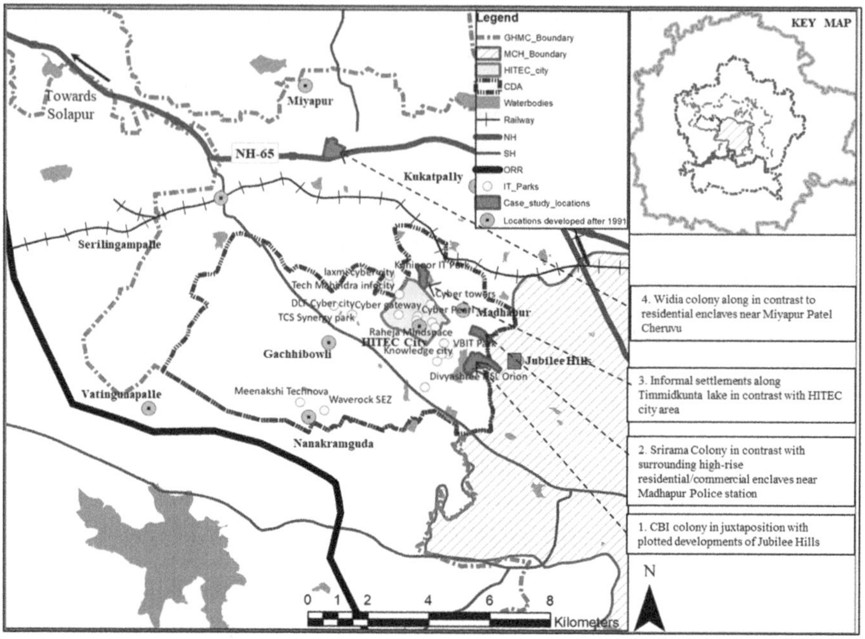

Figure 6.5 Location of case study areas in Hyderabad

(*Source:* Google Earth images)

Figure 6.6 Jubilee Hills area with plotted developments on one side and temporarily built structures on the other side of the road

(*Image credit:* Authors, 2022)

Figure 6.7 Non-liveable houses of Srirama colony lying beside the high-rise apartments of Madhapur

(*Image credit:* Authors, 2022)

like irregular water supply, unhygienic sanitation facilities, and narrow lanes, unlike their elite surroundings that receive 24/7 basic services.

The third case study area was a ragpickers' colony in the eastern part of Hitex Charminar (Figure 6.8). Similar to the former case study areas, the people in the colony were rural migrants from Telangana and Andhra Pradesh. The residents are mainly migrants from the Kurnool district of

Figure 6.8 Top images: Rag pickers' colony on the eastern side of HITEX Charminar. Bottom images: Artisan's colony near HITEX Charminar

(*Image credit:* Authors, 2022)

Andhra Pradesh, who are not skilled enough to participate in highly productive work. Therefore, they are involved in waste collection in the HITEC city area and earn their living by selling scrap materials in the market. The neighborhood has non-serviceable temporary shelters without any water supply or sewage connections, which portrays its socio-economic difference from the elite surroundings of the HITEC city area.

Near the ragpickers' colony, we found another colony of migrated artisans from Uttar Pradesh making aesthetic stone products for the global communities. They mostly have single-room, unhygienic houses that lack water supply, sanitation, or drainage facilities. They lie next to the high-rise gated communities (like Exotica Hitech City and SV Heights).

Similar spatial variances were observed in our fifth case study area, i.e., Widia Colony. We found small informal houses built of permanent or semi-permanent materials on one side of the degrading Miyapur Patel Cheruvu (pond in Telegu). In contrast, high-rise apartments developed by real-estate developers flourished on the other side of the water body (Figure 6.9). The informal dwellers primarily work as construction or service workers in tiffin centers or nearby commercial areas. Some are still engaged in animal rearing (Figure 6.10), showing their economic uncertainty. The dwellers are skeptical that the government or real estate developers will grab their lands and convert them into enclaves.

The case studies suggest a growing inconsistency in the newly developed parts of Hyderabad that provides evidence of the ever-increasing social polarization between neighborhoods and their spatial manifestation in terms of fragmentation of the urban geography. The neoliberal reforms in Hyderabad mainly emphasized the development of IT parks and an elitist environment in the urban peripheries, resulting in gentrification mostly along its western fringes. These gentrifiers often prefer living in gated and well-serviced settlements due to their safety, security, services, and similar socio-economic statuses (Anilkumar, et al., 2022). The growing demand for gated enclaves thus affects the land market. The land developers grab lands from the poor

Figure 6.9 Disparity in development across Miyapur Patel Cheruvu
(*Image credit:* Authors, 2022)

Figure 6.10 Slum settlements practicing animal rearing in Miyapur Patel Cheruvu (*Image credit:* Authors, 2022)

and evict them to a faraway land to construct gated communities for more profit, as evident in the case of Widia Colony.

The case studies further demonstrate how the city's expanded economic prospects have drawn impoverished rural migrants from surrounding districts. These poor immigrants cannot participate in the pricier formal housing market, which is more aligned with the elites, so they rely on the informal housing market. They flock around the existing vacant places around the IT parks or residential enclaves and provide housekeeping and domestic activities to these neighboring affluent areas (Sood, 2016). Similar to the luxurious enclaves, the densification of these non-well-off rural people in certain parts of the urban landscapes creates enclaves of migrants that do not have a formal boundary but bear a very different spatial identity from their affluent surroundings (Figure 6.11).

6.6 Conclusion

The chapter explores the emerging trend of spatial polarization in Hyderabad in the post-1991 period. A comprehensive literature review reveals that following the neoliberal reforms, the former Andhra Pradesh government adopted different policies and initiatives, bringing an extensive spatial restructuring to Hyderabad. This spatial restructuring had three major aspects:

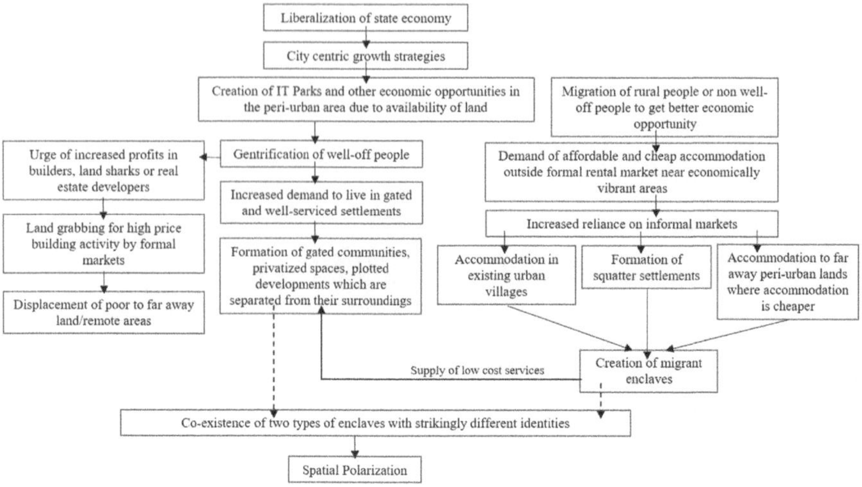

Figure 6.11 Urban processes leading to spatial polarization
(*Source:* Authors derived from He (2013))

i. The policies primarily emphasize the construction of specialized knowledge enclaves in the urban peripheries without making them a substantial part of the inner city areas;
ii. Growth of separate IT parks and their related enclaves was made an integral part of the development process with better incentives; and
iii. The development in the urban peripheries, especially around the Cyberabad area, was made more inclined to the needs of the elite, making it restrictive to the rural migrants migrating to the city.

Over time, these restructurings have significantly driven spatial polarization in the city at different spatial scales. Firstly, we can observe an increasing slum population within the erstwhile MCH boundary compared to the relatively affluent urban periphery that portrays a city-scale spatial polarization in Hyderabad. Secondly, the recent growth of poverty patches alongside the residential enclaves illustrates a spatial manifestation of the microscale social polarization process within the city. The case studies that were carried out in Hyderabad provide evidence of these growing impoverished patches along affluent enclaves. They highlight the increasing interdependencies between the global communities of the high-rise enclaves and the rural migrants of the informal settlements. Such spatial divergence is driving neighborhood-scale polarization in the city, thereby making the urban landscape more fragmented.

This chapter employs a qualitative approach and a discursive method to present its argument on the emerging trend of spatial polarization. It opens up a broader avenue in the research related to spatial polarization, which has mostly remained less explored in the Indian context. However, the study only covers Hyderabad city as a case area, but future research may also focus on other Indian cities and integrate their local contexts to understand the variations in polarization trends across different cities.

References

Anarock Property Consultants Pvt. Ltd. (2018). *HITEC City, Hyderabad: The Epicenter of Hyderabad's IT-ITeS Developments*. Anarock Property Consultants Pvt. Ltd.

Anilkumar, R., Bhowal, T., Gani, U., Gupta, A., Khandekar, A., Konda, G. R., . . . Trimukhe, A. (2022). *City profile: Hyderabad. Cool infrastructures: Life with heat in the off-grid city*. Cool Infrastructures (UKRI GCRF) Publications. http://dx.doi.org/10.7488/era/2181

Chacko, E. (2007). From brain drain to brain gain: reverse migration to Bangalore and Hyderabad, India's globalizing high tech cities. *Geojournal, 68*(2/3), 131–140.

Chadchan, J., & Shankar, R. (2009). Emerging Urban development issues in the context of globalization. *Institute of Town Planners, India Journal, 6*(2), 78–85.

Das, D. (2015a). Hyderabad: Visioning, restructuring and making of a high-tech city. *ELSEVIER, 43*, 48–58. http://dx.doi.org/10.1016/j.cities.2014.11.008

Das, D. (2015b). Making of high-tech Hyderabad: Mapping neoliberal networks and splintering effects. *Singapore Journal of Tropical Geography, 36*(1), 231–248. https://doi.org/10.1111/sjtg.12112

Das, D., & Lam, T. (2016). High-tech utopianism: Chinese and Indian science parks in the neo-liberal turn. *BJHS Themes, 1*, 221–238. https://doi.org/10.1017/bjt.2016.11

Department of Industries and Commerce, Government of Andhra Pradesh, India. (2001). *Biotechnology Policy 2001, Andhra Pradesh*. Department of Industries and Commerce, Government of Andhra Pradesh, India.

Greater Hyderabad Municipal Corporation. (2013). *Slum Free City Plan of Action for Greater Hyderabad Municipal Corporation*. Slum Free City Plan of Action for Greater Hyderabad Municipal Corporation.

Greater Hyderabad Municipal Corporation. (2021). *About GHMC*. Retrieved July 22, 2022, from https://csr.ghmc.gov.in/AboutGhmc.aspx

Haynes , K. (2020). *The Urban morphology of Hyderabad, India: A Historical*. Western Michigan University.

He, S. (2013). Evolving enclave urbanism in China and its socio-spatial implications: The case of Guangzhou. *Social & Cultural Geography, 14*(3), 243–275.

He, S., & Wang, K. (2019). Enclane Urbanism. In A. Orum (Ed.), *The Wiley Blackwell Encyclopedia of Urban and Regional Studies* (pp. 1–5). Wiley Blackwell. https://doi.org/10.1002/9781118568446.eurs0089

Henley & Partners. (2023, April 18). *World's Wealthiest Cities Report 2023*. https://www.henleyglobal.com/publications/wealthiest-cities; https://www.henleyglobal.com/publications/wealthiest-cities

Hyderabad Metropolitan Development Authority. (2018). *About HMDA*. Retrieved August 4, 2022, from https://www.hmda.gov.in/About.php

Information Technology and Communications Department, Government of Andhra Pradesh. (2005). *Information & Communications Technology (ICT) Policy of the Government of Andhra Pradesh – ICT Policy 2005-2010*. Government of Andhra Pradesh.

Jadhav, D., & Baragade, D. (2019). *Impact of globalisation Indian IT and ITES industries*. Neville Wadia Institute of Management Studies & Research .

Kamraju, M., & Vani, M. (2018). A study on growth and distribution of population in Hyderabad city. In *Sustainable development a dynamic perspective* (1st ed., pp. 3–14). Anjan Publisher.

Kennedy, L. (2006). Regional industrial policies driving peri-urban dynamics in Hyderabad, India. *Elsevier, 24*(2), 95–109. https://doi.org/10.1016/j.cities.2006.06.001

Kennedy, L., & Sood, A. (2019). Outsourced urban governance as a state rescaling strategy in Hyderabad, India. *Elsevier, 85*, 130–139. https://doi.org/10.1016/j.cities.2018.09.001

Kennedy, L., & Zérah, M. H. (2008). The shift to city-centric growth strategies: Perspectives from Hyderabad and Mumbai. *Economic and Political Weekly, 43*(39), 110–117.

Markandey, K. (2011). Hyderabad: From the Feudal City to a Hi-Tech metropolis. In *Urbanisation in South Asia* (pp. 199–226). http://dx.doi.org/10.1017/9789382993087.008

Markandey, K. (2020). Slums of Hyderabad-A spatio-temporal analysis. *Population Geography, 42*(2), 19–32.

Markandey, K., & Alam, S. M. (2020). Consequences of unplanned growth: A case study of metropolitan Hyderabad. In *Urban and regional planning and development* (pp. 203–219). https://doi.org/10.1007/978-3-030-31776-8_13

Matlovic, R., Klamar, R., Kozon, J., Ivanová, M., & Machilko, M. (2018). Spatial polarity and spatial polarization in the context of supranational and national scales: Regions of Visegrad countries after their. *Bulletin of Geography. Socio–economic Series, 41*, 59–78.

Metropolitan Policy Program, Brookings Institution; LSE Cities, London School of Economics and Political Science; Deutsche Bank Research. (2010). *Global Metro Monitor.* Massachusetts Avenue: The Metropolitan Policy Program, The Brookings Institution and LSE Cities, London School of Economics and.

Mohan, D. (2007). Urbanisation and globalisation in the twenty first century: Emerging challenges. Rockefeller Foundation's Urban Summit.

Osolen, R. S. (2010). *Social spatial polarization in the Toronto Metropolitan Area.* University of Waterloo.

Parthasharathy, S. (2016). *Reimagining Necklace road: Exploring new forms of public space for Hyderabad City.* ETSAB Barcelona School of Architecture.

Ramakrishnaiah, B., Ramamoorthy, D., & Kumar, D. S. (2020). Improving the slum conditions in Hyderabad area. *Anveshana's International Journal of Research in Engineering and Applied Sciences, 5*(2), 8–13.

Rees, M., & Harvey, P. (2020, Spring). India's Hyderabad story. *The International Economy*, 52–55 & 71–72.

Sam, J. S. (2012). Globalization and layered spaces: The case of Hitec City in Hyderabad, India. *Perspectives on Global Development and Technology, 11*(4), 480–512. https://doi.org/ 10.1163/15691497-12341237

Sassen, S. (1991). *The global city: New York, London, Tokyo* (NJ ed.). Princeton University Press.

Sassen, S. (2001). *The global city: New York, London, Tokyo.* Princeton University Press.

Sassen, S. (2005). The global city: Introducing a concept . *The Brown Journal of World Affairs, 11*(2), 27–43.

Shaw, A. (1999). Emerging patterns of Urban Growth in India. *Economic and Political Weekly, 34*(16/17), 969–978. Retrieved April 5, 2022, from https://www.jstor.org/stable/4407880?seq=8

Sood, A. (2016). The speculative Frontier: Real estate, governance and occupancy on the metropolitan periphery. *South Asia Multidisciplinary Academic Journal*, ;(26) 72–98.

Telangana State Industrial Infrastructure Corporation Limited. (2020). *Industrial Area Local Authority (IALA) in the industrial parks*. Retrieved July 4, 2022, from https://tsiic.telangana.gov.in/about_iala.html

Venables, A. J. (2018). *Globalisation and urban polarisation*. University of Oxford, CEPR and International Growth Centre.

Wulff, M., & Reynolds, M. (2010). *Housing, inequality and the role of population mobility*. Australian Housing and Urban Research Institute.

Zwiers, M., Kleinhans, R., & Ham, M. V. (2015). *Divided cities: Increasing socio-spatial polarization within large cities in the Netherlands*. IZA Institute of Labour Economics.

7 Neoliberal Spatial Policy and Social Inequality in South Korea

Hwajin Lim

7.1 Introduction: National Land Balance Policy and Development of Sejong City

Approximately 120 km inland from Seoul, the capital of South Korea, lies a newly planned city, Sejong City (official name: Sejong Special Self-Governing City), which could be called the 'Brasilia' of Asia. Sejong City is the administrative center of the city complex. Its name in South Korean is Haengbok, which means 'happiness'. This project symbolized the central government's willingness to lead in priming the country for a balanced national spatial structure and improving its overall competitiveness.

Sejong City has an area of 72 km^2 and a population of approximately 350,000 as of June 2020, with a target population of 500,000 by 2030. The central facilities of Sejong City include 40 central government offices. Approximately 15,000 civil servants work in these offices. The average age of the population in Sejong is 32 years, making it a unique city with a young population. Sejong has the highest birth rate in South Korea, which is notable because South Korea suffers from a declining birth rate. It has a well-developed infrastructure with a favorable living environment, public facilities, and private-sector-led infrastructure, such as commercial facilities (Figure 7.1).

What is the impact of Sejong City on the country as a whole? Sejong City appears to play a role in the inter-regional population movement in South Korea. According to the South Korea National Statistics Office, in 2015, 29,548 people moved out of the metropolitan area to Chungcheongnam-do, where Sejong City is located. This amounts to two-thirds of the total number of people who moved out of the metropolitan area to other regions.

However, this is not only about effectiveness. Some issues arose early and continue to surface even now. Initially, due to the lack of educational infrastructure and living environment in the region, many public employees commuted from the metropolitan area. However, this trend has reduced in recent years. Nevertheless, as the National Assembly and other central institutions are located in Seoul and the majority of private companies' headquarters and other central functions are located in the metropolitan area, conducting important tasks incurs travel time and costs. Population movements in recent

DOI: 10.4324/9781003280866-7

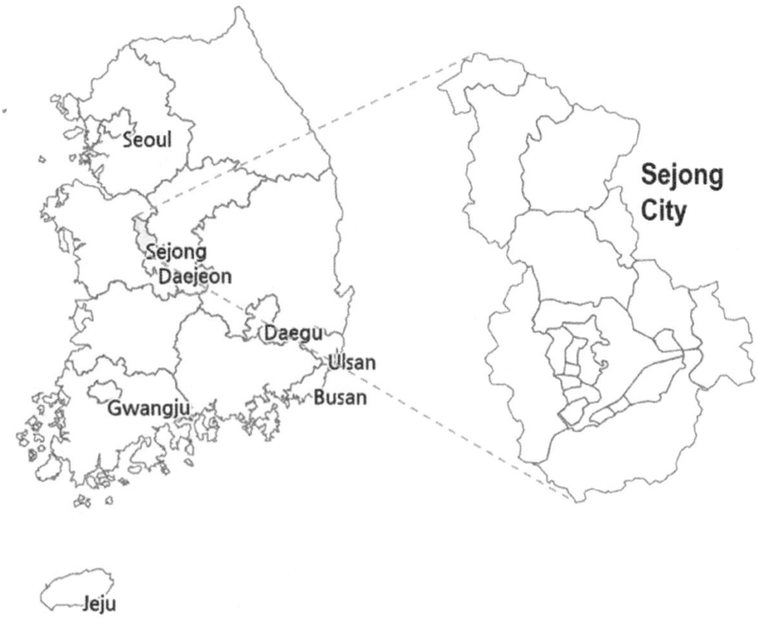

Figure 7.1 Location of Sejong City

years have had little effect on the entire land area. Some argue that the population of Sejong City comes not only from Seoul but also from neighboring areas, such as Daejeon, Chungcheongnam-do, and Chungcheongbuk-do, and that it is merely a redistribution within the regions rather than a balance of the nation's land mass.

Sejong City has been promoted as the most important regional development project for balanced national land development to correct the concentration of people in Seoul as its founding goal. After the announcement, setback, and revival of the plan by the Roh administration, the project continued in the next administration—the Lee administration. At first glance, the debate seems to center on the relocation of central ministries and agencies from Seoul to Sejong City. However, it was originally a conflict with political forces over the interests of the Seoul metropolitan and non-metropolitan areas, including Sejong City (Choi, 2016). This chapter provides an overview of the national land and urban policy trends in South Korea and their relation to neoliberalism. The study is based on historical policy trends and focuses on recent cases and initiatives. The next section provides an overview of how national land and urban policies in South Korea have evolved over time and examines how the insistence on correcting Seoul's monocentric and balanced national development has been realized.

7.2 The National Land and Urban Policy Stream in South Korea during Neoliberalism

To discuss the elements of neoliberalism in South Korea's national and regional policies, it is necessary to examine the economic flow and urban development of East Asia as a whole. Within East Asia, Japan achieved economic development at an early stage, while the emerging economies of South Korea, Taiwan, Singapore, and China had different types of development. One thing in common is that, unlike capitalist growth in the West, they went through a developmental stage in which the national government (central government) distributed various resources and space with the aim of achieving country-driven economic development. The spatial nucleus driving such developing nations is the metropolitan area, which refers to large cities and their surrounding areas. For instance, Tokyo and Seoul metropolitan areas have resulted in more than half the concentration of the national economy and nearly half the population. However, this spatial imbalance and rapid urbanization have created social disparities. As a result, the top 10% of income has become increasingly concentrated, with some studies showing a difference of more than 20 times that of the bottom 10%. In South Korea, these spatial and social inequalities are complex and intertwined. One of the causes is national land and urban policies based on neoliberalism, which was introduced in earnest after the International Monetary Fund (IMF).

7.2.1 National Land and Urban Policies during the High-Growth Period

South Korea experienced rapid economic development in the 1960s. The five-year economic development plan, which began in 1962, led to significant growth in the South Korean economy. Infrastructure development was prioritized under this five-year plan. The Comprehensive National Land Development Plan was launched in 1972, which is similar to Japan's National Comprehensive Development Plan. The infrastructure, urban and land use systems that were in place at the time are still the physical foundations of economic development.

After the Park Chung-hee administration (1961–1979), which actively pursued economic development policies through national land development, the Jeon Doo-hwan administration (1980–1988) maintained a trend of continuous economic growth. The National Land Use Plan aimed to develop small- and medium-sized regional cities through the development of state-led industrial complexes to maximize economic and spatial efficiency. In addition, the Settlement Area Development Plan, which is similar to the Settlement Area Concept, was established to facilitate balanced national development and became the foundation for the creation of new regional cities. While these policies have triggered growth not only in Seoul but also in other large regional cities, the rapid urbanization of the region has also led to a scattering of problems (Choi, 1996, 1999; Kim, 1999).

7.2.2 *Conversion to a Neoliberal Policy*

In the 1980s, a full-fledged neoliberal policy emerged in South Korea. The global spread of neoliberal policies was led by the Thatcher administration in the United Kingdom and the Reagan government in the USA in the 1970s. Liberalism appeared in East Asia, including South Korea, approximately ten years after these trends. Initially, neoliberal policies were introduced gradually through the liberalization of capital and the reform of the industrial structure.

This was followed by full-scale development of neoliberal policies from the late 1980s to the mid-1990s, which was further accelerated by the IMF Asian economic crisis of the late 1990s. The end of the Cold War, the prioritization of economic over ideological considerations, and the gradual easing of the conflict with North Korea provided a tailwind for policies that prioritized economic development. Under these circumstances, government intervention led to significant growth in the residential real estate market. The construction industry, which has been growing since 1960 because of infrastructure and development projects, continued to increase its share of the industrial structure (in terms of value-added) from 4.6% in the 1970s to 12% in 1991 (World Bank, 1993). This rapid growth of the construction industry can be attributed to the 'Two Million Housing Units Construction Project' at the Roh Tae-woo government (1988–1993). The focus of this project was to build five major cities in the metropolitan area. With the development of new cities, the construction market in South Korea became a source of capital flow and accumulation, attracting real estate speculation (World Bank, 2009).

The civilian government that followed the Kim Young-sam government (1993–1998) followed a new ideology of free markets and economic growth, seeking workers' understanding of economic development and actively opening the domestic market to global capital. These radical neoliberal policies later weakened the government's ability to control the market, triggering the 1997 IMF Asian economic crisis.

7.2.3 *Mixed Aspects of Neoliberal Policies and Developmentalism since the Economic Crisis*

In South Korea, the IMF's proposed neoliberal policy could not completely replace the developmentalist national model. The Kim Dae-jung government (1998–2003), which started immediately after the economic crisis, overcame the economic crisis using neoliberal policies; however, the main actor that promoted such policies was not the private sector or local governments but the central government, that is, the state. Similarly, the subsequent Roh Moo-hyun government (2003–2008) strategically introduced neoliberal policies. One example is the deregulation of the labor market to provide preferential treatment to corporations and employment reforms, which increased the number of non-regular employees and made the labor market more flexible.

In addition, the government spearheaded large-scale national land development projects and actively implemented policies for regional innovation by local governments under the agenda of balanced development. However, the Seoul metropolitan area grew remarkably, particularly during the emergence of new urban poor due to employment instability and widening social and spatial disparities became more pronounced (Choi, 2012).

Kim Dae-jung government's urban policies aimed to implement neoliberalism as a developmentalist state, including deregulation of land transactions, repeal and suspensions of laws related to the public concept of land, land tax exemptions or adjustments, relaxation of restricted development zones (green belts), construction of international investment free cities, permission for foreigners to acquire domestic land, liberalization of condominium sales prices, and revitalization of condominium reconstruction and transactions. These policies were designed to provide the private sector with new investment and profit opportunities under the deregulation of the development of urban space, which was to be built either jointly by the public and private sectors or by private capital. In addition, the government actively pursued the sale of state-owned assets and the privatization of public corporations.

Under the subsequent Roh Moo-hyun government, clearer policies were developed, which sought balanced national land development to eliminate excessive concentration in the metropolitan area and deregulation of land use to eliminate the shortage of habitable land. Although these two policies may seem unrelated at first glance, both the development of Sejong City and Innovation City for balanced development had the objective of stabilizing the land and housing markets by expanding the total habitable land area by a factor of two or more. The National Balanced Development Policy, which appears to be distanced from the neoliberal policy, is related to the neoliberal policy. Furthermore, recent urban construction projects have been linked to development projects not only by the central but also by local governments, aiming at development through the transfer of authority and financial support. This policy sparked the emergence of entrepreneurial local governments in South Korea, with Seoul at the forefront of this movement (Table 7.1).

Although Sejong City grew to 300,000 residents, the development of Sejong, Innovation City, and other areas, which was the centerpiece of the Roh Moo-hyun government's decentralization policy, has not achieved its goal of decentralizing the population of the Seoul metropolitan area. Initially, regional policies were led by the central government and aimed at decentralizing government agencies in the metropolitan area. However, in the latter half of the period, the trend changed to promote decentralization. Economic and real estate policies were linked, aiming to revitalize the economy through public investment in Sejong City and the Innovative City Project.

Conversely, the Lee Myung-bak government (2008–2013) accelerated the promotion of economic blocs through regional economic zones and liberalization of housing policies. Furthermore, it undertook large-scale civil engineering projects associated with the development of the four rivers. The

Table 7.1 Major land policy flows in South Korea (since 2000)

Fiscal year (April 1–March 31)	*National Land Policy*	*Contents*	*Remarks*
2000	The Fourth Comprehensive National Land Plan (2000–2010)	Realization of an integrated national land in the 21st century	20-year plan
2003	New National Land Idea	Regional policies of decentralization, division of labor, and decentralization for an era of regionalization and balanced development	Roh Moo-hyun Government
2003	Law on Special Measures for the Construction of a New Administrative Capital, Special Law on Decentralization, Special Law on Balanced National Development	Establishment of the Presidential Commission for National Development and introduction of the Special Account for Balanced National Development	
2004	Enterprise Urban Development Special Act	Development of corporate cities	
2004	Special Act on Construction and Support of Innovative Cities	Building and supporting innovative cities by relocating public institutions	
2005	Special Act on the Construction of an Administrative Center Complex	New Administrative Capital Subsequent Measures	
2008	Vision and Promotion Strategies for New Regional Development Policies	Three-dimensional regional development policy	Lee Myung-bak's government
2009	Revision of the Special Law on Balanced National Development	Regional Development Committee, renamed Regional Treasurer, and established Regional Economic Area Development Committee	
2009	First Three-Year Regional Development Plan	Vision for regional development by broad economic region	Statutory plan according to the Equal Special Law
2013	Presentation of the Hope for the Community (HOPE) Project	Community-based Community Living Area Policy	

(*Continued*)

Table 7.1 (Continued)

Fiscal year (April 1–March 31)	*National Land Policy*	*Contents*	*Remarks*
2014	Revision of the Special Law on Balanced National Development	Modification of the Broad Special Account, creation of a new Special Account for Regional Development, and 56 Regional Well-being Spheres	
2014	Second Five-Year Regional Development Plan	Regional development plans for 17 regional cities and provinces and 18 departments	
2015	Phase 2 Regional Hope (HOPE+)	9 Generation Promotion Agenda for the Era of National Happiness Experience	

Source: Regional Development Commission (2017).

administration shifted its policy objectives to emphasizing selection and concentration rather than balance and decentralization. In addition, a large quantum of public funds was added, and financial investment was made for the four major civil engineering projects, termed the Four Great Rivers Development.

In particular, the policy of dividing the country into several regions and developing growth strategies for some of those regions, such as the policy of regional economic zones, relied on the neoliberal philosophy of selection, concentration, and productivity, which are based on the theory of comparative advantage.

The Park Geun-hye government (2013–2016), which appeared to follow in the footsteps of the Lee Myung-bak government, took a completely different direction and did not promote large-scale development, concentrating on maintaining existing policies. In other words, spatial and urban policies were not very active, and the main urban policies were job creation and housing policies, mainly through the Creative Economy Support Center. In this sense, this period was a dark age for spatial urban policies. After three years, many problems emerged, and the policy came to a standstill.

The slogan of the Moon Jae-in administration was a 'people-centered' policy to depart from the Park Geun-hye administration. The Moon Jae-in administration attempted strong regulations to contain rising real estate prices. However, this resulted in real estate prices jumping.

What is the current state of South Korea's spatial policy after experiencing these changes? The current Yoon Suk-yeol administration came into power after the Moon Jae-in administration. Although it has just departed, the

Yun government advocates for more developmentalism and neoliberalism. In addition, there are indications that the Yoon government will attempt to deregulate real estate finances.

Policies in Seoul metropolitan area, where the population is concentrated, are closely related to the central government. Currently, South Korea is in an era of decline in small- and medium-sized cities and concentration of large cities. Urbanization in South Korea is already at a world-class level, and rural areas are experiencing a drastic population decline. Although the concentration in Seoul has reached its peak, migration to large cities continues, particularly in small- and medium-sized regional cities. There are predictions that the population of regional metropolitan areas may decline in the future. This phenomenon is similar to Japan, and the concentration of people in Seoul is likely to continue to increase in the coming decades (Kim, 2015).

Considering this context, the Moon Jae-in government has decided to promote urban regeneration projects to halt the decline of small- and medium-sized local cities. A new Moon Jae-in administration policy named the urban revitalization policy provides support for urban development activities in more than 200 cities across the country. South Korea's urban revitalization policy was modeled on the policies of the United Kingdom and drew heavily on Japan's Urban Revitalization Special Measures Law (Kwon, 2013).

As urban policy and administration are politically influenced in South Korea, the policy tends to evolve according to the direction of the central government rather than the change in administration every five years. While each administration may take advantage of its own unique characteristics, there is also a tendency for each administration to seek effectiveness and achieve results by formulating policies that differ from those of the previous administration. Policies based on neoliberalism have been significantly advanced since the IMF economic crisis in 1997, as the government was forced to adopt market-oriented policies to promote the economy of the country.

In other words, South Korea's real estate policy has been changing rapidly since the Asian financial crisis (IMF crisis). In particular, the increase in household debt due to foreign capitalization of the housing finance market and rapid increase in real estate prices are progressing and are the bane of the current government. This policy is said to have been initiated by neoliberalists. The current macro-spatial disparity in South Korea is further aggravated by the complex pattern of the concentration of the Seoul metropolitan area, spatial division of the Busan metropolitan area, and regional decline. There is a growing awareness from the central government that regional policies, including the current urban regeneration policy, should be bottom-up rather than top-down.

As discussed, neoliberal urban policies in South Korea emerged in the 1990s and increased after the IMF economic crisis. Neoliberal urban policies have been promoted since the Lee Myung-bak administration, and their characteristic feature is hybridity, that is, their eclecticism with neoliberalism while maintaining the national system of developmentalism. In other words, neoliberal policies function based on the developmentalist state. In particular, the most significant characteristic of neoliberal policies is that they are led by the state rather than the private sector, although the policy contents are based on neoliberalism.

7.2.4 Widening Spatial and Social Disparities due to Neoliberal Policies

Under national and regional policies based on neoliberalism, spatial and social disparities are widening and becoming increasingly complex. In South Korea, the concentration in metropolitan areas is remarkable, while the crisis of population decline is expected to emerge in other regions. There is a significant increase in the number of cities in danger of disappearing in the Sejong City neighborhood, which is a national project aimed at balanced national development (Lee, 2018).

Although the population inflow to the Seoul metropolitan area has not increased significantly, the pattern of population inflow indicates an increase in the number of potentially extinct cities due to the concentration of the population in neighboring central cities. In other words, regional disparities in population have not changed significantly when viewed in a wide region, such as the province level, and the frame of metropolitan areas versus other regions can be interpreted to achieve the goal of stopping concentration in the Seoul metropolitan area. However, the disparity between provincial subregions is widening. The Gini coefficient of the population disparity between municipalities increased from 0.46 in 2001 to 0.49 in 2017. In addition, the Gini coefficient for municipal tax revenues declined from 0.52 in 2008 to 0.48 in 2013 but rose quickly to 0.52 in 2014 and has remained at a high level of 0.52–0.53 through 2018. Not only the population gap between municipalities but also the tax revenue gap is widening. These trends are expected to continue in the future (Lee, 2018).

7.2.5 South Korean Real Estate Policy under the Neoliberalism

After the IMF, the metropolitan market changed dramatically from wild swings in apartment prices in Seoul and downtown amid neoliberalization. In 1998, foreign finance became more closely associated with housing finance. This led to exacerbated real estate market conditions in South Korea, to an extent that real estate income accounted for 70% of the country's GDP. During the IMF economic crisis of 2005–2006, real estate income ascended to more than double its previous level.

Since then, housing prices have increased steadily, especially in areas expected to benefit from nationwide development and redevelopment. In addition, the new town projects promoted by the South Korean government since 2010, mainly in Seoul and metropolitan areas, have caused soaring real estate prices. In particular, the redevelopment of housing for one-person households and low-income earners. The supply of family-oriented and

100-sq. m-centered apartments has also caused the eviction and gentrification of former residents.

7.3 State-Led Neoliberal Policy: Development and Results of the Recent Urban Regeneration Policy

As mentioned, South Korea preferentially implemented central government-led housing and real estate policies over policies that capture the realities of cities and regions. Urban and regional policies have taken a back seat due to their strong policy tone to prevent real estate speculation. To compensate for this, the Moon Jae-in administration is implementing urban regeneration policies and smart-city projects. This section introduces these urban policies, particularly mixed neoliberal, and development policies, and summarizes their characteristics (Yeung, 2000).

7.3.1 Urban Regeneration Policy

7.3.1.1 Background and History of the Emergence of Urban Regeneration Policies

The principal urban and regional policy of the current Moon Jae-in administration is the urban regeneration policy. This policy calls for a five-year investment of 10 trillion won (8 million USD) per year to develop urban regeneration projects in 100 locations nationwide per year. In the initial phase, the policy was expanded to regional cities across the country, drawing on the experience of excellent practices in Seoul, which has a proven track record in urban regeneration. The background of this policy was Seoul City's urban regeneration policy, which was the exit strategy of Seoul Mayor Park's New Town policy. Instead of completely rebuilding new towns, the Seoul Metropolitan Government is conducting small-scale, community-based development in the Yongsan and Guro districts with an awareness of preserving the landscape and maintaining the community. In addition, the '2030 Seoul Living Area Plan', which fosters relatively underdeveloped commercial areas in the northeastern and southwestern regions of Seoul, has become a model for integrating urban regeneration policies with a variety of other policies.

7.3.1.2 Discussion and Overall Composition of the Urban Regeneration Policy

The urban regeneration policy, otherwise known as the Urban Regeneration New Deal Policy, is characterized by the inclusion of two keywords: urban regeneration to revitalize old urban areas and the New Deal to revitalize the economy. This policy uses urban regeneration tools to promote a central government-led regional development strategy, termed the New Deal. This is a clear indication of a developmental state based on neoliberalism, in which the national government leads in implementing measures like emergency measures for urban regeneration in Japan.

The Urban Regeneration New Deal policy targets old small-scale urban areas on a district or community basis and provides housing infrastructure services like large-scale housing complexes. The strategies commonly used in South Korea include the construction of housing, parking lots, and welfare facilities. It is hoped that this project will improve residents' quality of life and revitalize downtown areas, thereby advancing the country's overall urban policy. The project framework is based on the five urban regeneration types promoted by the Seoul Housing and Urban Development Corporation (SH): complementary development projects, low-rise residential development and sales, station-front space development, common property utilization, and innovation space creation. It adds agricultural, mountain, and fishing village welfare types.

The policy goal is to strengthen financial support and promote small-scale projects, with policy development focused on solving housing problems. On the housing welfare side, approximately 170,000 public rental housing units, housing support for newly married couples (a measure to reduce housing costs, which are a major burden), and 300,000 youth rental housing units will be provided annually. In addition, the government is committed to promoting the Urban Regeneration New Deal policy, which provides low-income residents with housing welfare.

In addition to the two trillion won (1.5 million USD) per year from the national treasury, the Housing and Urbanization Fund, which has a fund of 100 trillion won (80 million USD), provides five trillion won (3.8 million USD) per year for the project through loans, investments, and equity contributions. Furthermore, local governments, Land and Housing Corporation (LH), South Korea Asset Management Corporation (KAMCO), national public corporations such as South Korea Railroad Corporation and South Korea Railway Facilities Corporation, and local public corporations such as Seoul Housing and Urban Development Corporation (SH) invest approximately three trillion won (2.3 million USD) annually. There is a strong influence of central government-led projects with the local governments and public corporations.

The project was conducted by the Urban Regeneration Project Planning Agency. This organization officially started on July 4, 2019, as an agency under the Ministry of Land, Infrastructure, Transport, and Tourism. The Planning Commission stated that regeneration that improves residents' quality of life is more important than the physical regeneration of the city. The commission adopted a policy of using appropriate measures to prevent gentrification in the project process, recognizing the importance of site-centered urban regeneration.

Thus, the urban regeneration policy is a socially integrated housing policy and aims to expand the role of public institutions, such as LH and SH, as funding institutions and promote it as an urban regeneration project that residents can experience firsthand. Although the urban regeneration policy is large scale, the overall urban and regional planning framework was maintained by promoting it in parallel with existing regional development policies. However, due to concentrating on smaller-scale projects than in the past, there have been fewer plans for large-scale regional development projects. The concentration in South Korea's metropolitan areas continues to grow, with more than half of the nation's population living in metropolitan areas, including Seoul, Gyeonggi Province, and Incheon. Although changes in the degree of concentration and disparity in economic power have slowed, the size of metropolitan areas remains extremely large. There is a significant disparity in the quality of work, living infrastructure, and cultural services between metropolitan and regional areas, with metropolitan areas accounting for more than 70% of the high-value-added business and service sectors. Moreover, South Korea has an aging society with a declining birthrate, and it is feared that the country's rural areas will become even less vibrant in the future.

In terms of job creation and economic growth, the main objective of urban regeneration policies is the creation of quality jobs through social and economic revitalization linked to urban regeneration and the solution of local social problems to secure future growth vitality. Specifically, the policy includes the integration of (a) housing, childcare, and work; (b) culture, creative industries, and housing; and (c) tourism, food, and communities. Another important goal is to strengthen decentralization and further aim for nationwide balanced development of land.

Furthermore, the urban regeneration policy aims to promote the renewal and revitalization of existing urban areas for balanced development of innovative cities and cities with metropolitan public institutions and old urban centers. While most large-scale infrastructure investment and construction have been completed in innovative cities and most government agencies have been relocated, there are still some scattered issues regarding settlement requirements. Therefore, a unique regional development vision and inter-regional cooperation are required, and the urban regeneration policy includes strengthening support for start-up companies.

7.3.2 Smart City Project

There are large-scale urban development projects that differ in character from the urban regeneration policies described above. The 'smart city', which has been the subject of much global attention in recent years, is one such example. This section introduces new urban development projects that integrate smart cities with urban regeneration policies.

Currently, South Korea's smart city policy divides urban space into three major areas, as shown below, and differentiated projects are underway in each area (Figure 7.2).

Figure 7.2 Location of Sejong 5-1 Living Area and Busan Eco-Delta City

1. Greenfield areas are the development of areas that will become testbeds for the introduction of cutting-edge technologies. They aim to create cities that will serve as a showcase for the world, such as Sejong 5-1 Living Area and Busan Eco-Delta City.
2. Brownfield areas add smart city policies to existing cities, such as industrial and innovative cities with relocated research institutions including existing urban development areas and medium and small cities.
3. Smart urban revitalization areas are living labs with co-creation activities, in which users and citizens participate in the development of new technologies and services to revitalize old city centers and other areas. The project will use user-oriented technology to revitalize the community, together with the people of the city.

The first green field smart city project is a typical testbed type of regional development that introduces state-of-the-art technology. For instance, the South Korea Land and Housing Corporation (LH) is a quasi-market-based public corporation under the Ministry of Land, Infrastructure, Transport, and Tourism, that oversees the development, maintenance, and management of land, housing, and cities, and is a stakeholder in Sejong. The 'Shared Vehicle City' theme was introduced to enable self-driving transportation and purchasing goods with blockchain technology-based cryptocurrency. A smart city project called 'Sejong 5-1 Life Zone' is planned under the theme of 'Shared Vehicle City', which will enable deliveries and emergency medical services through drones and robots. In addition, K-water, a government agency for water resource development to provide water for both public and industrial use, is a stakeholder in the 'Water Specialized City'. This project will utilize coastal land, such as the Nakdong River, and generate green energy, such as 'hydrothermal energy', which uses river water to convert the temperature difference between water and air into heat. Furthermore, a 'Busan Eco-Delta City' is planned under the theme of 'Eco-Delta City'.

These new urban developments are characterized by a top-down approach with few regulations, aiming to showcase cities to the rest of the world. They are also called 'national model cities' or 'model cities' like the 'National Strategic Special Zones'. There are also projects that are designed in a game-like manner, and some of the images are similar to the 'Virtual Singapore' in Singapore. The concept is that the near-future city is being developed on an empty plot of land, like a large sheet of paper.

The second area of redevelopment has attracted considerable attention. Until September 2017, there were restrictions regarding the size of cities to be developed, such as limiting the area to 900,000 m^2. However, laws regarding area regulations have been relaxed, making it possible to introduce smart cities in medium and small cities, which are one-fifth the size of conventional cities. Today, even small- and medium-sized cities can utilize existing and new technologies and break away from traditional industrial cities.

Smart urban regeneration is being planned in Busan, Daegu, and other cities. However, as it is led by a government agency that differs from the urban regeneration policy, coordination with the urban regeneration policy has been identified as a hindrance.

7.4. New Developments in Seoul: Inner City Development Projects and Public Housing Projects for Young People

7.4.1 *Development Dispute and Its Resolution in Seoul's Sewoon Plaza*

This subsection describes Seoul's urban development plan and the recent case of the Sewoon Plaza. This project is in a semi-industrial area in the city center. This project began in earnest in July 2018, with the approval of the Sewoon Plaza Reconstruction Promotion District 4 (Sewoon 4 District) development project by Jongno-gu local government. However, the redevelopment plan was abandoned. It is a large-scale project to subsidize a complex centered in the Seung shopping district and Jongno 4-ga and is part of the Seung reconstruction project. According to the plan, the development was to construct

9 buildings of up to 18 stories in an area of 32223.70 m^2, and the complex consisted of business, residential, and commercial facilities.

The project had a long history, having been promoted for 30 years, and was designated as a downtown redevelopment area in 1982. However, redevelopment efforts failed several times due to the subdivision of the site and complicated landowner relations. Although the first phase of the project went smoothly, the progress of the plan was slowed down due to the opposition of historical buildings and long-established businesses in the second phase of the development of Ulji-ro Rd. In particular, the project in the Seung 3 area faced difficulties due to the large number of long-established stores. The first phase of this project was promoted during the administration of Mayor Lee Myung-bak. However, the development of the second-phase project was put on the brakes due to a different policy stance during the administration of Mayor Park Won-soon.[1] In 2021, the change in the mayor of Seoul brought dramatic alteration to the plans for the Sewoon Plaza. This is another potential return to neoliberalism with aggressive redevelopment in the future.

7.4.2 *Minimizing the Side Effects of Neoliberal Policies: Seoul City's Public Housing Policy for Young People*

Housing prices in Seoul have become completely unstable and are escalating frequently due to the growing neoliberalism in housing finance policy. Under these circumstances, there is severe housing poverty, especially among young people. Young households are increasingly living in inferior housing of less than 5 m^2 for economic reasons due to stagnant wage growth, and the possibility of purchasing a home of their own is becoming even rarer. In fact, according to the South Korea Statistical Office, the average monthly income of all households in the April–June 2019 period was 4,530,510 won (approximately US$3,480), up 4.2% from the same period last year; however, the monthly average income of households whose head of household is 39 years old or younger was 4,490,163 won (approximately US$3450), which increased only 0.5% over the same period last year. There is a large disparity between the average monthly income of young households and that of households in their 40s (3.8%) and 50s (7.3%). The disposable income, which excludes taxes, social insurance premiums, and other non-consumption expenditures, was 3,615,000 (approximately US$2780) won in the April–June period of the same year. This was 1.1% lower than that in the previous year and was the only negative figure among all age groups.

The absolute amount of income is relatively low for those in their 20s and 30s, who have only recently entered the labor market. Generally, the income growth rate of those in their 20s and 30s is higher than the overall growth rate. However, this phenomenon no longer applies in South Korea due to the employment instability since the financial crisis of 2009. Meanwhile, housing prices have continued to escalate. According to a survey by the South Korea Appraisal Institute, the median price of condominiums for sale in the Seoul area was 660.03 million won (0.5 million USD) as of June 2019. A young household with a disposable annual income of 15.3 years can afford to buy a mid-priced condominium in Seoul. In the January–March quarter of 2004, this period was 10 years. However, in the October–December quarter of 2003, it increased to 12.3 years. In the October–December period of FY2021, it was 13.7 years and has been increasing annually. This is because the average monthly income of young households increased by only 7.6% during the same period, while average housing prices in Seoul increased by 28.8% over the past five years. Housing prices have risen much faster than incomes.

The Seoul Metropolitan Government created a policy to supply properties near subway stations that are convenient and open to young people, called the 'Youth Station Rental Housing Project' to prevent the further acceleration of these problems. The draft plan for this project was announced in the second half of 2019, with a goal of supplying 15,000 housing units by FY 2019 and 50,000 units by FY 2020. Youth station rental housing can be divided into public (in this case, Seoul City) or private rental housing, called 'Newstay', with priority given to young people. Currently, the city is accepting applications for tenants. However, the distinctive feature of this program is that priority is given to those who can afford to live in a convenient location in the city center. University students, newly married couples (within seven years), and young adults who have been employed for five years or less are eligible for public housing. In the case of private rental housing, the target population is non-housing residents aged 19–39 and newly married couples (within seven years). For 20% of them, priority is given based on income criteria.

Thus, the current Seoul City government promotes inclusive housing and urban policies, whereas autonomous regions are considering profitable development projects, and examples such as the Sewoon commercial district will be seen in the future.

7.5 Summary: Returning of Neoliberalism and Inclusive Urban Policies

In recent years, South Korea's long-standing idea of balanced development has seen contrasting outputs in the population growth of Sejong City and the population decline of Seoul City. This has led to a shift from the discussion of regional disparity toward spatial inequality and social disparity. In addition, the concentration of the region's central cities and the movement of new wealth to the city center area are being discussed. The fact that the Seoul city government and others were interested in social revitalization is a sign of mature debate. However, questions are being raised regarding the results of urban revitalization policies. Some argue that many budget-related problems have occurred and that there are no visible results.

South Korea is characterized by its neoliberal real estate policy while redistributing space through the balanced development of the nation's land. In fact, the construction of Sejong City, which included more concerns than expectations, proceeded smoothly. It is commendable that the government continued its efforts to decentralize to the countryside through the corporate city policy of relocating the headquarters of major companies and the innovative city policy of relocating public institutions. Although both policies remain a challenge due to the required support for the settlement. It is expected that the overall structure of the country will change depending on future developments.

Considering the recent policies and projects and the relationship between national land and urban policy trends and neoliberalism in South Korea, it can be stated that its urban policies are a mix of different traits aiming to maintain the national system of developmentalism and neoliberal policies. This trend will be maintained in the future, and policies that result from the contention between developmentalism and neoliberalism will emerge with the public opinion. South Korea will develop as a flexible developmentalist society based on competitive corporatism, falling somewhere between a national model based on socialist developmentalism, such as China, and a social-democratic national model centered on corporatism, such as the Nordic model. In terms of urban policies, the country will increasingly face the challenge of building social consensus while promoting urban policies of industrial and economic development.

Two major issues in South Korea's national land and urban policies are the decentralization and revitalization of large-scale new towns located in the suburbs of the metropolitan area. Decentralization will increase the urban planning authority of basic local governments, leading to differential development trends. In addition, there is concern that redevelopment and other measures will lead to a return to the city center, then the population of Seoul the metropolitan area will increase again.

The first COVID-19 outbreak in South Korea occurred in Daegu in February 2020, while the Seoul metropolitan area avoided serious impact for some time. The Omicron variant caused a large number of infections in the metropolitan area and threatened human lives. However, the peak of the outbreak was not long. Therefore, offices and other business sectors continued to operate face-to-face with little change. Nevertheless, there were significant changes in the food, beverages, and commerce industry with the closure of many businesses. The new normal during the COVID-19 pandemic has not had a significant impact on Seoul's urban structure. Hence, Seoul's value remains high. The impact of regime change is more significant than that of COVID-19. The change in administration was immediately followed by changes in the real estate market. Depending on future policies, urban space and people's lifestyles may change drastically, requiring a careful eye on the future trends.

Although cities have functioned as engines for national economic development, they should be places where people live. While weakening conventional developmentalism, South Korea's current urban policies, which address welfare and inequality correction, are at a turning point in a major reorientation that calls the nature of cities into question.

Note

1 Seoul City has also suspended the Spyo Urban Environmental Improvement Area, which is next to the Seung 3 Area, without comprehensive measures, such as relocation of merchants and compensation. In particular, in January 2019, small businesses and landowners gathered to express their opposition to the project suspension, and the conflict between residents who oppose and those who support Seoul City's policy of postponing development is deepening.

References

Choi, B.-D. (1996). Political economy and environmental problems in Northeast Asia. In D. Rumley et al. (Eds.), *Global geopolitical change and the Asia-Pacific: A regional perspective.*Avebury, Brookfield.

Choi, B.-D. (1999). *The East Asian economic crisis and its social and environmental impacts.* Paper presented at a conference on 'The Asia-Pacific Economy in 1997 and into the 21st Century: Analyses of the Crisis and the Prospect from Economic Geography', 18–20 December 1999, Tokyo, Japan.

Choi, B.-D. (2012). "Developmental Neoliberalism and hybridity of the Urban Policy of South Korea." *In Locating Neoliberalism in East Asia: Neoliberalizing Spaces in Developmental States*, edited by B. Park, R. C. hill and A. Saito, 86–113. West Sussex: Wiley-Blackwell. https://doi.org/10.1002/https://doi.org/10.1002/

Kim, W.-B. (1999). Developmentalism and beyond: Reflections on South Korean cities. *South Korea Journal, 39*(3), 5–34.

Kim, Y. (2015). Neoliberal Urbanization and Urban Enclosure (I): A theoretical intervention. *Journal of South Korean Geographer, 50*(3), 431–449-.

Kwon, T.-j. (2013). *Historical review of modern Urban planning to guide directions for the 21st century Urban regeneration. Journal of the South Korean Planning Association, 48*, 6.

Lee, S.-H. (2018). *South Korea's local disappearance 2018 report.* South Korea Employment Information Institute.

Regional Development Commission. (2017). Basic research on repentance and prospects of national land and regional policies (in South Korean), ;https://doi.org/10.1002/9781444346657.ch4.

World Bank. (2009). *Reshaping economic geography: World development Report 2009.* IBRD and WB.

World Bank. (1993). *The East Asian miracle: Economic growth and public policy.* Oxford University Press.

Yeung, H. (2000). State intervention and neoliberalism in the globalizing world economy: Lessons from Singapore's regionalization programme. *The Pacific Review, 13*(1), 133–162.

8 Urban Inequality Modeling as Storytelling

Using Simulation as a Narrative of Studying Bengaluru's Inequality

Kristi Verma and Arindam Biswas

8.1 Introduction

Inequalities in a city exist in various dimensions and are broadly categorized as physical inequalities and social inequalities. Physical inequalities relate to spatial mismatch, access to housing, environmental imbalances, and social inequalities, to economic, political, and educational disparities. Social inequalities are often associated with capital movement because of market access. This affects the disparities between rural and urban areas in an urban agglomeration or metropolitan region, leading to spatial inequalities. Hence, both physical and social inequalities are interdependent. These inconsistencies are, in turn, proliferating because of the lopsided influences of open trade and globalization. Therefore, cities must focus on promoting policies that ensure fair distribution of services, especially infrastructure and public resources. The predominance of extreme poverty and income inequality in developing nations is a major concern in achieving equitable development goals for all. This income divide often gives rise to urban informality and peri-urban agglomerations across the cities and hence further augments spatial inequality. Since spatial inequality directly aligns with geographical disparities rooted in ethnic, lingual, political, and religious divisions, it is of great concern for a nation's growth.

The Global South is advancing in terms of economic vibrancy, innovation, and enterprise as we enter the third decade of the 21st century. The global shift in power has led to the rise of the middle class, as observed in the United Nations Development Programme report 2013, titled 'The Rise of the South: Human Progress in a Diverse World'. This report also exemplified gentrification as an emerging phenomenon in the Global South. More than land valuation, gentrification deals with the loss of value of spaces because of economic and political forces. In India, gentrification is often linked with slum removal, urban renewal, and land privatization. This transformation is dominant in major metropolitan cities, e.g., Mumbai, Hyderabad, Bengaluru, Ahmedabad, Kolkata, and Chennai. These fundamental changes in Indian cities are directly associated with replacing economically weaker sections of the society with relatively higher-income groups. 5.41% of India's

DOI: 10.4324/9781003280866-8

population live in slums, which accounts for approximately 65.4 million people or approximately 13.9 million households.

> Spatial inequality is ubiquitous.
>
> (Tan & Zeng, 2013)

This chapter is an account of a study of the spatial inequalities in Bengaluru,[1] the capital of the state of Karnataka, due to urban infrastructure using statistical and spatial analytics techniques. Almost 3.3 million people reside in slums in the state of Karnataka, which raises more concerns about widespread inequality and homelessness (Census of India, 2011). This chapter investigates the temporal growth of the study area over the past four decades and examines the spatial inequality through the accessibility of infrastructures.

The study investigates the two key questions:

(a) How has Bengaluru grown over the past?
(b) Does the urban growth pattern of Bengaluru experience inequality in the distribution of urban infrastructure?

The study hypothesizes that the location choices of urban infrastructure not only conform to the demographic demand but also adhere to the financial capacity of the population residing in its proximity. The objectives of this chapter are

(a) To study the temporal growth of the Bengaluru metropolitan area over the past four decades;
(b) To examine the spatial inequality through the accessibility of urban infrastructures.

The chapter focuses on the Bengaluru metropolitan area as empirical research to respond to the principal objectives. Bengaluru is chosen due to its distinct urban character and diverse population structure creating a visible divide between the affluent class and the poor, especially after the advent of neoliberalism. The urban fabric of the city is extracted by using high-resolution temporal imageries to understand the startling differences in the built density. Temporal data is captured for three decades, from 1989 to 2021, to understand the growing differences in these areas (Figure 8.2). Machine Learning models are trained to capture the extent of emerging inequality by integrating remotely sensed and statistical data. The results aid in understanding the underlying causes of inequalities and the expressions of spatial segregations.

8.2 Literature Review

8.2.1 Inequality

The United Nations mentions 'inequality' as the state of not being equal in status, rights, and opportunities. It is a concept parallel to social justice theories

(United Nations, 2015). It is a prejudicial circumstance where a few have more resources and opportunities than others in society. Inequality may broadly be categorized into social and economic domains, which are interdependent.

8.2.1.1 Economic Inequality

Economic inequality affects the nature of economic growth in a region. One may calculate it by measuring the disparities in income and wealth. On the contrary, the uneven distribution of resources in each community causes 'social inequality' that affects the specific social functioning of the residents of an urban area. Yet, economic and social inequalities are interdependent. We may refer to Kuznets's hypothesis, which dominated the early literature on income inequality, to support this notion. It shows an inverted U-shaped relation between the disparities because of income and Gross National Product (GNP) per capita. It implies a definitive relationship between structural transformation and income distribution. It may be observed that inequality appears to bear a dynamic relationship with the advancements in urbanization and industrialization. Researchers make a case for a reversal of the Kuznets curve in many developed countries since the 1970s (Paul, 2018).

Economic inequality may be measured by studying two key attributes – wealth and wage. The inequality may rise to the extent that it may jeopardize the city's growth when the capital markets are heterogeneous (Aghion, Caroli, & Garcia-Penalosa, 1999). Demonetization in India in 2016 has noticeably contributed to the income capacity of the informal sector and thus the increasing economic inequality. Moreover, the pandemic has led to a major shock on the livelihood opportunities of a large section of society. These two crusades are bound to affect the overall inequality pattern of the country in the short to medium term.

8.2.1.2 Social Inequality

Social inequality arises because of the unequal distribution of rights and resources between various classes, races, and genders, causing disparities in society. It is closely linked to economic inequality and results in spatial disarrangements. For this chapter, we refer to measuring social inequality by understanding the conditions of inhabitants and the opportunities available around them. This may be categorized into two theories. The first is the functionalist theory, which deems the inevitability of inequality. The other is a conflict theory, which perceives inequality because powerful groups dominate the less powerful ones. Thus, social inequality has three dimensions – structural conditions, ideological supports, and social reforms (Crossman, 2020).

8.2.1.3 Spatial Inequality

The disparity in economic and social indicators of well-being across the administrative units within a city contributes to 'spatial inequality'. Spatial inequality may exist both within an urban area and between urban and rural areas. Therefore, urban planners and policymakers must ensure a spatially fair allocation of infrastructure and services in cities. Spatial inequality causes high regional disparities, leading to political instability affecting economic and social scenarios. This notion is based on the aspects of 'proximity' to services and opportunities and linked with the development over time. It occurs when different individuals experience different standards of living.[2]

8.2.1.4 Effects of Socioeconomic Inequality on Spatial Inequality

Spatial inequality is an element of complete inter-personal inequality. However, in combination with political and ethnic tensions, it may destabilize societies. The distribution of spatial inequalities varies as per the anomalies of geography and the susceptibility of activities to cluster together. This clustering of economic activities causes unbalanced development scenarios, leading to spatially concentrated growth, which in turn may create income disparities depending on labor migration from rural to urban and peri-urban regions. Hence, capitalizing on the infrastructure required for such areas to let the migrants reside is a policy option that planners must explore (Venables, 2013). India's Gini coefficient[3] for the year 2011 was 35.7% (World Population Review, 2022), which shows a very high inequality. This income inequality is observed spatially through income-based segregation, especially in residential areas. Hence, it becomes imperative to study spatial inequality to understand how this inequity affects the urban development of a region (Tal & Maarten, 2018).

8.3 Navigating the Study Process

The process used in this study is shown in Table 8.1.

The study achieved the two key objectives through a structured process to collect, compile, and synthesize information. These are explained in detail as follows.

8.3.1 Extraction of Data

The authors extracted the satellite imageries through Landsat satellite for spatial analysis and cross-referenced them with the updated Google satellite imageries. The relevant shapefiles of administrative boundaries were obtained from the Karnataka Geographic Information System, an open-source platform by the Government of Karnataka (Government of Karnataka, 2020).

8.3.2 Digitization

The authors digitized the built cover of Bengaluru's urban region using ArcGIS 10.3 software. The maps, once overlaid, elucidated a crucial understanding

Table 8.1 Analytical frameworks

	Deliverable	*Analysis and methodology*	*Data*
Objective 1: To study the temporal growth of the Bengaluru metropolitan area over the past four decades	A land cover map for temporal growth of the study area since 1980	Obtaining land cover data from satellite imagery separately for all four decades Digitizing and analyzing the land cover on ArcGIS 10.3.1	Land Cover Maps for 1980–1990, 1991–2000, 2000–2010, 2011–2020 from Landsat and Google Earth
	Identification and mapping of factors of the selected parameter to be considered for the inequality study	Data Collection Research to identify parameters for measuring inequality Spatial Mapping Identifying locations of each facility within the selected parameters on ArcGIS 10.3.1 Logical analogy Comparison between economic and spatial inequalities and their factors	Data from open-source websites, urban data portals, Census of India, and Google locations
Objective 2: To examine the spatial inequality through the accessibility of urban infrastructures	Availability of infrastructures in each municipal ward	Analyzing the number of geo-locations for the factors of the selected parameter to map inequality per ward of the study area	Empirical analysis from the generated dataset
	Accessibility of infrastructures in each municipal ward	Analyzing the weightage for the number of geo-locations for the factors of the selected parameter to map inequality per municipal ward of the study area	Empirical analysis from the generated dataset
	Accessibility and availability of infrastructures to gated communities	Selecting wards on the basis of the weightages given in the previous step and zooming in the study area to highlight the aspect of gated gentrification	Empirical analysis from the generated dataset

of the temporal growth trend of the city across four decades: 1981–1990, 1991–2000, 2001–2010, and 2011–2020.

8.3.3 *Temporal Growth in Municipal Wards*

The first objective of the study is to calculate the temporal growth of the Bengaluru metropolitan area. The authors analyzed the temporal growth at the municipal ward level on ArcGIS 10.3 software by using spatial join of the shapefiles of the Bruhat Bengaluru Mahanagara Palike (BBMP) wards.[4]The output of these exercises is achieved in the form of built cover maps of four decades indicating the growth pattern. Afterward, the average percentage growth per municipal ward is computed and presented on a map (Figure 8.2).

8.3.4 *Data Collection of Infrastructure Attributes*

The data collection process primarily forms the basis for examining spatial inequality addressing the final objective of this research. The major urban infrastructures in the study area were primary and secondary schools, hospitals, Bengaluru Metropolitan Transport Corporation (BMTC) bus depots, metro stations, and public roads. The authors extracted the required locations for these urban infrastructures from open-source platforms, such as OpenCity and Mapcruzin, and cross-referenced them with Google Maps to avoid potential errors. The study only considers city-level infrastructures in the transportation, health, and educational institutions categories. Therefore, the calculations do not involve local medical shops, dispensaries, ward-level gurukuls, anganwadis, etc. Other data, such as population and household data, were obtained from the Census of India (Census of India, 2011).

8.3.5 *Measuring Spatial Inequality*

The second part of the chapter required careful calculation of the spatial inequality using the procured data. The authors considered three parameters, i.e., availability of infrastructure, accessibility of infrastructure, and presence of gated community, to quantify the spatial inequality across the city.

8.3.5.1 *Availability of Infrastructure*

Since inequality is a general term and is commonly discussed as a qualitative attribute, it is crucial to specify the parameters for measuring it. One such parameter is the availability of resources/utilities. The chapter focuses on the availability of the relevant urban infrastructure selected in this study. The availability was measured by considering the number of households per municipal ward given by the Census of India (Census of India, 2011).

8.3.5.2 Accessibility of Infrastructure

The second parameter to measure spatial inequality is the accessibility to the resources/utilities. Accessibility is calculated for each selected urban infrastructure using the average distance between the centroid of a municipal ward and all the urban infrastructure inside the ward.

8.3.5.3 Gated Communities within Municipal Wards

The third parameter identified to measure inequality is the presence of gated communities within the municipal wards. The areas for the gated communities in selected municipal wards are recorded to understand the effect of inequality. The authors focused on four municipal wards located in different locations of the metropolis for this process. The municipal wards are selected based on the weighted average obtained by combining the abovementioned parameters. Therefore, one municipal ward within each identified range has been considered.

8.3.6 Extent and Constraints of the Study

The study assesses within the BBMP boundary and does not extend to the regional level. For studying the temporal growth, the chapter spatially assesses all the municipal wards within the BBMP boundary and creates a database for further research. It identifies city-specific spatial inequality factors useful for future studies and proposals. While examining the spatial inequalities, the study creates a database on GIS for further research. It links the smallest administrative unit with factors of measuring spatial inequality and statistical assessment of the necessary attributes/infrastructure. It also links the aspects of gentrification with spatial inequality.

The study is based on secondary data, including remotely sensed satellite imageries. The authors conducted the study during the second wave of COVID-19 and nationwide lockdown and hence used online research methods (ORMs) as a tool for this research. The study does not imply other cities.

8.4 Study Area

Since the mid-20th century, the globalized world has been undergoing industrial advancements, focusing on the computer industry. The 1970s witnessed knowledge education deeply rooting itself in the curriculum of Ivy League and equivalent institutions of the world. Hence, the interest of the then workforce grew toward knowledge-based industries, and the IT (Information Technology) sector was a significant part of this industrial setup. This has led to a human capital shift from production to knowledge-based development. IT sector-centric cities have become a lucrative destination for professionals to move, in turn, adding to economic inequality and spatial polarization in many cities (Natarajan & Biswas, 2019). Bengaluru also depicts a similar pattern of industrial and spatial development. It is crucial to investigate the master plan of the city to understand its spatial pattern against the backdrop of knowledge-based industry. The stakeholder consultation process for the city's master plan document suggests that the implementation needs attention, especially at the municipal ward level showing the non-realization of the 74th Constitutional Amendment Act, 1992.[5] The process suggests a dire need for enhancing adequate government educational infrastructure, public health centers, and other urban infrastructures in peripheral extents and the physical accessibility to them. The review of the master plan suggests an immediate need to provide additional and alternate public transport systems to augment last-mile connectivity by integrating different travel modes. This requires integrated planning at micro- and macro-levels (BDA, 2017). Hence, there is a need to shift the focus on the city's infrastructure, starting at the municipal ward level.

Bengaluru, a metropolitan city and the capital of Karnataka, is known as the 'Silicon Valley of India'. The city has grown into a cosmopolitan territory, attracting businesses and people nationally and globally. It is the largest city in Karnataka and ranks fifth in population in the country with 11.7[6] million people (Karnataka, 2017). It is the fastest-growing city in India and ranks first in the Ease of Living Index (2021), an index for millions of populations in cities in the country.

8.4.1 *Revised Master Plan for Bengaluru 2031 (RMP-2031)*

The Local Planning Area (LPA) of the Bengaluru Development Authority (BDA) comprises Bruhat Bengaluru Mahanagara Palike (BBMP) and 251 peripheral villages. The unprecedented population growth in the city is the leading cause of the degrading urban land management issues. The preparation and revision of RMP-2031 (Revised master plan for Bengaluru 2031) are bestowed to BDA under the Karnataka Town and Country Planning (KTCP) Act of 1961. The census 2011 records that BBMP accommodates 8.50 million people. RMP-2031 aims to achieve adequate infrastructure services for continuing the growth. Therefore, a city-wide sustainable transportation system is proposed to be implemented. Few land parcels are also earmarked for public transport stations (BDA, 2017). However, the city has shown higher inequality in terms of the distribution of infrastructure services, especially among lower-income groups. Therefore, it becomes crucial to study the dynamics in terms of spatial distribution.

8.4.2 *Details of the Study Area*

The Bruhat Bengaluru Mahanagara Palike (BBMP) is the fourth biggest Municipal Corporation in India. It is accountable for the infrastructural resources of the Greater Bengaluru metropolitan area. Bengaluru Metropolitan Region Development Authority (BMRDA) is a self-governing organization established by the Government of Karnataka (GOK) under the BMRDA Act of 1985 to supervise the systematic development of the Bengaluru Metropolitan Region (BMR). It includes Bengaluru urban district, Bengaluru rural district, and Ramanagara district. Bengaluru Development Authority (BDA) is the principal planning authority of Bengaluru ((BBMP), 2021). Bengaluru has three administrative parallels – a district comprising 1,082 urban villages and taluks, Bengaluru Metropolitan Area (BMA), and BBMP Area comprising 198 municipal wards (Figure 8.1).

The population of BMA was 8,520,435, with 52% males and 48% females. The city has an average literacy rate of 88.69% (Census of India, 2011). The sex ratio is 922, and the child sex ratio is 942. Bengaluru was the most populated city in the very first Census of India. The city had grown intensively since 1949, with a 5.7 million population between 1871 and 2001. It is known as the Garden City of India because of its tree-lined streets and lavish greenery. It is home to numerous technical learning and research institutions like the Indian Institute of Science (IISc), Indian Institute of Management (IIM), Institute for Social and Economic Change (ISEC), Indian Institute of Information Technology (IIIT), National Institute of Advanced Studies (NIAS), Tata Institute for Fundamental Research (TIFR), Jawaharlal Nehru Centre for Advanced Scientific Research (JNCASR), Indian Space Research Organisation (ISRO), Hindustan Aeronautics Limited (HAL), National Aerospace Laboratories (NAL), Central Power Research Institute (CPRI), Central Manufacturing Technology Institute (CMTI), various research centers of the Defence Research and Development Organisation (DRDO). The Bengaluru urban district has a comparatively higher per capita income than the rest of the state. Regardless of its economic opportunities, the number of the urban poor is steadily progressing in the city. Moreover, the ever-increasing involuntary migrant seems to contribute to the increasing spread of slums and informal settlements in the city.

8.5 Data and Analysis

8.5.1 Spatial Inequality

8.5.1.1 Temporal Changes over the Past Four Decades

Bengaluru has developed notably as an IT hub from a fortified settlement in 1537. The economic growth in the city contributes to maintaining the country's national and global connections. Urban planning in the city received statutory backing with the KTCP Act of 1961. The government of Karnataka constituted BDA in 1976, now responsible for the city's fourth master plan (RMP-2031) (BDA, 2017). In the past four decades., Bengaluru has been growing along with the major transportation links, primarily the National Highways (NHs). The city is particularly growing toward northwest (along NH 48), southwest (along NH 275), and south-east (along NH 44) directions. The authorities extended the BMA boundary in the east direction in 2017. The growth in this direction may be the result of the development of

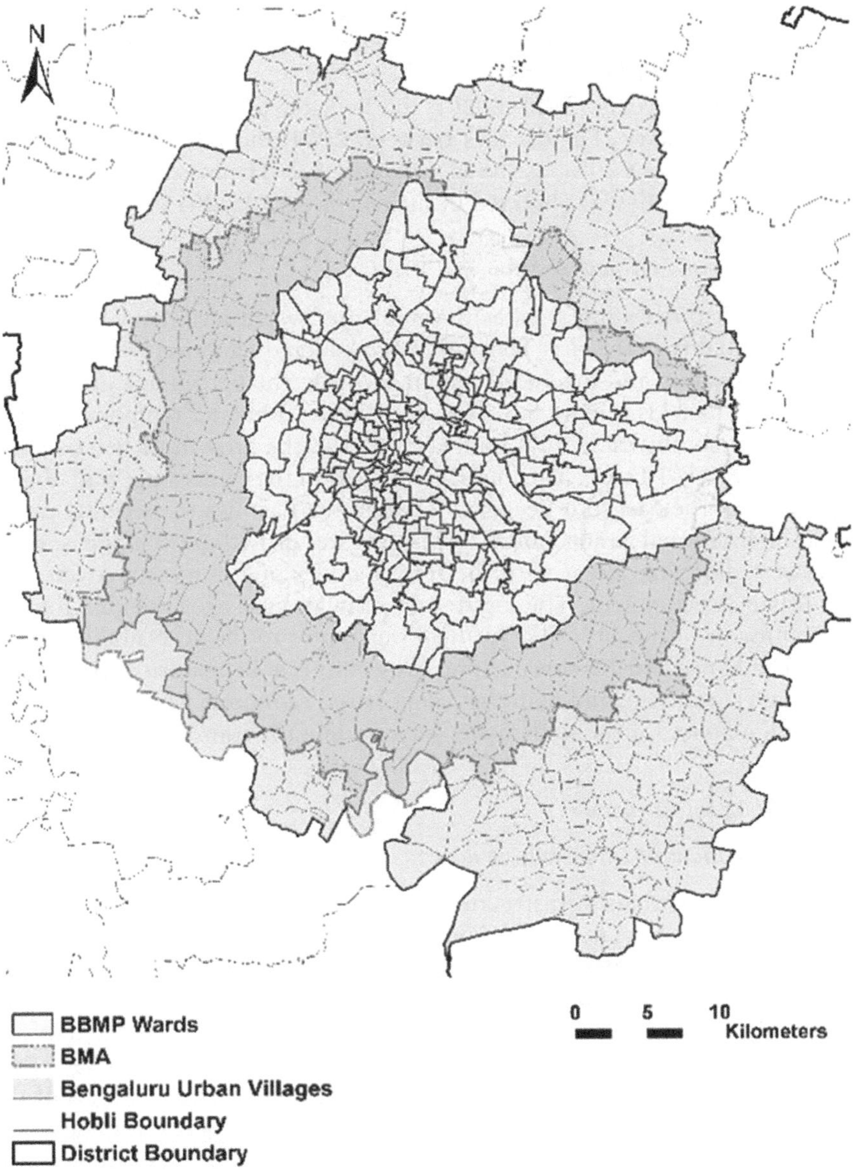

Figure 8.1 Administrative boundaries of Bengaluru urban district

the International Tech Park (ITPL). ITPL is the first multi-national funded technology park (Natarajan & Biswas, 2019) in India.

The Bengaluru Government trusts that the city has an elaborate road network (BBMP, 2015). A key transport node is the road leading to Mysuru that lies toward the south of Bengaluru and forms an entrance to the city. The

Government has also planned the metro expansion along the east-west corridor. There are 13 new metro stations proposed beyond the Baiyappanahalli metro station toward the east.

In the last ten years (2011–2020), the Bengaluru urban area has grown beyond its boundary. The decades between 2001 and 2010 had the lowest growth rate of about 20%, as shown in Figure 8.2. The maximum growth of approximately 47% was observed in the recent decade (2011–2020).

8.5.1.2 Temporal Growth in Municipal Wards

The research further investigates the municipal ward level data to identify spatial inequality in the city. The authors considered temporal growth as one of the parameters and produced a map showing the percentage growth for all municipal wards (Figure 8.3). The map shows a greater temporal growth in the west, southwest, south, and east. Hence, the growth of Bengaluru is majorly in Anekal Taluk. The municipal wards in the center have had almost no growth in the past four decades.. Though the East has the recently established International Trade Park (ITPL), a greater growth percentage is in the southwest direction along with the transit nodes and is mostly covered by peri-urban development. The metro and railway lines are extended toward the southwest of the city. This further contributes to the accessibility of services. The Bengaluru-Mysurue expressway connects Bengaluru with another booming IT, tourism, and manufacturing-based economy, Mysuru. It acts as a growth magnet for the settlements surrounding the transit link.

8.5.2 Urban Infrastructure

8.5.2.1 Locations of Urban Infrastructure

Fundamentally, urban infrastructure may be classified into nine sub-types: education, healthcare, transport, community support, public space, access to information, public safety, recreation, sports, arts, and culture. Out of these, this research considers three important urban infrastructures that are education, healthcare, and transport. The technical data needed for the analysis was obtained through the Karnataka government's website (kgis.ksrsac.in/kgis/). The analysis was performed with the help of the geo-locations of the selected urban infrastructure: schools, hospitals, bus stops, metro stations, and existing road networks. Figure 8.4 shows the distribution of these urban infrastructures across the city in each municipal ward. Below are the details of the data for the selected parameters.

8.5.2.1.1 SCHOOLS

An open-source platform called OpenCity, an urban data portal, is used to obtain the shapefiles for schools in Bengaluru (Oorvani & DataMeet, 2013). The data last updated in 2013 shows that 1885 public and private schools are located in Bengaluru.

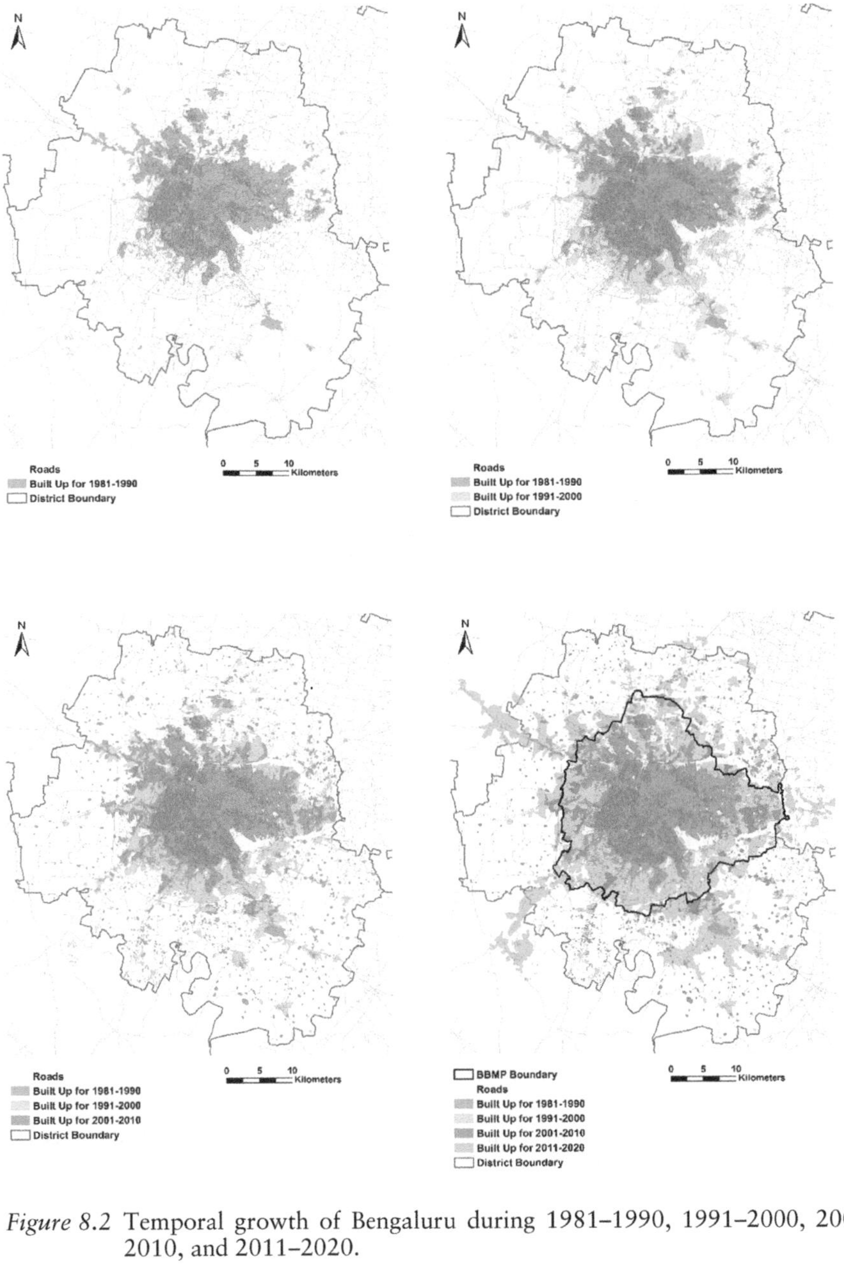

Figure 8.2 Temporal growth of Bengaluru during 1981–1990, 1991–2000, 2000–2010, and 2011–2020.

8.5.2.1.2 HOSPITALS

An open-source platform called 'Maps Bengaluru' is used to obtain the shapefiles for hospitals in Bengaluru. The geographic locations of these were verified with satellite imagery. There were 159 major hospitals in the city in 2020 (Hospitals in Bengaluru, 2020) (Maps Bengaluru, 2020).

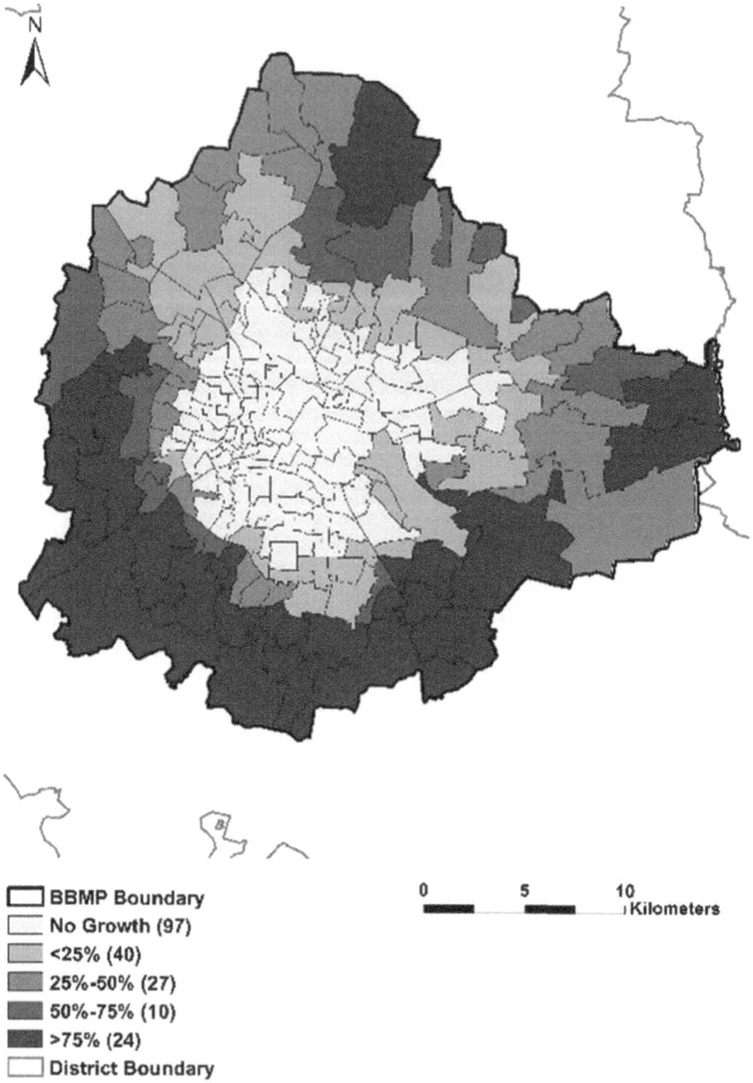

Figure 8.3 Percentage of growth in municipal wards of Bengaluru (BBMP Area) in the past four decades

8.5.2.1.3 BUS DEPOTS

An open-source platform called OpenCity, an urban data portal, is used to obtain the shapefiles for bus depots in Bengaluru (Oorvani & DataMeet, 2013). As per the data last updated in 2008, there were 44 bus depots in Bengaluru.

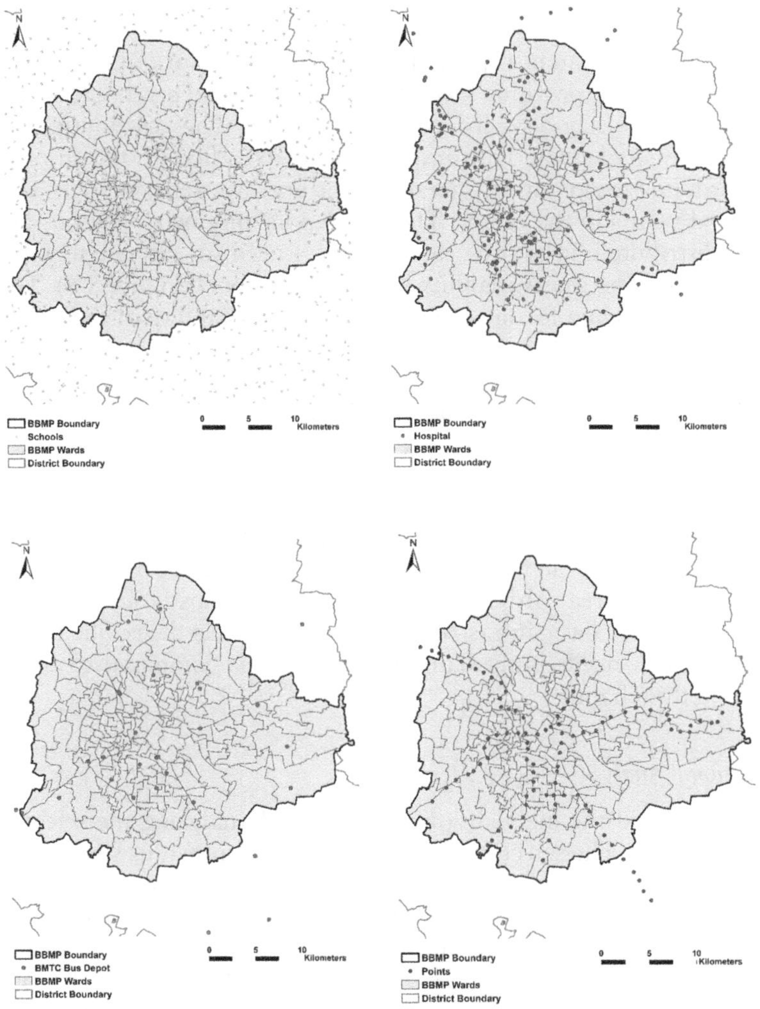

Figure 8.4 Locations of urban infrastructure in Bengaluru (BBMP area)

8.5.2.1.4 METRO STATIONS

The open-source Google Maps helped obtain the shapefiles for metro stations in Bengaluru (Bengaluru Metro, 2020). As per the data last updated in 2020, there were 96 metro stations in Bengaluru.

8.5.2.1.5 EXISTING ROAD NETWORK[7]

An open-source platform called Mapcruzin is used to obtain the shapefiles for the existing road network in Bengaluru (MapCruzin, 2020).

8.5.2.2 ANALYSIS OF AVAILABILITY

The authors analyzed urban infrastructures per municipal ward in the BBMP area, as discussed in the previous section. The study found a relatively balanced distribution of schools across the study area. The distribution of hospitals is largely inadequate with respect to the given households in each municipal ward. It is comparatively greater in the northwestern, western, and a few municipal wards in the center. The bus depots and metro stations are inadequately distributed, indicating that there is a need for city administrators to shift the focus on the availability of public transport (Figure 8.5). The authors used the following formula to calculate the availability of the urban infrastructures in the BBMP area.

$$N = \frac{\text{Count of urban infrastructure in a municipal ward}}{\text{Total Households in a Ward}} * 100$$

Where N is the availability factor of infrastructure per municipal ward.

Considering that the central city is densely populated, the lack of availability of urban infrastructures in the area is alarming and calls for reconsidering the distribution in the area. Although the central area is mostly non-residential, it is crucial to have basic infrastructure services such as the public transport network, which needs immediate improvement as compared to other areas studied in this chapter.

8.5.2.3 Relational Analysis

The authors measured the inequality by relating and analyzing the selected urban infrastructures. The selected parameters from the previous section are spatially combined and derived conclusive maps, as shown in Figure 8.6. The inequality is measured by the availability of urban infrastructures in the study area. The spatial map of the combined analysis[8] indicates that the urban infrastructures follow the temporal growth patterns of the city, thus demonstrating an organic relationship between growth, urban infrastructures, and transport links and proving the hypothesis of this research. Each ward was given a rating as a measure of the indicative inequality. This inequality is measured in two ways: firstly, by taking a simple average for all parameters and, secondly, by taking a weighted average[9] for these parameters. These are calculated as per the following formula:

$$\text{Average} = \frac{\text{As\%} + \text{Ah\%} + \text{Ab\%} + \text{Am\%} + \text{Ar\%}}{5}$$

$$\text{Weighted Average} = \frac{0.4\text{As\%} + 0.2\text{Ah\%} + 0.14\text{Ab\%} + 0.14\text{Am\%} + 0.12\text{Ar\%}}{5}$$

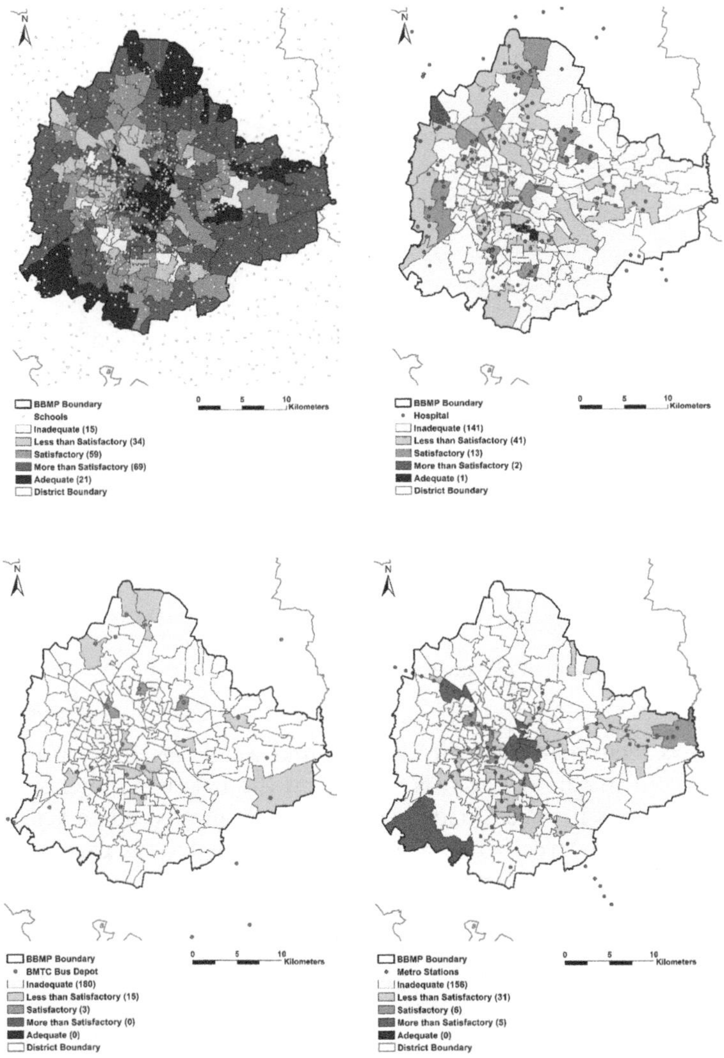

Figure 8.5 Availability of infrastructure in Bengaluru (BBMP area)

where

As% is the availability factor of schools,
Ah% is the availability factor of hospitals,
Ab% is the availability factor of bus depots,
Am% is the availability factor of metro stations,
Ar% is the availability factor of road length.

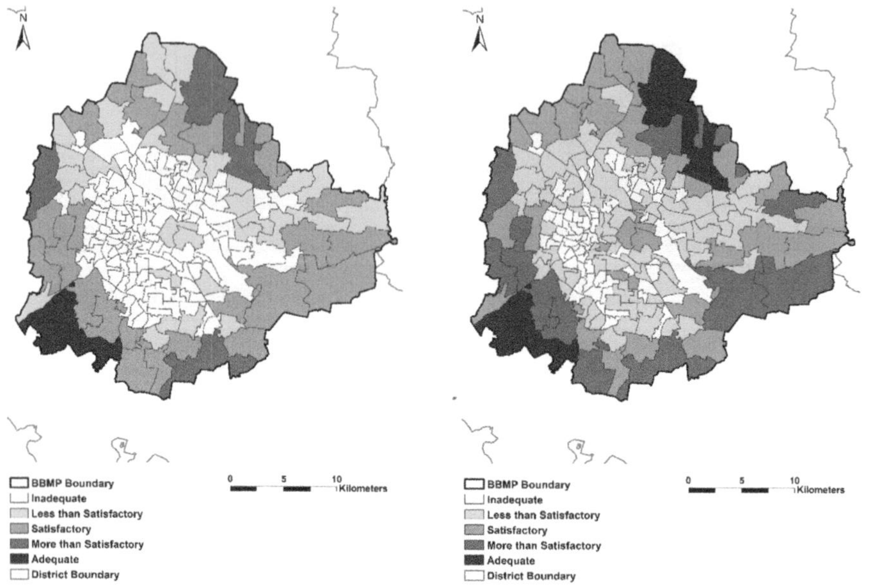

Figure 8.6 Averages per ward of all the availability factors

Figure 8.6 shows relational inequality when equal weightage is given to all parameters covered in this research is shown on the left. It highlights distinct radial boundaries between inadequate and other graded adequacies in the existing wards. However, when a more detailed analysis is carried out and weighted averages are assigned for each parameter, it produces a map, as shown on the Figure 8.6 (right). This highlights specific wards at each level of adequacy and reveals a tilted north-south axis of comparative better infrastructure services. This axis is illustrated in Figure 8.7. This virtual axis houses a major railway segment toward the northern half. The virtual tilt toward southeast is indicative of a major divide because of Bengaluru Mysuru Infrastructure Corridor Area Planning Authority's (BMICAPA) layouts as shown in.

8.5.2.4 Analysis of Accessibility (Distance)

The second key derivative for measuring inequality is the accessibility of available resources. The authors calculated the accessibility for each ward by obtaining the average distance between the centroid of the ward and the total count of the urban infrastructure present in the ward. The authors used the following formula to calculate the accessibility of the urban infrastructures in the BBMP area (Figure 8.8).

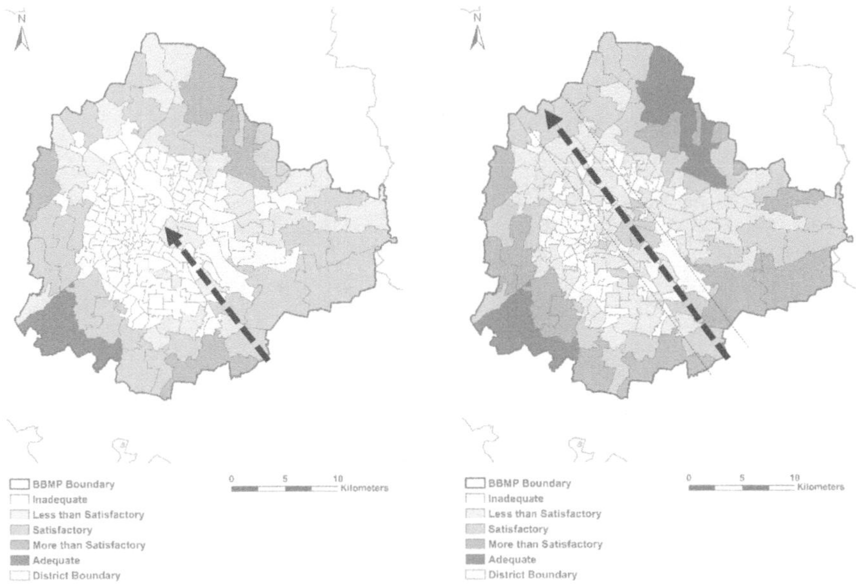

Figure 8.7 A virtual tilted north-south axis of comparative better infrastructure services

$$M = \frac{\text{Distance of Urban Infrastructure in a Ward from the centre of the Ward}}{\text{Total Count of the Urban infrastructure in a Ward}}$$

where *M* is the accessibility factor per ward.

The study finds that the municipal wards on the northwest to southeast axis have better accessibility to the schools than the other municipal wards in the vicinity, highlighting convenient accessibility of education. The municipal wards experiencing rapid development over the past couple of decades have greater adequacy of urban infrastructure. The accessibility of health infrastructural facilities is inadequate in the periphery and the city center. The wards toward the east lack health infrastructure altogether. The accessibility of public transport is better in the center as compared to those in the periphery.

8.5.2.5 Gated Communities

This section indicates urbanization along highways in northwest, southwest, and southeast directions. The development along these transit routes is residential in nature. The study finds gentrification in the form of gated residential colonies clustered principally in the peripheral areas of the BBMP. Figure 8.9 shows enlarged snips in the northeast, east, southeast, and west directions.

Figure 8.8 Accessibility of infrastructure in the municipal ward of Bengaluru (BBMP area)

In Bengaluru, gated communities and educational and health infrastructures generally proliferate in the peripheral municipal wards but lack the distribution of public transportation linkages. However, there is some exception like ward number 149, which is relatively well accessible but lacks in urban infrastructures. In some municipal wards, the availability of hospitals is also very few, e.g., ward numbers 84 and 193 (as shown in Figure 8.9) each has

Figure 8.9 Gated communities

only one city hospital. The findings suggest widespread deprivation of mobility and urban infrastructure across the BMA area.

8.6 Conclusion

The focus of this chapter is to understand the spatial inequality of Bengaluru through the accessibility and availability of urban infrastructures, namely schools, hospitals, bus depots, metro stations, and road networks. Bengaluru has grown from the center in different directions owing to the key factors involved in catalyzing this growth. In Bengaluru, this growth is further influenced by the presence of transportation linkages and prime knowledge-based institutions, e.g., ITPL. The study finds a virtual axis formed by the municipal wards having greater adequacy of urban infrastructure and mobility than the surrounding areas. This axis is a diagonal belt between the northwest and the southeast directions. The city's temporal growth over the past two decades also coincides with this axis. The analysis of the availability and accessibility of urban infrastructures also supports the existence of this axis.

The analysis at the municipal ward level finds a notable inequality distribution moving outwards from the city center. The peripheral municipal wards have a comparatively adequate distribution of services. The spatial aspects of this inequality were further examined by selecting a few wards at the fringes of the BBMP boundary. It is observed that these municipal wards with predominant residential land use at the periphery have relatively better availability of urban infrastructure. The settlements at the periphery are gradually gentrifying toward the rural hinterlands. However, these municipal wards have inadequate public transportation networks and thus limited accessibility. Even though education and health infrastructures are distinctly available in the peripheral municipal wards, their accessibility needs significant improvement. On the contrary, the city center has predominantly commercial land use distribution and near to inadequate availability of education and health infrastructure. However, the connectivity to public transport is better in these areas.

This research aids in understanding the complex nature of the relationship between the expressions of spatial inequalities and the presence of urban infrastructures and mobility. It focuses on the municipal ward to show these two variables' interdependence and the correlation between inequality and urban development. The study concludes that inequality, in turn, bears a dynamic relationship with urbanization through the process of gentrification and urban expansion.

The authors recommend further studies on spatial inequality of infrastructure and other related amenities that influence these disparities in a city, at a micro-level. The data from this research may help categorize the key spatial attributes of Bengaluru and similar metropolitan areas. Hence, the present research becomes crucial in discussing urban renewal and redevelopment at both micro- and macro-levels.

Notes

1 For information regarding the South Karnataka Region and Bangalore Metropolitan Region, refer to the Final Report for Revised of Structure Plan – 2031, Bangalore Metropolitan Region (BMRDA, 2016).
2 There are a few known indicators to measure the standards of living, e.g., Gross Domestic Product (GDP) per capita, Human Development Index, Satisfaction with Life Index, Happy Planet Index, etc. Each of these is used by different countries.
3 A measure of income inequality where 0 means perfect equality and 1 indicates perfect inequality. It is often written as a percentage.
4 As per the BBMP Act, 2020, the BBMP area is supposed to have an additional 45 municipal wards thus summing up to 243 from the previous 198 wards. The current municipal ward boundaries are yet to be finalized as this chapter is written, so this research is based on the earlier municipal ward boundaries.
5 74th Constitutional Amendment Act, 1992, addresses the provision of Urban Local Self-government by constituting three types of municipalities depending upon the size and area.
6 As stated by Bangalore Development Authority updated in 2017.
7 Since roads are basic infrastructure, directly influencing the urban development, the authors only used the data for the road network while conducting the relational analysis and did not do an independent evaluation.
8 This is including the temporal growth pattern mentioned in this chapter and the analysis based on the geographic locations of the selected social infrastructures.
9 The weighted percentages for the selected social parameters are based on the contribution of education, health, and transportation, overall economy of the city, and the quality of life as per the references used for this chapter. The authors determined the values of the percentages used for the relational analysis by considering the contribution of education, health, and transportation to the overall

economy of the city, and the quality of life of the people living in the study area. The authors explored the well-being aspect for understanding this distribution by reviewing the references mentioned in this chapter.

References

Aghion, P., Caroli, E., & Garcia-Penalosa, C. (1999, June). Inequality and Economic Growth: The Perspective of the New Growth Theories. *Harvard Library*. http://nrs.harvard.edu/urn-3:HUL.InstRepos:12502063

Bangalore Metro. (2020). Google: https://www.google.com/maps/d/u/0/viewer?msa=0&mid=1CthYvk35CpUtJ5GLoPIQFjq_32U&ll=12.979342494515555%2C77.58873159120735&z=14

BBMP. (2015). *Bruhat Bengaluru Mahanagara Palike*. www.site.bbmp.gov.in

BBMP. (2021). Bruhat Bengaluru Mahanagara Palike (BBMP): https://bbmp.gov.in/about-us

BDA, B. D. (2017). *Revised Master Plan for Bangaluru-2031 (Draft)*. Bangalore: Bangalore development Authority. https://opencity.in/pages/bda-revised-master-plan-2031-all-documents

BMRDA. (2016). *Revised of Structure Plan - 2031 Bangalore Metropolitan Region*. https://bmrda.karnataka.gov.in/storage/pdf-files/St%20report.pdf

Census of India. (2011). *Data on migration*. Census of India: https://censusindia.gov.in/2011census/migration.html

Crossman, A. (2020, January 28). *The sociology of social inequality*. ThoughtCo.: https://www.thoughtco.com/sociology-of-social-inequality-3026287#:~:text=One%20view%20aligns%20with%20the,an%20important%20function%20in%20society.&text=Social%20inequality%20and%20social%20stratification,a%20meritocracy%20based%20on%20ability.

Government of Karnataka. (2020). *Downloads*. Retrieved November 2020, from Karnataka Geographic Information System: https://kgis.ksrsac.in/kgis/downloads.aspx#

Hospitals in Bangalore. (2020). Google: https://www.google.com/maps/d/u/0/edit?mid=1WYVvkHzGGQcJtQaLYQNhMyzmpv8&ie=UTF8&hl=en&msa=0&ll=12.895248385835894%2C77.5960710846546&spn=0.160589%2C0.219727&z=17&source=embed

Karnataka, G. o. (2017). *History*. Bengaluru Urban District: https://bengaluruurban.nic.in/en/history/#:~:text=Bangalore%2C%20officially%20known%20as%20Bengaluru,populous%20urban%20agglomeration%20in%20India.

MapCruzin. (2020). https://mapcruzin.com/free-karnataka-country-city-place-gis-shapefiles.htm

Maps Bangalore. (2020). https://maps-bangalore.com/bangalore-map-hd

Natarajan, H. A., & Biswas, A. (2019, October 31). A Critical review of the Indian knowledge-based industry location policy against its theoretical arguments. *Regional Science Policy and Practice*. doi:10.1111/rsp3.12257

Oorvani, F., & DataMeet. (2013). OpenCity, Urban Data Portal: https://opencity.in/data

Paul, S. (Ed.). (2018). *Kuznets Beyond Kuznets*. Asian Development Bank Institute. https://www.adb.org/sites/default/files/publication/451936/adbi-kuznets-beyond-kuznets-income-inequality-globalization-asia.pdf

Tal, M.-S., & Maarten, v. H. (2018). Neighbourhood change and spatial polarization: The roles of increasing inequality and divergent urban development. *City*, 108–118. www.elsevier.com/locate/cities

Tan, L., & Zeng, D.-Z. (2013, April 12). Spatial inequality between developed and developing economies. *The Regional Science Association International*. doi:10.1111/pirs.12046

United Nations. (2015). *Concepts of Inequality: Development Issues No. 1*. Development Strategy and Policy Analysis Unit. Development Strategy and Policy Analysis Unit, Development Policy and Analysis Division, Department of Economic and Social Affairs. https://www.un.org/en/development/desa/policy/wess/wess_dev_issues/dsp_policy_01.pdf

Venables, A. L. (2013). Spatial inequality and development. https://www.wider.unu.edu/publication/spatial-inequality-and-development-0

World Population Review. (2022). *Gini coefficient by country 2022*. World Population Review: https://worldpopulationreview.com/country-rankings/gini-coefficient-by-country

9 Housing Inequality and Community-Based Counteracting in a Deprived Community in Taipei, Taiwan

Kojiro Sho and Tetsuo Kidokoro

9.1 Housing Inequality in Taipei

Spatial inequality in cities has accelerated with globalization and neoliberalism (Kidokoro et al., 2022, 2023; Sho et al., 2024). Housing inequality is one of the most critical issues driven by the neoliberalism-oriented housing market throughout the world in the context of spatial inequality. In recent years, previous welfare-oriented housing policies have been diminishing, and economic contexts have been increasingly emphasized in most Asian societies. Under this context, housing speculation has become a major housing problem and hence a major concern of social movements since the mid-1980s in Taiwan. Although the government has implemented various schemes to slow down housing prices, past policies have not challenged the fundamental structure of the system of housing provision, particularly its speculative tendencies. On the other hand, it is noted that a civil movement has been built up around the issue of affordable rented housing since the late 1980s resisting the tendency toward intensified housing commodification that benefits developers at the expense of the socially vulnerable groups (Ronald & Chiu, 2010; Chen, 2011; Tsai, 2018).

Hitherto, municipal public housing operated by the Taipei City Government is supposed to provide low-income households of the bottom two deciles of average income with affordable housing in Taipei, yet the provision of public housing is far less than needed (Hsiao, 2022). The Taipei City Government launched a new scheme of public rental housing called 'Social Housing' in 2014 to fill this gap (Hsiao and Iwasaki, 2021). Yet, its rent level is higher than the existing public rental housing and is therefore not affordable for socially vulnerable households. Although the 'Social Housing' scheme provides housing to a certain segment of lower-income households who are currently not properly served in the private rental market, the effect of this policy is limited in terms of the transformation of the housing market. It can be said that the trends of the commodification of housing itself should be challenged (Rietdijk, 2022).

All in all, the shortage of social housing in Taipei remains a major challenge. Public rental housing stock still accounts for less than 1% of the total housing stock in Taipei.[1] In 2017, the Taipei City Government claimed to

DOI: 10.4324/9781003280866-9

increase public housing stock to 5% of the city's housing stock. Even after this enhancement, the percentage of public housing is still about 2% of the total housing, including those currently under planning or under construction.

Reflecting the low rate of public housing stock, the housing ownership rate is quite high in Taiwan. The housing ownership rate in Taipei was 72.1%, while the average in Taiwan was 78.9% in 2020.[2] Under the neoliberal shift of urban development policies in Taiwan, housing prices have been experiencing a dramatic increase in Taiwan, especially in Taipei. Against this backdrop, many scholars claim that socially vulnerable households have become even more difficult to secure their houses (e.g., Chen, 2011, 2020; Sho et al., 2023).

Under the neo-liberalization shift, which places a higher priority on market mechanisms, various low-interest mortgage programs subsidized by public funding started in the 1990s and the rate of homeownership have been increased. And, at the same time, they have boosted housing prices dramatically because housing has largely become a target for speculation. Indeed, the real estate price/income ratio[3] in Taipei and New Taipei City (surrounding Taipei and comprises Taipei metropolitan areas with Taipei) has increased sharply after 2002 till today (Figure 9.1). Among the six major cities of Taiwan, New Taipei City has the highest value, followed by Taipei. It is noted that the ratios have almost doubled during 2002–2021 in Taipei and New Taipei City.

Another index to represent the trends of the housing market, namely, the mortgage burden ratio,[4] also shows a similar trend to that of the real estate/ price income ratio during the past 20 years in Taiwan. The ratios of Taipei and New Taipei City have increased sharply after 2002 till today (Figure 9.2).

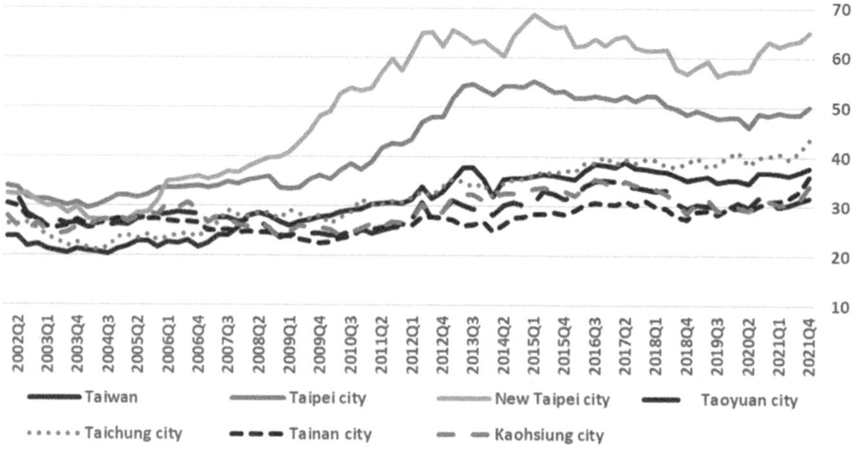

Figure 9.1 Real estate price/income ratio of six major cities in Taiwan during 2002–2021

(*Source:* Compiled based on the data of the Ministry of the Interior, 2022)

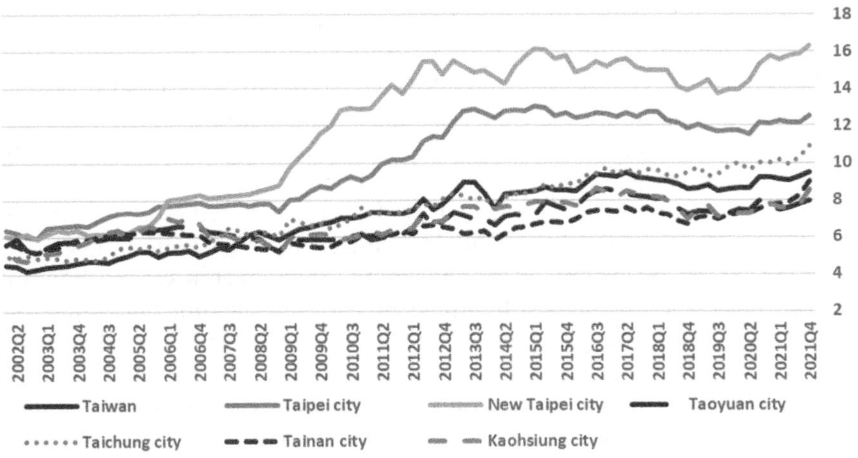

Figure 9.2 Mortgage burden ratio (%) of major cities in Taiwan during 2002–2021
(*Source:* Compiled based on the data of Ministry of the Interior, 2022)

Consequently, the ratios of Taipei and New Taipei City have almost doubled during 2002–2021.

Under this situation, housing affordability has naturally become a serious issue (Chen, 2020). Nowadays, the government primarily focuses on the growth of the housing market and homeownership with little control over speculation (Chen, 2019). Namely, the neoliberalism housing policy and the inadequacy of public housing policy evidently stimulated the jumping-up of housing prices ('housing bubble'), which led to the serious housing inequality in Taipei today. Consequently, socially vulnerable groups tend to concentrate in specific deprived areas where the level of rents is lower due to inadequate housing and living conditions, such as narrow dwelling units, deteriorated building conditions, security conditions, existence of nuisance, etc.

9.2 The Nanjichang Resettlement Housing Complex

Many social movements have recently emerged in Taipei to counteract the housing inequality caused by the neoliberal shift in housing policies. Community-based voluntary activities are particularly important because they would provide direct and immediate support to socially vulnerable groups. In what follows, we will examine the community-based support activities, taking the case of the *Nanjichang* Resettlement Housing Complex in Taipei.

Most of the existing public housing stock in Taipei was constructed around the 1960s. The deterioration of the public housing and its living environment due to aging has therefore become one of the major housing issues these days in Taipei. Among them, the resettlement housing settlements prepared for residents who have been relocated due to public construction projects came to attract attention recently[5] (Hsiao, 2019).

The *Nanjichang* Resettlement Housing Complex (hereinafter called NRHC) is a community composed of about 6,000 households, which lies across *Wanhua* District and *Zhongzheng* District (Figure 9.3). Originally, NRHC was constructed as a relocation settlement for the residents of illegal settlements along the river which had been abolished to construct the river levee. The construction of NRHC started in 1964 and completed in 1975. Five-story apartments were built by the then most advanced building method. They were the highest buildings in Taipei at the time of completion. The neighborhood unit principle, which was the most creative urban planning theory at the time, was applied and rich public space as well as facilities were provided, including parks, children play lots, schools, markets, emergency evacuation rooms, etc. The apartment buildings built in NRHC were indeed regarded as a model of modern apartments. However, after more than 50 years since its completion, apartments of NRHC suffer from many drawbacks, including deterioration of buildings, small unit size, deteriorated living conditions, vulnerability to fires and earthquakes, etc. Many first-floor units have been illegally converted to night market shops or restaurants, which have caused nuisance such as fire, foul smells, wastes, noise, etc. (Figure 9.4). Due to these problems, the rents of the apartments of NRHC have been decreasing, and thus socially vulnerable households have been increasingly concentrating on NRHC. As a result, the rates of various socially vulnerable groups residing in NRHC became significantly higher than the average in Taipei (Table 9.1).

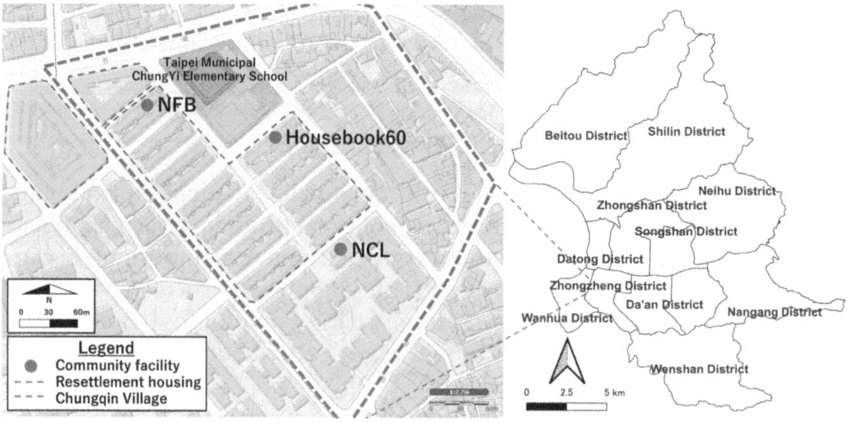

Figure 9.3 Map of The *Nanjichang* Resettlement Housing Complex (NRHC)

(*Source:* Created based on the data of Taipei City Government (2021) and National Development Council (2021))

Figure 9.4 Current view of NRHC: Deterioration is progressing
(*Image credit:* Authors).

Table 9.1 Concentration of socially vulnerable groups in Zhongqin *Li*[a]

Socially vulnerable groups	*Number*	*Rate to the total of Zhongqin Li*[b]	*Average rate of Taipei City*[c]
Low-income households designated by Taipei City	175	5.8%	2.0%
Low-income elderly households[d]	73	2.4%	0.5%
Elderly population	1,230	18.6%	14.1%
Single elderly population households	65	2.1%	1.29%
Households with handicapped people	536	17.6%	4.47%
Households with foreign spouses	More than 400	5.8%	1.01%

Source: Compiled based on Fang (2018)

[a] *Li* is the smallest administrative unit in Taiwan. There are 456 *Li* within 12 districts in Taipei City, and the average population of *Li* is 5,514 people in 2022. NRHC is located at Zhongqin *Li* (see Figure 9.1).

[b] The total population of Zhongqin *Li* is 6,599 (male 3,104, female 3,601), and the total number of households in Zhongqin *Li* is 3,019.

[c] As of May 2018, some of them are as of 2016.

[d] Over 65 years old.

9.3 Development of Community Facilities in NRHC

Community development activities have been conducted at the level of *Li* in Taipei. The chief of Zhongqin *Li* has been very keen on supporting socially vulnerable residents in NRHC and has played a leading role in community development. The present chief of Zhongqin *Li*[6] has been in the office for more than 20 years since he was elected as the chief of *Li* for the first time. Mutual trust among residents has been nurtured through various community development activities organized under the present chief of *Li* through active participation by residents (Teng, 2021).

As the outputs of continuous community development activities to support socially vulnerable groups in the community, several community facilities have been developed: the *Nanjichang* Community Land (hereinafter called NCL), the *Nanjichang* Food Bank (hereinafter called NFB), and the 'Housebook 60' community Café (Figure 9.5).

NCL is a multi-service center located at the center of Zhongqin *Li*. It works as an important social space for residents and provides various child-care and welfare services. It is a renovated building of an abandoned residence of an ex-military officer. Before the renovation, the deterioration of this building became a problem for the community, and thus it was proposed to renovate the building and reuse it as a facility for socially vulnerable groups residing in NRHC. To realize this vision, the negotiation was done with the government agencies that own the property, and permission for renovation and conversion was issued in 2010. Subsequently, a series of workshops participated by residents were held and designed under the assistance of experts from the National Taiwan University and other organizations. The renovation of the building was completed in July 2011. NCL provides various community facilities, including a branch of the city library, after-school teaching for children, a community restaurant, a food delivery service facility, and a community café (left of Figure 9.5).

NFB is located in the northwest area of NRHC. It introduced the local currency system in which residents can obtain points by participating in community volunteer activities, and those points can be exchanged for various daily necessities collected from various charity/social organizations. A post

Figure 9.5 Community facilities in NRHC

(*Image credit:* Authors)

office which had not been used for long was renovated after the permission of the related government agencies through a similar process of NCL. NFB started operation in December 2013 (middle of Figure 9.5).

'Housebook 60' Café opened in September 2016 to provide a genuine café space in the community, in which unused foodstuffs of NFB can be utilized to avoid food loss and, more importantly, to provide job training/opportunities for delinquent youths of the community. It is also intended to attract customers from outside so that profits can be utilized to maintain other community facilities (Teng, 2021). A vending machine-type community refrigerator, which stocks the foodstuffs unused in NFB and close to the expiration date, is placed at the entrance of 'Housebook 60' Café. Anyone can take them for free (right of Figure 9.5).

9.4 Food Bank as a Tool to Counteract Poverty

Food security is one of the important aspects in reducing poverty. Food bank is a system to redistribute donated, surplus food to socially vulnerable groups and it has emerged as one of the key frontline responses to the growing problem of food poverty and inequality (Riches, 2002; Kim, 2015; MacLeod et al., 2019). Indeed, in the past 20 years, many food banks have been established and it is one of the fastest–growing charitable institutions in the world.

NFB initially started as an activity of the Zhongqin *Li* office. As the size of operation has grown significantly, a new community-based non-profit charity organization called Jen *Ji Shian* Social Service Institute of Taipei City was established in March 2014 to operate NFB. Foodstuffs and other daily necessities are donated and collected from various supporting organizations including wholesalers, religious organizations, the Red Cross Society, etc. Members of NFB can obtain points by engaging in community voluntary activities and those points can be exchanged to items stocked in NFB. By combining the 'community currency', the point system in NFB, with voluntary activities in NCL, it is possible for a socially vulnerable household to help others rather than only accepting support or help from others. This model sustains the operation of both NFB and NCL and empowers the community to support not only the residents but also more vulnerable people and households outside the community (Hsiao et al., 2016).

By 2018, the number of members had reached 385 households. Among them, 121 members were from low-income households, and 161 were those who required urgent food support. Regarding items of foodstuffs taken by members, essential foodstuffs account for large shares: rice (18.4%), cooking oil (9.4%), canned food (8.2%), and milk powder (8.0%). If we estimate the possible amount of rice obtained from the average points acquired through community activities, households with three household members can obtain enough rice to consume from NFB. It is evident from the estimate that NFB strongly supports the daily life of socially vulnerable groups.

Importantly, NFB supports the improvement of the quality of life of socially vulnerable groups not only by offering daily necessities but also by providing an opportunity to enter the circle of mutual trust among community members by incentivizing them to participate in community activities. Furthermore, as an important aspect of NFB, socially vulnerable people themselves can play an important role in community development through participation in community activities. It will enhance the sense and pride of the community where they live. In the interviews with residents, many voices point out the virtuous cycle in the community. For example, Ms L, who is an immigrant from a foreign country and moved to NRHC after she married a Taiwanese citizen, said:

> Rice, food oil and other daily necessities are well serviced in this community. Though residents are poor, I am proud of this community because this is a warm community and residents all help and support each other.[7]

9.5 Conclusion

In conclusion, we try to distill some important lessons from the case of NRHC in this section. Firstly, the social, political, and institutional setting of the community in Taiwan plays an important role, i.e., Li acts as the smallest administrative unit, and, at the same time, it acts as a representative organization of the community. In particular, the chief of Li, an elected officer by the residents, can act as a community leader and, simultaneously, as an intermediary between the community and the city government. Under this context, voluntary community activities are successfully supported through smooth consultation and coordination with related city and government agencies.

Secondly, the real needs of socially vulnerable groups will vary substantively. Community-based initiatives can develop community activities directly responding to the unique and urgent needs of the socially vulnerable groups living in the community. In the case of NRHC, they include: after school teaching support to children, job training and creation for the delinquent youths ('Housebook 60' café), support for health and social life (the food bank and the community restaurant), involvement of socially vulnerable groups to the circle of mutual trust in the community (participation to community activities through points exchange system of the food bank), provision of the space to connect the community and people outside the community ('Housebook 60' café).

Thirdly, it is important that various voluntary activities should be deployed together in a complementary manner. In the case of NRHC, through the points exchange system of NFB. Enough number of participants in various voluntary community activities are secured, and, at the same time, socially vulnerable groups are effectively and smoothly included in the circle of mutual trust and help in the community. The community restaurant and cafe in NCL not only provide food with proper nutrition and social space to community members but also provide a job training function to delinquent youths. Additionally, professional job opportunities (barista) for delinquent youths are provided in 'Housebook 60' Café. Further, profits earned by the 'Housebook 60' Café, which targets customers from outside the community, are used to support the operational costs of NCL and NFB.

Fourthly, it is noted that the link with the outside should be developed. In NRHC, relationships with outside support organizations have been developed through the activities of NFB. 'Housebook 60' Café, which became popular as the first café operated in relation to the food bank in Taiwan, seems to act as a social place to link the community and the outside world. It can be said that the above-mentioned experiences of NRHC provide many important lessons for community-based voluntary activities in deprived areas in other cities in the world.

Notes

1 This percentage is about one-tenth of that of the average of OECD countries by 2021.
2 These are much higher than the average of OECD countries (43%) or the United Kingdom (34%), Australia (31%), and the USA (25%), according to OECD (2021).
3 Real estate price/income ratio is defined as Median of real estate price/Median of household disposable income.
4 Mortgage burden ratio (%) = Median of monthly mortgage repayment/Median of household disposable income * 100%
5 There are about 20,000 resettlement housing units in Taipei.
6 The chief of Li is elected directly by residents through the official election. The chief of Li becomes an officer of the city government. Each Li has a Li office.
7 Interview in November 2018.

References

Chen, Y. L. (2011). New prospects for social rental housing in Taiwan: The role of housing affordability crises and the housing movement. *International Journal of Housing Policy, 11*(3), 305–318.

Chen, Y. L. (2019). 'Re-occupying the state': Social housing movement and the transformation of housing policies in Taiwan. In Y. L. Chen & H. Shin (Eds.), *Neoliberal Urbanism, contested cities and housing in Asia. The contemporary city*. Palgrave Macmillan. https://doi.org/10.1057/978-1-137-55015-6_2

Chen, Y. L. (2020). "Housing prices never fall": The development of housing finance in Taiwan. *Housing Policy Debate, 30*(4), 623–639. https://doi.org/10.1080/10511482.2020.1714691

Fang, H. S. (2018). From community meal delivery to food sharing network: Pioneer practices in Nanjichang (South Airport Community). Retrieved July 20, 2021, from https://www.ur-plaza.osaka-cu.ac.jp/wp1/wp-content/uploads/2018/07/S2-2_5.pdf

Hsiao, H. W., Kidokoro, T., & Seta, F. (2016). Research on welfare-oriented *machizukuri* approach in a housing complex. *Journal of Architecture and Planning (Transactions of AIJ), 81*(729), 2463–2473.

Hsiao, H. W. (2019). Study on consensus building process and method of public sector-led process of mass housing complex: Case of urban regeneration project of Lanzhou-Sien resettlement housing in Taipei city. *AIJ Journal of Technology and Design, 25*(60), 887–892.

Hsiao, H. W., & Iwasaki, A. (2021). Study on the new supply of public rental housing in Taipei city, Taiwan-. *AIJ Journal of Technology and Design, 27*(66), 1009–1014.

Hsiao, H. W. (2022). From squatter settlements to cultural heritage: The preservation and revitalization as "group of buildings" based on the case experience of Treasure Hill Art Village in Taipei City, Taiwan. *Journal of Asian Architecture and Building Engineering, 21*(2), 644–661.

Kidokoro, T., Fukuda, R., & Sho, K. (2022). Gentrification in Tokyo: Formation of the Tokyo West Creative Industry Cluster. *International Journal of Urban and Regional Research, 46*(6), 1055–1077.

Kidokoro, T., Sho, K., & Fukuda, R. (2023). Urban suburbia: Gentrification and spatial inequality in workers' communities in Tokyo. *Cities, 136*, 104247.

Kim, S. (2015). Food bank systems in Korea and the USA. *International Journal of Social Welfare, 24*, 145–158.

MacLeod, M., Curl, A., & Kearns, A. (2019). Understanding the prevalence and drivers of food bank use: Evidence from deprived communities in Glasgow. *Social Policy and Society, 18*(1), 67–86.

National Development Council. (2021). DATA.GOV.TW. Retrieved May 9, 2022, from https://data.gov.tw/dataset/7441

OECD. (2021). OECD Affordable Housing Database. Retrieved May 10, 2022, from https://www.oecd.org/housing/data/affordable-housing-database/

Riches, G. (2002). Food banks and food security: Welfare reform, human rights and social policy. Lessons from Canada? *Social Policy & Administration, 36*, 648–663.

Rietdijk, C. E. (2022). Affordability of social housing for youth in greater Taipei: Justice for whom? *International Journal of Housing Policy. ;(23).*

Ronald, R., & Chiu, R. L. H. (2010). Changing housing policy landscapes in Asia Pacific. *International Journal of Housing Policy, 10*(3), 223–231.

Sho, K., Chen, Y. L., & Oshima, K. T. (2023). Alternative gentrification: Coexistence of traditional and new industries in historic districts through transfer of development rights in Dihua Street, Taiwan. *International Journal of Heritage Studies, 29*(12), 1299–1314.

Sho, K., Fukuda, R., Lim, H., Kim, S. M., & Kidokoro, T. (2024). Self-consciousness inequality under spatial polarization: Evidence from growing and declining neighborhoods of Osaka City, Japan. *Cities, 148*, 104846.

Teng, C. (2021). *A Utopian vision for Nanjichang: Borough Chief Fang Hesheng* (S. Williams, Trans.). Taiwan Panorama.

Tsai, I. C. (2018). Housing price convergence, transportation infrastructure and dynamic regional population relocation. *Habitat International, 79*, 61–73.

10 Capturing Regional Inequality of Knowledge-Based Innovation Activities by the USA-Based Multinational Enterprises in a Globalized World

Arun Natarajan Hariharan and Arindam Biswas

10.1 Introduction

Competitive growth and survival in this dynamic environment need continuous amelioration in business processes, including products and services. To address this scenario, organizations turn toward innovation as one of the primary drivers in the present globalized era (Ireland & Web, 2007). Research and Development (R&D) is the cornerstone of any economy that drives innovation to the forefront in the current economic scenario, leading to global welfare in social and economic conditions. Capital investments in R&D stimulate solutions to climate change, resource optimization, and address a sustainable financial future (Govindarajan & Ramamurti, 2011) (Pece, Simona, & Salisteanu, 2015).

At a global level, the increasing access to research in science and engineering (S&E) education has paved the way for incremental growth in R&D expenditure among developed and developing nations (NSB, 2018). Figure 10.1 shows the concentration of activities and spending related to R&D in global regions. North American and European countries spent more than 40% of total expenditure on R&D during the year 2000 but have gradually reduced their R&D spending between 20% and 30% by 2017. China leads R&D performance growth in Asian countries with an annual average R&D expenditure of 20.5% and 12.8% between 2000–2010 and 2010–2017, respectively. Subsequently, the average yearly growth of R&D spending in South Korea is 10.9% and 8.3% between 2000–2010 and 2010–2017, respectively (NSB, 2020).

The numerous R&D location options available for MNEs in deciding and investing in R&D activities present opportunities and risks in different countries across emerging regions. The most frequent analogy of geographical proximity used traditionally was the location choice of industries, which is superseded by 'The World Is Flat' (Friedman, 2005) and 'The Death of Distance' (Cairncross, 2002). These analogies and the dynamic business environment marked the distribution of economic activities geographically.

DOI: 10.4324/9781003280866-10

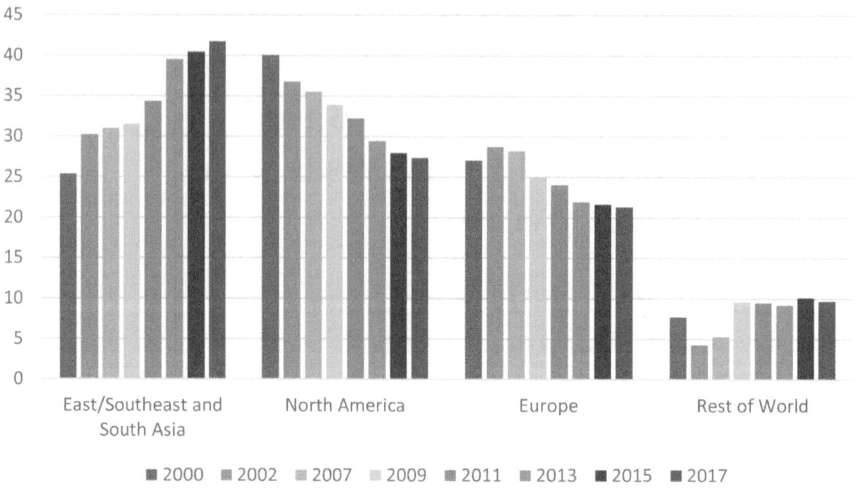

Figure 10.1 Regional share of global expenditure on R&D activities

(*Source:* Compiled by the authors based on data from the US National Science Foundation, National Centre for Science & Engineering Statistics (Various Years))

Michael Porter postulates that knowledge-based activities require location choice between geographies rather than intermediate input in the product development (Cantwell, 2009).

The primary purpose of this chapter is to understand the regional inequality of knowledge-based innovation activities by USA's multinational enterprises. This chapter utilizes the (Dunning, 2009) Ownership, Location and Internationalisation (OLI) framework in determining the role of Foreign Direct Investment (FDI) in mitigating regional inequality in the production of innovation activities. This framework defines the conduct of the MNEs based on benefits gained through OLI. This chapter analyzes the location choice of R&D expenditure based on the following aspects. These are:

- To analyze the dominant nature of MNEs in the globalization of knowledge-based R&D innovation expenditure;
- To determine the location choice of USA's MNEs through R&D expenditure in developed and developing S&T innovation centers in the Knowledge-Based Information and Communication Technology (KBICT) sector.

10.2 The Dominance of the USA-Based MNEs in Knowledge-Based Industry R&D Expenditure

A firm pursuing FDI and adding value through owning and controlling activities in more than one country is classified as a multinational or transnational enterprise (MNE) (Dunning & Lundan, 2008). MNEs play the controlling role in configuring the global economic environment and enhancing FDI distribution graphically (Kim & Aguilera, 2016) (Beugelsdijk, McCann, & Mudambi, 2010). MNEs invest through subsidiary companies owned by the enterprise in a greenfield manner or jointly by acquiring existing resources in a host country. They are responsible for over half of the global R&D expenditure (Patra & Krishna, 2015). The gradual shift in the location choice of production activities over time depends on increasing knowledge and sophistication in product development leading to increasing distance from an enterprise's home country (Vernon, 1979) (Selemun & Sundqvist, 2018).

The life cycle of any innovation is mapped for five years or even less, with 15% spending on the research domain in R&D. Development and commercialization domains spend the remaining 85%. Between 2001 and 2018, research on the top 1,000 enterprises spending on R&D has emphasized an annual growth of 4% (Jaruzelski, Dehoff, & Bordia, 2005). Figure 10.2 represents the growing R&D expenditure of the top 1,000 global enterprises between 2001 and 2018. In the past four decades, the control of innovation and R&D centers focused on home locations handling the maximum activities of R&D, and the host locations adapt these products or technologies for local needs by enterprises from the USA, the EU, and Japan (Doz, Wilson, Veldhoen, Goldbrunner, & Altmann, 2006). Two aspects assess the dynamic globalization of R&D activities. Firstly, the increased R&D diffusion has provided access to large markets and significantly internationalized the civilization of R&D activities. Secondly, disseminating knowledge among the developed and developing regions, especially the economic beginning of

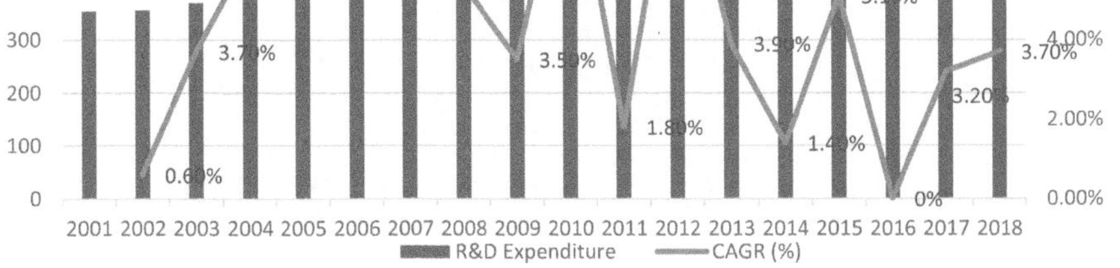

Figure 10.2 R&D expenditure by the top 1000 enterprises globally between 2001 and 2018.

(*Source:* Compiled by the authors based on data from the Global Innovation 1000 Study, various years).

India and China, has resulted in building organizational capabilities of efficient networking. These centers of innovation and R&D have risen from 45% to 66% between 1975 and 2004, respectively (Doz, Wilson, Veldhoen, Goldbrunner, & Altmann, 2006). Figure 10.4 depicts R&D expenditure by the top 1000 Global Innovation MNEs between 2012-2018.

The enterprises from North American countries represent the highest representation in the global Innovation 1000 survey between 2005 and 2018. The number of North American and Japanese enterprises spending on R&D activities has reduced negatively to 2.07% and 3.84% globally between 2005 and 2018. In contrast, during the same period, enterprises in China and Europe spending on R&D activities increased by 23% and 2% globally. The R&D diffusion index of knowledge-based sectors, namely automotive and electronics, was at 3.7 and 3.5, respectively, between 1975 and 2004 (Doz, Wilson, Veldhoen, Goldbrunner, & Altmann, 2006). Figure 10.3 represents the annual R&D expenditure attracting the top nine industrial sectors globally among the top 1000 enterprises. The KBICT sector, including software and internet, computing, and electronics and telecommunication services, registered a compound annual growth rate (CAGR) of 9.74%, 3.37%, and 1.94%, respectively, between 2004 and 2015. Sectors like industrials, healthcare, aerospace, and defense account for the top five industries with a CAGR of 10.73%, 4.41%, and 4.12%, respectively, between 2004 and 2015.

The substantial shift in product manufacturing between 1970 and 1980 required mechanical, chemical, or electronic conversion of processes. In the 1990s, product manufacturing processes controlled the KBICT process

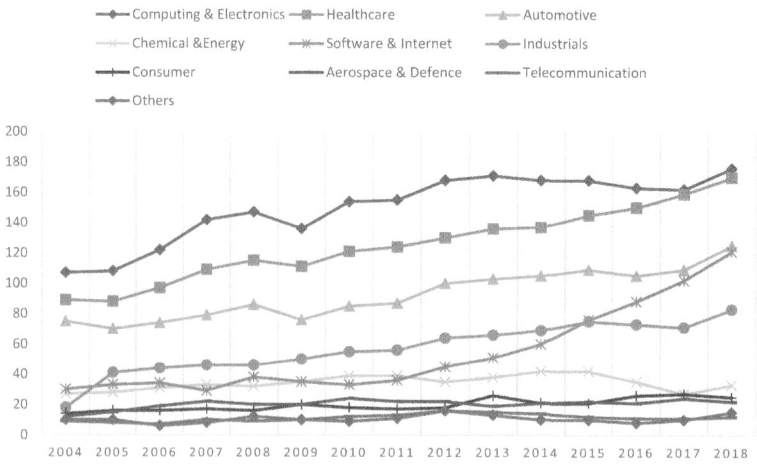

Figure 10.3 Dominant industrial sectors attracting R&D expenditure from global innovation 1000 enterprises.

Source: Compiled by the authors based on data from the Global Innovation 1000 Study, various years.

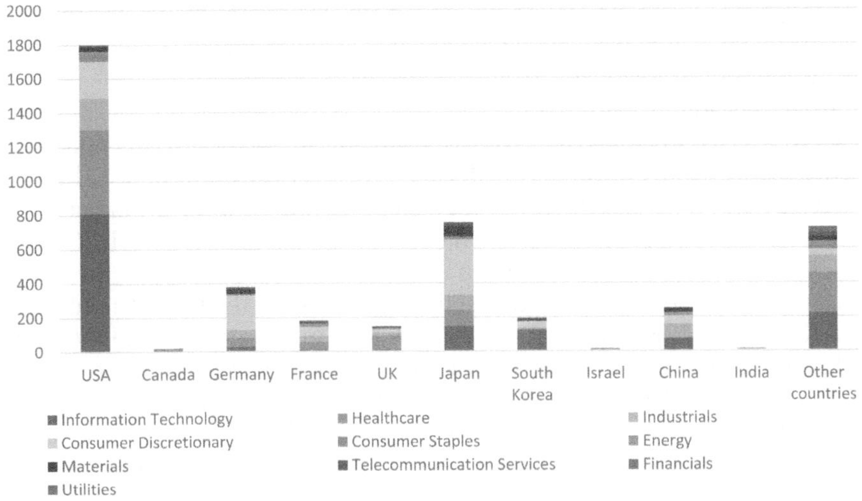

Figure 10.4 R&D expenditure by the top 1000 Global Innovation MNEs between 2012 and 2018.

Source: Author calculations based on data from the Global Innovation 1000 Study, 2018.

involving electronic control systems, sensors, and microprocessors. These KBICT processes, artificial intelligence, and machine learning applications were decisive in product manufacturing, traditionally enabling cost-effective and sophisticated product and service development through R&D innovation (Branstetter, Drev, & Kwon, 2018).

MNEs of the USA have been at the forefront of technological innovation since the early 1960, achieving a prominent position in the world economy. In the early 1990s, these MNEs distributed their R&D activities from their home locations to other industrialized countries like Canada, Germany, and Japan, and developing regions like China, India, Israel, etc. Between 2012 and 2018, KBICT industries received the highest R&D investments at 32% of all sector R&D investments with US$ 1,514 billion. Figure 10.4 depicts the R&D expenditure by the top 1000 global innovation MNEs between 2012 and 2018. Globally, the USA-based MNEs' R&D spending was the highest at US$ 821 billion, dominating at 54% compared to other countries from 2012 to 2018. The following section illustrates the location choice of R&D investments in knowledge-based industries.

10.3 The Augmentation of Innovation R&D Activities in Developing S&T Centers due to R&D Expenditure by the USA-Based MNEs

The growing demand for KBICT processes in both product and non-product-based R&D activities and pertinent skilled labor led to the search for alternative locations by the USA-based MNEs. The intellectual quest for knowledge in conducting R&D across the globe by enterprises advocates the availability of assets in the host locations as a significant factor in their location decisions (Hall, 2011). The USA-based MNEs dominate the area of KBICT, strengthening their role as leaders in innovation R&D and technological advancement on a global scale. The access to international talent reserve by the USA-based MNEs augments the rate of innovation activities without any geographical barriers (Bloom, Jones, Reenen, & Webb, 2020).

The Bureau of Economic Analysis estimates that the average worker compensation in the USA for the R&D activity pertinent to the KBICT industry is considerably higher than their subsidiaries in China and India and attracted as favorable destinations for innovation activities. The primary criteria of the USA-based MNEs in selecting novel S&T centers to diffuse R&D activities required an abundance of low-cost and superior human capital supply compared to the conventional S&T centers (Branstetter, Glennon, & Jensen, 2018). With a considerable measure of cost-effective skilled labor and their economic convergence policies from the early 1990s, India and China led to their attraction as location choices of R&D activities related to KBICT sectors by the USA-based MNEs.

The USA-based MNEs R&D spending on computer and electronic product manufacturing and professional, scientific, and technical services has experienced a CAGR of 4.45% and 5.45% in China and India, respectively, between 2008 and 2017. R&D innovation activities serve as the cardinal point of motivation in maintaining the engines of economic growth (Schumpeter, 1950). Patents signify a physical measure of any country's national innovation capability over time and determine the basis for the R&D expenditure in that country (Furman, Porter, & Stern, 2002). The inventor of patents registered with the United States Patent and Trademark Office (USPTO) is used in this chapter to determine the augmentation in R&D innovation by the USA-based MNEs.

The aggregate number of USPTO inventors' publishing patents has grown by 6% between 1985 and 2019 and a CAGR of 5.3%. Figure 10.5 illustrates the growth of inventors in the publication of USPTO patents for different sectors between 1985 and 2019. The electrical engineering sector was dominant in the evolution of inventors, with a CAGR of 7.88% between 1985 and 2019. This sector grew by 14% compared to other industries represented by inventors between 1985 and 2019. In the present study, the KBICT industries like computer technology, semiconductors, telecommunications, basic communication processes, digital communication, and IT services impart novel technologies that augment innovators in the electrical engineering patents of USPTO. Figure 10.6 illustrates the USPTO inventor growth of different sectors of KBICT industries. The IT services industry exhibits an increase of 260 times and a growth rate of 17.22% compounded annually. Digital communication and computer technology are the other KBICT industries where USPTO patent inventors grew 84 and 43 times between 1985 and 2019.

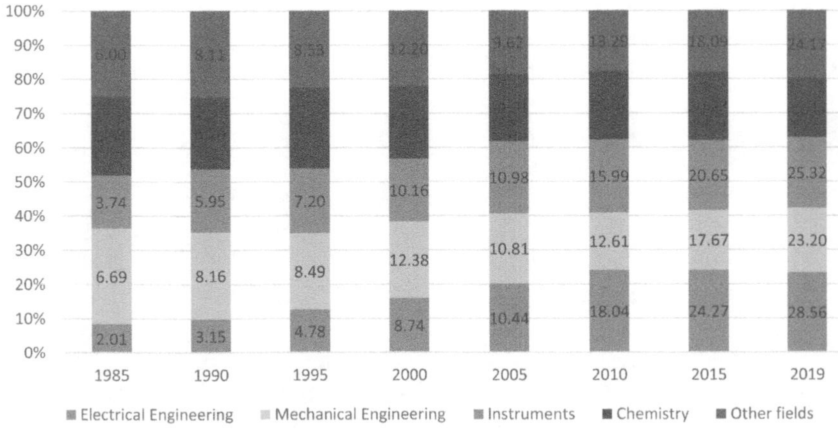

Figure 10.5 Growth of inventors from various sectors in USPTO patent publication between 1985 and 2019.

Source: Author calculations based on data from USPTO (2020).

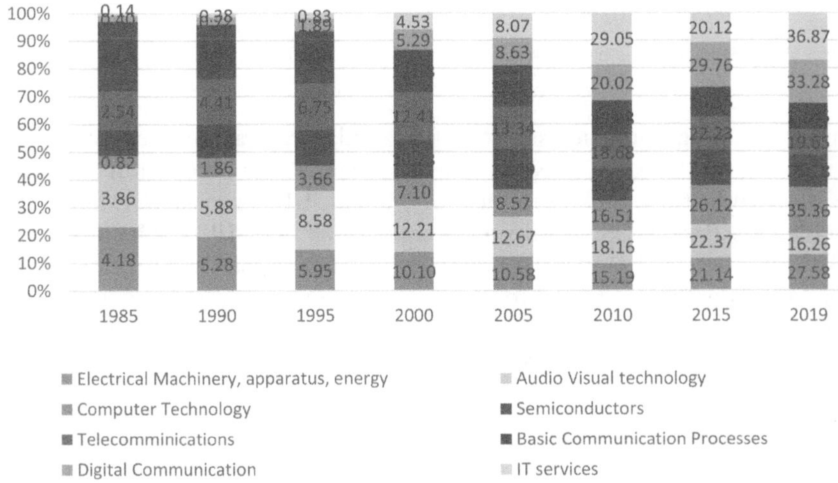

Figure 10.6 Growth of USPTO inventors in KBICT industries under the electrical engineering sector between 1985 and 2019.

Source: Author calculations based on data from USPTO (2020).

The local demand for technological innovations and lower input costs enable endogenous growth in economic development. Traditionally, developing countries had less emphasis on R&D innovation due to technology transfer agreements from developed nations (Timmer, 2003). Figure 10.7 depicts the growth of USPTO inventors in the KBICT sector in developed and developing countries between 1985 and 2019. At the beginning of the millennium,

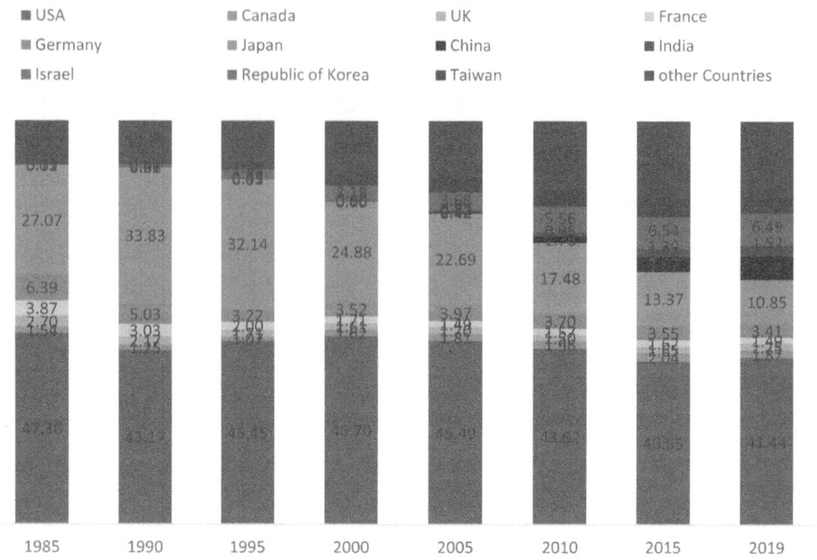

Figure 10.7 Growth of KBICT USPTO inventors from different countries between 1985 and 2019.

Source: Author calculations based on data from (USPTO, 2020).

many developing countries set S&T knowledge capital and regional centers focusing on the KBICT sector. The dominant R&D innovation locations in KBICT industries, including the USA, Japan, UK, France, Germany, and Canada, possessed a USPTO inventor share of 89% in 1985, which reduced to 60% in 2019. Subsequently, countries like China, South Korea, Taiwan, India, and Israel have started to race ahead compared to other countries in KBICT sectors, from less than 1% in 1985 to 20% in 2019 (Branstetter, Glennon, & Jensen, 2018) (USPTO, 2020).

10.4 Discussion and Conclusion

R&D activities exhibit the innovative capacity of any enterprise to sustain itself in the present competitive global economic scenario. The geographic distribution by MNEs in locating R&D activities has helped them gain opportunities in knowledge-based innovation, exhibiting their competitiveness among their counterparts. The economic liberalization in developing regions, conducive trade policies and the shifting of R&D activities from the manufacturing sector to service activities, including digitally traded services, has increased global growth in R&D innovation. The advent of ICT and the globalization of production activities have impeded offshoring R&D activities into developing economies. MNEs in emerging nations have changed from utilization to exploration in recognizing knowledge resources from the late 1990s to the early 2000s (Erken & Kleijn, 2010). The present study has limited its focus toward USA MNEs in expediting innovation expenditure globally. Cost-effective skilled human capital is one of the major driving points of the globalization of R&D activities. Countries like China and India have joined Taiwan and South Korea in augmenting knowledge production through patent publication in the KBICT industries. Further research on the spatial location of KBICT R&D innovation clusters would help augment regional development in these developing countries.

Acknowledgment and Funding

Any remaining errors are solely the responsibility of the authors. The Chord Division of the Department of Science and Technology, Government of India, with grant no. DST/NSTMIS/05/123/2017-18 has fully supported this research.

References

Beugelsdijk, S., McCann, P., & Mudambi, R. (2010). Introduction: Place, space and organisation - economic geography and the multinational enterprise. *Journal of Economic Geography, 10*(4), 485–493.

Bloom, N., Jones, C., Reenen, J. V., & Webb, M. (2020). Are Ideas getting harder to find? *American Economic Review, 110*(4), 1104–1144.

Branstetter, G., Drev, M., & Kwon, N. (2018). Get with the program: Software-driven innovation in traditional manufacturing. *Management Science, 65*(2), 1–19.

Branstetter, L. G., Glennon, B. M., & Jensen, J. B. (2018). *The it revolution and the globalisation of R&D*. National Bureau of Economic Research.

Cairncross, F. (2002). The death of distance. *Royal Society for the Encouragement of Arts, Manufactures and Commerce, 149*(5502), 40–42.

Cantwell, J. (2009). Location and the multinational enterprise. *Journal of International Business Studies, 40*(1), 35–41.

Doz, Y., Wilson, K., Veldhoen, S., Goldbrunner, T., & Altmann, G. (2006). *Innovation: Is gLobal the way forward? A joint study by Booz & Company and INSEAD*. Booz & Company and INSEAD.

Dunning, J. (2009). Location and the multinational enterprise: A neglected factor? *Journal of International Business Studies, 40*(1), 5–19.

Dunning, J., & Lundan, S. (2008). *Multinational enterprises and the global economy*. Edward Elgar Publishing.

Erken, H., & Kleijn, M. (2010). Location factors of international R&D activities: An econometric approach. *Economics of Innovation and New Technology, 19*(3), 203–232.

Friedman, T. (2005). *The world is flat: A brief history of the twenty-first century*. Holtzbrinck Publishers.

Furman, J. L., Porter, M. E., & Stern, S. (2002). The determinants of national innovative capacity. *Research Policy, 31*, 899–933.

Govindarajan, V., & Ramamurti, R. (2011). Reverse innovation, emerging markets, and global strategy. *Global Strategy Journal, 1*(3–4), 191–205.

Hall, B. H. (2011, October 12). The internationalisation of R&D. SSRN: https://papers.ssrn.com/sol3/papers.cfm?abstract_id=2179941

Ireland, D., & Web, J. (2007). Strategic entrepreneurship: Creating competitive advantage through streams of innovation. *Business Horizons, 50*(1), 49–59.

Jaruzelski, B., Dehoff, K., & Bordia, R. (2005). The Booz Allen Hamilton Global Innovation 1000: Money isn't everything. Strategy+Business, *41*, 1–16.

Kim, J., & Aguilera, R. (2016). Foreign location choice: Review and extensions. *International Journal of Management Reviews, 18*(2), 133–159.

NSB. (2018, January). National Science Board Science & Engineering Indicators. Overview of the State of the US S&E Enterprise in a Global Context: https://www.nsf.gov/statistics/2018/nsb20181/report/sections/overview/r-d-expenditures-and-r-d-intensity

NSB. (2020, January). Science & Engineering Indicators. The state of US Science and Engineering 2020: https://ncses.nsf.gov/pubs/nsb20201/global-r-d

Patra, S., & Krishna, V. (2015). Globalisation of R&D and open innovation: Linkages of foreign R&D centers in India. *Journal of Open Innovation: Technology, Market, Complexity, 1*(7), 1–24.

Pece, A., Simona, O., & Salisteanu, F. (2015). Innovation and economic growth: An empirical analysis for CEE countries. *Procedia Economics and Finance, 26*, 461–467.

Schumpeter, J. A. (1950). *Capitalism, socialism and democracy*. Harper & Brothers.

Selemun, N., & Sundqvist, M. (2018). *A study comparing R&D clusters in India*. Umeå University.

Timmer, M. (2003). Technological development and rates of return to investment in a catching-up economy: The case of South Korea. *Structural Change and Economic Dynamics, 14*, 405–425.

USPTO (2020, March 31). Comparisons. Trends in Innovation: https://www.patentsview.org/web/#viz/comparisons&cmp=all/state/numDesc/2020

Vernon, R. (1979). The product cycle hypothesis in a new international environment. *Oxford Bulletin of Economics and Statistics, 41*(4), 255–267.

Index

For Product Safety Concerns and Information please contact our
EU representative GPSR@taylorandfrancis.com Taylor & Francis
Verlag GmbH, Kaufingerstraße 24, 80331 München, Germany